12 $^{25}_{n}$

Mastering Your Moods

RECOGNIZING YOUR EMOTIONAL STYLE AND MAKING IT WORK *FOR* YOU

Dr. Melvyn Kinder

SIMON & SCHUSTER
New York   London   Toronto   Sydney   Tokyo   Singapore

SIMON & SCHUSTER
Rockefeller Center
1230 Avenue of the Americas
New York, New York 10020

Designed by Irving Perkins Associates
Manufactured in the United States of America

10   9   8   7   6   5   4   3   2   1

Library of Congress Cataloging-in-Publication Data
Kinder, Melvyn.
    Mastering your moods : recognizing your emotional style and
making it work for you / Melvyn Kinder.
        p.   cm.
    Includes index.
        1. Personality and emotions.   2. Emotions—Physiological aspects.
    3. Mood (Psychology)—Physiological aspects.   4. Temperament.
    5. Self-help techniques.   I. Title.
    RC455.4.E46K55   1994
    152.4—dc20   93-26169
                                                              CIP

ISBN 0-671-78223-1

For Sara, Eric, and Alexandra

Acknowledgments

To MY EDITOR, Marilyn Abraham, whose wise and masterful dealings with my emotionality enabled us to keep this work flowing and on track. I am enormously grateful for her understanding and good cheer.

To Laura Daltry whose editorial assistance was sharp and focused and contributed greatly to the final version of the manuscript. Likewise, Clayton Rich's perceptive observations about temperament and psychology always proved to be valuable and provocative.

To my literary agent, Richard Pine, for his enthusiasm, humor, and ironic observations about the role of emotions in everyday life.

And finally to Laurie Conniff, M.A., for her research skills and her ability to fluidly come from the university world and yet understand the task of writing for the lay public.

Contents

PART ONE

THE MYSTERY OF YOUR EMOTIONS

Chapter 1

GOOD PEOPLE, BAD MOODS

Do you often feel apprehensive, but you can't pinpoint any reason for your anxiety? Do you tend to experience intense feelings and think you're going to explode unless you express them immediately? Or, are you the kind of person who secretly wonders why you're so restless, so quickly bored with jobs or romances?

If you're like most people, you may find that your emotions and moods are baffling. We *want* to feel good. A thousand different voices tell us we *should* feel good. Yet often we find ourselves feeling terrible! What is wrong with us? The answer may be surprising.

You can argue that feeling moody or out of control at times has always been part and parcel of the human condition. But somehow in this era of so-called psychological enlightenment, being at the mercy of our emotions seems intolerable.

We compare our own inner turmoil to the appearance of people around us, and we're convinced they're not experiencing the emotional ups and downs we suffer. Everything we read tells us we should be able to control our emotions, but we can't seem to do it. For example, if we are prone to feeling anxious or angry, *it's our fault!* We are convinced we are unenlightened, or bad, or emotionally ill, or dysfunctional. The gap between what we feel and what we're told we *should* feel is a constant condemnation.

We may lose ourselves in work or relationships, trying to soothe or inspire ourselves. We may drink too much or use illegal drugs. We may try therapy to "work through" the early childhood experiences that (popular psychology tells us) are causing our present emotional pain. Millions of us go to the pharmacy each month to refill the prescriptions for antidepressants or tranquilizers that (our doctors tell us) will balance "abnormalities" in our brain chemistry. Millions more of us are joining "adult child" or twelve-step recovery groups to recover from the adult "dysfunctions" brought on by our "dysfunctional" families.

We're told that if we're courageous and open patients, if we "work through the painful memories," "gain insight," "let go," "grow," and "change," we'll start feeling better. The message is that our emotions will change for the better when we think about things from a new perspective, or take the right pill, or work the recovery program in the right way. If we *don't* feel better, *it's our fault.*

If you want to feel happy, confident, resilient, able to cope with whatever life throws in your path, and you wonder why your emotions are so turbulent, so resistant to all your efforts to change them, you're like many people today who are confused and frustrated by the inability *to feel the way you think you should.* What's worse, you're likely to be compounding your agitation by berating yourself for experiencing "weak" or "negative" moods and emotions. You are suffering not one, but two, levels of distress. First, you're feeling bad. And then, *you're feeling bad about feeling bad.*

EMOTIONAL "MASTERY" IS POSSIBLE

In this book, I will share with you the startling new findings in brain chemistry and human behavior that, together with my twenty-four years of experience with my patients, led to my theory of *why we feel the way we do.* In the near future, I believe we are going to change almost everything we had believed about emotions. We make radical changes in how we approach psychotherapy: how much we can expect to change, and *how to make that change come about.* In this book, I will share with you new answers to questions that have baffled us until now:

- Why do we blame ourselves for emotional distress?
- Why does psychotherapy frequently fail?
- Why do people with "normal" innate natures think they have an emotional illness?
- Why are some people "numb" or "cut off" from their emotions?
- Why might you be prone to despondency despite years of therapy (inner change), and despite changing your life radically (external change)?
- Why must some people take risks or pursue extreme passions to feel alive?
- Why do some couples stay together and what is their real chemistry?

You will learn to master your emotions and shape your emotional destiny—free from blaming others, and, most importantly, free from self-blame, pessimism, and despair. As you read on, you will come to understand what's truly sparking your emotions and moods. You will discover which of the four temperament types you are, and your emotional ups and downs will become understandable and predictable. You will learn step-by-step, doable techniques that will help you short circuit dark moods, anger, restlessness, worrying. You will find ways to expand your emotional comfort zones. You will gain not only emotional self-confidence but you will be able to bring your new understanding to more successful interactions with your loved ones and your associates in the work world.

FEELING BETTER ABOUT YOUR "SELF"

People say, "I just want to feel good about myself." But, they believe they can't feel good about themselves because they are burdened with uncomfortable feelings. In my view, what has happened in the psychological boom of the past thirty years is that we have come to confuse self-esteem with emotional ease—*feeling good about oneself is predicated on "feeling good."* Undeniably, we experience our "self" with our emotions. Unfortunately, we then go on to judge our "self" on the basis of our emotions—

and we don't feel good about ourselves if we experience what our culture tells us are "bad" or "sick" emotions.

In the past thirty years, we have seen the psychologizing of America. We've been bombarded with theories, books, magazine articles, television and radio "shrinks." It's pervasive: personality tests as part of the hiring process; management seminars as you move up the ladder; marriage encounters at church or synagogue; self-help books and self-help groups, support groups, and twelve-step groups for a spectrum of psychological problems.

All of these programs include notions and techniques about ridding ourselves of unwanted emotions that get in the way of our self-esteem—feelings such as anger, anxiety, sadness. The experts urged us to scream them away in encounter groups and primal therapy, analyze them away in psychoanalysis, think them away with cognitive and behavioral therapy. Outside of treatment, we could sweat them out of our system with jogging, aerobics, or pumping iron. But all of these approaches are flawed, for they are based on misconceptions about our emotional life.

As a therapist, I have always been intrigued by psychological myths that develop periodically in our society based on trendy yet false notions about why we are the way we are. I believe these psychological myths give us misleading information and unrealistic expectations, including how we *should* feel, how we should *control* our emotions, and as a result, they cause our essential good natures to become buried and distorted. It is these psychological myths that cause us to find our feelings intolerable or shameful, that cause so many of us to have low self-esteem.

I believe the core dilemma in our relationships, our work, and our sense of self is that we have neglected the emotional cornerstone of "self." Under the layers of "shoulds" and "shouldnots" about our feelings, which we've gotten from parents, peers, society in general, is the source of our true, visceral, instinctive emotional response. This source is our innate and biologically based temperament—what I call the *natural self*.

The exciting news, as we'll explore in this book, is that our emotions are largely biochemical—not a product of childhood traumas, moral deficiencies, character defects, the wrong husband, the wrong job, and so forth. But we're still operating on old ideas and outdated theories about why we feel the way we do. As a result, we're left confused and disheartened by the puzzling and enigmatic nature of our emotions.

PROFILES OF EMOTIONAL TURMOIL: DENYING THE NATURAL SELF

Mark

Mark sells complex investments to pension-fund managers. He is sitting outside a prospect's office, going through his usual tense ritual. "What's wrong with me? I know my product. I know it's good, but I feel so uptight." He tries the visualization exercise he learned in motivational seminars, visualizing the prospect signing the contract, but the picture fades as Mark feels his hands. "Oh, no," he thinks, hating himself. "They're sweating like crazy!"

Mark is not a cool guy, the smooth closer he wants to be. He may be fooling most of the people most of the time, but Mark knows his insides don't match his outsides. He has felt like an imposter for years. He keeps trying to remake himself into the slick image on which he fixated as a teenager. But the truth is, Mark is still the anxious, sensitive person he was as a first-grader.

Leon

Leon is driving home after a horrible day at his job at an aerospace firm. "I've blown it!" He curses himself, angry, ashamed, dreading what his wife will say and do when he tells her what happened.

During a meeting with five other design engineers and their project supervisor, Leon lost his temper when his supervisor turned down a suggestion that Leon knew would simplify a pivotal process in a $20-million project. "But you haven't even bothered to hear me out!" he impulsively shouted at the supervisor.

Leon then apologized and quickly tried to smooth things over. "Sorry, I'm just so excited about this." But the atmosphere in the conference room had become poisonous. The supervisor wrapped up the meeting and dismissed them. Leon fears he'll be "laid off" within a few weeks, just like he was before when he lost his temper on the job.

Leon lives a life filled with bouts of self-loathing because of his short fuse. He senses his anger is something over which he has no control, and he feels doomed to flaring up and damaging his work life in the process. He's confused because he sees himself as good natured for the most part. What Leon has never known is why he is prone to these outbursts, and why his response to frustration is so predictable. His attempts at willpower just never work because he doesn't understand his basic temperament.

Katy

Katy is sick of endless therapy sessions, sick of endless prescriptions for antidepressants, sick of being sick. She has played the emotional illness game for five years, and she's finally worn it out. Katy has come to the end of her interest and patience with the interminable antidepressants that make her feel "zoned out." She's weary of being the good patient who somehow never gets better enough to let go of her ill and chemically imbalanced self-image. She's ashamed of the never-ending excuses she gives to her husband and her children as to why she is too tired to go with them on family outings.

Katy is fed up with being labeled "depressed," but she is at a loss to figure out why she feels the way she does. Katy has never really understood why she is prone to moodiness and certainly no one has ever helped her with this understanding.

Christie

Christie is crunching the final numbers on a marketing report that will bring in $145,000 to her company. Today her boss told her that she is on track for a partnership in the firm—if she wants it. She was thrilled, for about an hour. Now, alone in her office at close to 9 P.M., she wonders, "Why am I feeling so empty?" She then smiles wistfully at the memory of illicit meetings she had with Sam, her married boyfriend—the excitement, the intrigues, even the danger.

She catches herself. "One year sober, finally have credit cards and a good job again, and . . . I am so bored! What's wrong with me?" Christie feels disillusioned. After squandering her twenties living "on the edge," Christie has spent the last few years laboring assiduously at becoming "normal": a responsible, productive, respectable person. But, the truth is, Christie is not a security-driven personality; she is a sensation seeker. She still craves the drama, excitement, and intensity she felt in high-risk situations.

What do these four basically healthy, intelligent, well-intentioned people have in common? They don't know why they feel the way they do. They don't like the way they feel. They're frustrated by their inability to feel the way they think they should.

Perhaps you identify with Mark. Do you tend to be nervous in new situations or with strangers? Do you find yourself wishing you were less sensitive to other people, less emotional? If so, you may be the sensitive but anxiety-prone *sensor.*

Maybe you're like Leon. You're full of feelings and you have to express them, whether it's delight over an accomplishment or irritability over that nut in the next traffic lane. You often feel remorse over expressing your anger, but you just can't seem to hold your temper no matter what you promise yourself. You may have the expressive, but often angry, temperament of the *discharger.*

Are you prone to bouts of sadness, or to waking up in the middle of the night and worrying for hours about something that seems trivial the next day? Do you fear not keeping busy because you're prone to start thinking sad thoughts and working yourself into a depressed state? If this strikes home, like Katy, you may have the temperament of the reflective, often melancholy, *focuser.*

Or, do you feel you need constant challenge? Do you quickly

lose interest when novelty wears off, whether in a job, a hobby, or a romantic situation? Are you drawn to excitement, thrills, and even danger? Like Christie, you may have the restless, striving temperament of the *seeker*.

Mark, Leon, Katy, and Christie are typical of the four temperament types we'll be exploring: the sensor, the discharger, the focuser, and the seeker. Like many of us, these four people have tried both conventional and trendy "solutions" to rid themselves of unwanted emotions: positive thinking, therapy, recovery groups, pills, willpower. But these paths are not delivering the desired emotional well-being.

SEARCHING FOR EMOTIONAL RELIEF

Everyone who seeks therapy or buys books such as this one obviously wants to transform his or her life. Typically, we are feeling emotions we find distressing. If we felt fine, we wouldn't seek therapy—we would solve our problems on our own. It is uncomfortable emotions that drive us into counseling. What so many people want today is some respite from emotional turmoil, but we are unsure of the path. Unfortunately, many of the conventional solutions available make us feel worse about ourselves instead of better!

All of the ways we come to understand ourselves are insights from academic psychology and psychiatry based on learning models of behavior and identity. If we are inclined to "feel badly" it is because we grew up with "bad experiences" or our inner child was made to "feel badly." We are told, "Let's look at how your parents raised you," to understand why we feel the way we do. As a result, in the last few decades we may have gotten the message that we should blame our parents for not giving us the unconditional love we needed to become confident, loving adults.

I believe this kind of therapy is often ineffective because it is based on unlearning maladaptive patterns of behavior. These theories assume who we are is learned—*nurture* or environment rather than *nature* or inheritance—is our self-developmental influence. So, if in the past we supposedly learned to react with particular emotions, we now, supposedly, can "unlearn" these reactions using insight, discipline, and will power.

The problem is, unlearning simply doesn't work in attempting to control or subdue our emotions; therefore, this guidance inadvertently sets us up for enormous self-blame. Suppose our feelings remain resistant to psychotherapy. Does this mean we're emotionally ill due to chemical imbalances or abnormalities in our brain? Are medications, then, the answer?

Here, too, many people are bewildered. Some family doctors and internists believe strongly in tranquilizers and antidepressants and prescribe them routinely, whereas other doctors denounce such drugs as addicting, ineffective, or bad for people due to their dampening effect on perceptions and responses. Our faith in these drugs is further eroded by news reports. It seems that nearly every month the media will proclaim a new tranquilizer or antidepressant a miracle drug, and a few months later indict the same medication as insidious and addictive, with toxic side effects.

Similarly, medication is controversial among mental health professionals. Psychiatrists may, too quickly, put patients on medications, whereas conventional or "talk" therapists may blindly espouse "mind over matter" with patients who would be better served by medication. And, significantly, health-care regulations dictate that a person must be labeled "disordered" or "ill" for a doctor to prescribe antianxiety medications or antidepressants for him or her. Such labels make people feel ashamed and inherently defective.

Without question, there are problems and controversies concerning the modern "miracle mood drugs." If you're like most people, you don't know when to try them, when not to, when to stop taking them, or, most importantly, why they work in the first place.

As an alternative, millions of people are now turning to the twelve-step recovery programs where members share their experience, strength, and hope with each other, and there is a sense of shared support and empathy. But this movement isn't the answer for everyone. Some find it too religious. Others find that the key concepts of surrender, powerlessness, addiction, or dysfunction are disempowering and shame-inducing. And, even after some recovery, sobriety, or abstinence from the problem behavior, when people find their emotions are still out of control, they may drop out, secretly feeling pessimistic and disillusioned.

Something is missing. It is true that today's complex lifestyles create more emotional turmoil. But something fundamental is missing! These haphazard ways we try to feel better are just not working!

MY QUEST FOR ANSWERS

In recent years, I have been intrigued and fascinated by the basic health and courage of my patients. Beneath the unrealistic expectations, unfounded beliefs, and psychological myths, I invariably found a core, an essence within each person, as I once characterized it, a "forgotten self." That realization led me to focus on the ways in which our essentially solid and good inherent natures become buried beneath myriad layers of trendy and false notions about why we are the way we are.

Because emotions are so basic, so central to what we do in life, I began to explore the reality and source of our feelings in earnest a number of years ago. A theory gradually emerged explaining why we feel the way we do, and why certain types of men and women are inclined to predictable patterns of emotions.

When patients relate their problems to me, I listen for two things: the way they *think* about the problem and how they *feel* about it. A few years ago, I began to ask myself: Why does my patient feel so intensely about this problem? The emotions often had a vividness that seemed almost independent of the particular issue. The emotions accompanying the presenting dilemma were so far out of proportion or inappropriate that they far outshadowed the problem. I began to suspect that the answer lay in emotional temperament. The person was feeling oversensitive, or angry, or depressed, or anxious in general and her interpretive mind was finding specific life problems to blame for her uncomfortable emotional state.

The scientific research into brain chemistry and inherited personality traits now supports what I long suspected: when you feel helpless about your emotions, it's probably because you really can't help feeling the way you do. What we've learned about brain biochemistry in the past few years is beginning to turn psychology on its ear. It is changing almost everything we had believed about emotions. For instance: how much of who we are is *nature* (inherited or innate, biologically-based) and how much of who we are is *nurture* (upbringing, parental love and teachings, social and cultural environment). Although dominant psychological theory of the past hundred years (since Freud) has focused on early childhood experience (nurture) to explain why we are the way we are, new research into the brain provides compelling evidence in a very different direction. The new findings point to the true source of our emotions:

- Our emotions have biological origins.
- Each of us is born with an innate and unique biologically driven emotional temperament.
- Who we are and how we react to the world around us is determined more by these inborn traits than by environment or our upbringing.

The answer then to the question of "what's wrong with me" may well be a combination of false expectations and denying your natural self.

WHAT IS TEMPERAMENT?

Temperament, as used in this book, refers to that part of our "self" or personality that is defined by our characteristic emotions. People, of course, differ greatly in their emotional sensitivity and expression. Our sensitivity, our emotional reactivity, and whether we're shy or social, timid or aggressive, inwardly focused or outwardly focused, shapes the way we experience and respond to our environment.

Without question, upbringing, education, and experiences will mold who we become. Our emotionality is certainly influenced by childhood messages we got from our parents, how hurt we have been in vital relationships, and the kind of conscious decisions we've made about our feelings.

Indisputably, life experiences can shape us in many ways, but they are not the most important determinants. Biology and genetics appear far more important. Our natural temperament will give the signature, the definitive mark, to who we are, how we psychologically navigate through the world. And, when you understand this, you will find that it is liberating rather than imprisoning—you will know exactly why you feel the way you do and what you need to do in order to feel better and how to feel more at ease with those around you.

Temperament predicts comfort or discomfort as we go through life in our work, with our loved ones, even in our moments of solitude. As therapists, we need to apply this new knowledge to people who experience distress, not necessarily from "mental illnesses," but from everyday problems in living.

Biologically based temperament explains why Mark, Leon, Katy and Christie are having a tough time: they are fighting their true natures (or are unaware of them). Each is attempting to change, deny, repress, their innate temperament. They're locked into narrow definitions of what is "normal" emotional expression. They're "in touch" with their feelings, but they disown them. As a result, they're each uncomfortable much of the time. Why? Because they are operating on old theories about human behavior and old answers that don't work.

Conventional theories of psychology and therapies simply aren't providing answers. Biologically-based temperament theory offers a new way of looking at our emotional life.

THE FOUR TEMPERAMENT TYPES

The four basic emotional types I have identified are the sensor, the seeker, the discharger, and the focuser. Very briefly stated, some defining characteristics include:

1. The sensor is prone to be extra sensitive to outer stimulation—sometimes wonderfully sensitive, other times overly anxious and fearful.
2. The focuser is prone to excessive awareness of inner feel-

ings or lack of them. The person can be delicately inwardly focused and aware, but is also prone to worry and sadness.
3. The discharger vents her feelings. She can be spontaneous, expressive, and passionate, but is also prone to anger and is easily set off by frustrations.
4. The seeker craves sensation and is emotionally satisfied with its quest. He can also be inclined to unhappy cravings and unsettling restlessness and boredom.

Each temperament type, as we'll explore in following chapters, has a biochemical base that dictates predictable emotional patterns and responses in any situation. Each temperament has an emotional comfort zone, a range of experiences, intensity, and stimulation that each of us finds tolerable. When we're pushed outside our comfort zone, we're vulnerable to unpleasant emotions and bad moods. For example, because sensors are so highly reactive to stimulation, so sensitive to other people, they are most comfortable in familiar surroundings. They're likely to become apprehensive and uncomfortable in situations such as cocktail parties or public speaking. Seekers, conversely, crave stimulation. They are most comfortable when they are pursuing novelty, risks, and goals. For the seekers, it is routine and familiarity—understimulation—that pushes them out of their comfort zone into what they dread the most: boredom. The biochemistry of each temperament type dictates a rather narrow comfort zone. Our goal is to expand our emotional comfort zone so that we are less vulnerable to unpleasant emotions and moods, and more comfortable with a broader range of experience.

BEYOND TRADITIONAL THERAPY

It is neglect of individual temperament, in my view, that explains why conventional therapy fails people so often. Conventional therapies ignore individual differences and hold out the promise that anyone can transform into whatever is the ideal. We set up false expectations based on the false premise that everyone is basically the same: what I call the *myth of emotional uniformity*. We want everyone to fit the same mold so we can use the same approach on them. But it's the lazy way and it doesn't work. Temperaments are stubborn: each responds to treatment differently because each perceives and responds to life differently.

Therapies that ignore temperament cannot explain why some patients continue to be sad or anxious or irritable even though, overall, they are feeling somewhat better about themselves. These treatments do not take into account that the patient has a natural self that cannot be changed. Even the newer therapies, such as *cognitive therapy,* in my view, fall short. Cognitive therapy works by helping the patient gain insight into his false or defeating beliefs. Next, those beliefs are challenged. Finally, the patient is offered a new set of beliefs that are more positive, more rational, more tolerant. Ideally, this new set of enlightened beliefs will result in more positive, more appropriate emotional responses. Thus, the patient will be more comfortable and will function more effectively in his life. Cognitive therapists today regard what they do as a kind of educational process: the patient "learns" something new that enables his emotional life to be happier while tracing feelings back to their source.

For example, the therapist might say, "I hear that you're angry with your husband because he's no longer providing the excitement you felt about him when you met. You feel that he's let you down and that you're stuck with a boring husband." The therapist then helps the patient to see that her thoughts and attitudes (a husband *should* be stimulating) are the *cause* of her anger. But what's missing in this approach is that the patient may be prone to irritability and anger *regardless* of whom she is married to! In other words, what's missing is an understanding of her innate temperament. When that component is included, the patient learns that her predisposition to anger may be hidden behind her conscious complaints, which are merely a convenient trigger for innate emotional expressiveness that she must learn to modulate regardless of the kind of man she is living with.

All too often in conventional therapies patients blame themselves or they blame the therapist. "Why do I still feel this way?" they ask, with the implicit accusation: "How come you're not helping me?" Along with this frustration, invariably comes disappointment, even self-loathing. For many people, the failure of therapy to produce desired personal change serves as a confirmation that something is wrong with them. Otherwise, why would they still be prone to feeling anxious, or worried, or depressed, or irritable—*after therapy?*

This was my experience, as well, before I began to integrate temperament theory into my work. I found that even when a patient gained insight, and tried out new suggestions for thinking and acting, too often he or she would come back and say, "But I still feel bad." My patients were still experiencing the same horrible or discomforting emotions that compelled them to seek my help in the first place.

In my practice I began to explain to these patients that this was their nature. They were simply sensitive, or prone to be irritable, or prone to be melancholy. I would suggest ways to work *with* their temperaments. Some patients resisted this method. They went shopping for another therapist who could magically change them—or at least promise to! Others sought medication that would change the way they felt.

But when patients stuck with me—patients who had tried so hard to change, had even gone to many therapists to alter their emotional life—and began to understand themselves and others in terms of their natures or temperaments, they began to arrive at greater peace within themselves and better relationships with family, friends, and coworkers. In addition, they were liberated from the additional layer of discomfort created from years of being unresponsive to admonishments to "Cheer up!' or "Get a grip!" When they understood the concept of the natural self, they could let themselves off the hook. They realized their emotional style was not their fault—and there was nothing wrong with them.

So much of therapy is ultimately about reassurance and self-acceptance. I was, in effect, saying to people, "You're okay. Let's work with your temperament." With enlightened acceptance, they could begin to carve out new goals in therapy, new strategies for feeling better—for truly *mastering* their emotional life rather than *controlling* or suppressing it.

I believe it is possible to discover your natural self, to become educated about the characteristics of your temperament, and how to work within that context to achieve greater self-acceptance, a more genuine sense of self, and emotional self-confidence. It is my belief that psychotherapy must begin to integrate both the learned and the natural in order to be effective. Without an understanding of underlying and innate emotional temperaments, therapy will fail.

In the absence of identification and understanding of your emotional temperament, it is impossible to:

Fully benefit from psychotherapy, because much of what therapists try to do is find historical causes for feelings that are actually innately and biologically determined.

Understand why and when medications might work, because so many of the drug industry messages really perpetuate the myth of emotional illness.

Understand your emotions in relationships at home and at work, because much of what causes discord, discomfort, or harmony is determined by the chemistry between temperaments.

Arrive at emotional well-being and genuine self-esteem, because the failure to accept oneself and to find emotional comfort stems from beliefs about emotions that are based on today's myths rather than today's science.

WHAT IF YOU'RE ON MEDICATION?

You may be one of the 30 million or so Americans who is taking pills to make you feel better, to correct chemical imbalances, to stabilize your emotional life. If you are, I want you to read this book, keeping your mind open to the possibility that you might be able to feel and function as well or better without the pills. Or, for that matter, without the booze, the pot, the overeating—whatever it is you are taking or doing to "medicate" your emotions.

I believe that most of my patients are acting and feeling in ways that I define as okay—normal and healthy. But they are certain there is something wrong with them! And, if a doctor has prescribed medication for them, this must mean the doctor concurs—they're being treated for an illness. I'm against the obvious economic motivations behind maintaining millions of people on expensive prescriptions year after year. And I'm against trendy notions of emotional illness and definitions of disorders that change from year to year. Although I have seen that psychotropic medication can be quite helpful in the short run or in crisis episodes, I believe a large percentage of the people on long-term psychotropic medication can learn to live comfortably and with more aliveness without the pills.

MY PROMISE

Knowing your genetic inheritance, identifying your emotional temperament, is not equivalent to a sentence in a tiny jail cell. Rather, it is not knowing why we feel the way we do and what our emotional tendencies are that imprisons us. Too many of us feel bad. We don't know why. We blame ourselves, our parents, our spouse, our boss. And we don't know how to feel better.

Although your basic emotional predispositions are fixed, you can learn to effect positive change within the parameters of your temperament. And doing this can empower you in ways much greater than those offered by simplistic theories that promise you unlimited psychological change. For example, if you're a sensitive sensor, prone to anxiety, there are doable techniques to broaden your emotional comfort zone so you are more comfortable and confident in situations that you've always avoided because they make you uneasy. If you're a discharger, you can learn to tolerate the irritations that usually throw you off track into a bad mood. If you're a focuser, you can discover how to short circuit your tendency to sadness or worrying. If you're a restless seeker, you can become more serene and stable.

You can learn to live more comfortably and with greater self-acceptance and self-love. You can learn to master your moods. Please note that by *master,* I do not mean control or suppress or contain. Mastery is about having the skill and the knowledge to work with your emotions, to modulate them, to orchestrate them.

As you read on, you'll discover what temperament type you are, and what truly is creating your emotions and moods. You will come to see why tolerance and acceptance of your natural self opens the way to a more vibrant experience in your daily life. You'll learn step by step the doable techniques that will empower you to create new and enlarged comfort zones.

As we complete the twentieth century—an era of scientific psychology—we know we must learn to listen to and honor our feelings. We know that emotions have their own logic and their own truth. And we know that a life without emotional vibrancy is, in the final analysis, half a life.

I believe my new perspective holds great promise for those of you who struggle with very normal but unpleasant moods and feelings. I will explore the link between biology and how we feel throughout this book. As we'll see, you cannot help feeling the way you do, but you can understand your innate temperament and learn to orchestrate your emotional life.

Chapter 2

EXPLODING MYTHS ABOUT EMOTIONS

IN THE FOLLOWING CHAPTERS, we'll explore the new discoveries about the biochemical basis of our emotions that are changing almost everything we have believed and point to a new understanding of why we feel the way we do. In this chapter, we'll clear the way for this new understanding by looking at what we have been taught to believe: the common, pervasive messages or psychological myths that we're bombarded with from infancy onward. These psychological myths, fueled by societal reinforcement, give us misleading information and false expectations about what and how we should and should not feel, reveal, express, and behave. As a result, our genuine feelings become buried and distorted under layers of judgments, shoulds and should-nots.

Here are six pervasive psychological myths which, taken together, define a narrow standard of "normal" emotion and emotional health. They espouse emotional conformity. These messages become deep-seated and internalized in our early childhood, and cause us to judge our feelings; they do a lot of damage:

1. The myth of uniformity: We are all alike in our emotional makeup. All "normal" and "healthy" people should feel and respond in the same ways.

2. The myth of good and bad: Feelings are either good or bad; unpleasant feelings are bad and should be eliminated.

3. The myth of control: We can and should strive to control our emotions.

4. The myth of perfectability: We can and should strive for psychological perfection.

5. The myth of emotional illness: Emotional distress is a sign of emotional or mental illness.

6. The myth of positive thinking: We create what we feel by what we think. We believe "it's all in our mind" and willpower can change our emotions.

As we explore these myths, try to acknowledge the ways in which you have made these myths part of your belief system. Accept as a working hypothesis that the first step in solving the mystery of why you feel the way you do is to clear away your misconceptions.

THE MYTH OF UNIFORMITY

We are all alike in our emotional makeup. All "normal" or "healthy" people should feel and respond in the same ways. The common belief is that humans are wired the same; that there is a normal range of feeling. Normal, healthy people respond alike. We think we must be going crazy or losing it if our feelings are different or more intense than what we've observed as normal in our own experience.

A basic problem for all of us is that we don't know for sure what the range of human feelings is because, so often, they are kept so private. We have private selves and public selves and the latter are encouraged to be devoid of intense expression. Typically, our most powerful emotions are experienced and expressed rarely, and then only in private to family members or close friends.

Because we don't know how others feel, we don't know what's in the "normal" range. We've never seen anyone sob their heart out, so when it happens to us, we think we must have lost control—we've lost our mind; we're having a nervous breakdown.

We don't know that catharsis is crucial to the human grieving process. We're alienated from each other by this secrecy.

Patients frequently are nervous, even ashamed, as they reveal feelings they judge as weak: anxiety, depression, grief, feelings of failure, hopelessness. "What's wrong with me—am I going nuts? Do you think I'm crazy for feeling this way?" One thing I do a lot of in my office is share my own emotional reactions and share anonymous anecdotes about other patients. My patients find this reassuring—they're not alone. My message is, "You're not crazy—you're human."

The myth of uniformity holds, for example, that a certain amount of anxiety is appropriate before a job interview. More anxiety than what is expected is considered inappropriate, abnormal, unhealthy, a sign that you're deficient. One woman may become extremely nervous before job interviews. They make her feel exposed, like her privacy is being invaded. Another woman can breeze through them. She loves talking about herself and she knows she can charm almost anyone. One woman is not healthier than the other. These women are just different. Certain people simply interview well. It doesn't mean they're better qualified or that they'll perform better on the job.

But, more to the point, the more anxious woman has learned to prepare for job interviews in a very diligent way. She makes a good impression with her informed questions about the company, her thought-out answers to anticipated questions about her career goals. She has learned to cope. Each emotional style leads to ways of coping. Extreme emotional styles can lead to even more ingenious and effective coping techniques.

The man who becomes tearful or despondent in the face of a loss or setback looks entirely different from the man who takes action immediately. Is one man weak, the other strong? Or are they just different? The more emotional man may be more empathetic, more compassionate. He also has access to intense joy as well as sadness. The more stoic man may cope better initially with a loss, yet he may never experience the intense emotions that reside on the extremes.

The myth of uniformity also leads us to accuse others of responding incorrectly when they don't respond the way we would. There's a huge gender gap in this area. Women bash men for not being more expressive of their feelings; men accuse women of being overemotional. "Why can't you get excited about this—you just don't care!" women complain. "Why can't you be rational?" men plead in frustration.

I frequently counsel couples whose core conflict is they don't feel the same. Martin and Samantha had been married for six months when they entered marital counseling. In tears, Samantha told me, "He doesn't love me." I asked why she felt that way. She said Martin didn't talk about their future with the same degree of excitement. "I don't think he really wants to be married—maybe we should get the marriage annulled."

A clash of temperaments is the issue. Samantha is emotional; Martin is reserved. In many ways, Martin is more committed to the marriage than his wife. He talks about their future in concrete ways, but he speaks in a practical rather than emotional manner.

I explained Martin's temperament to Samantha, but she remained anxious. As we explored her feelings, it became clear that she is frightened by any differences between herself and those upon whom she is emotionally dependent. She often becomes insecure when her women friends express emotions different from her own. Mirror images are most reassuring to Samantha. She is not alone in that feeling. We all want to feel a bond based on kinship or likeness. But her husband is not her emotional twin, and never will be. Samantha has to let go of the myth of uniformity if she is to build a happy marriage with Martin. I told her to reframe her assumptions and focus on appreciating Martin's unique temperament. What Samantha has to consider is that people don't respond incorrectly when they don't feel the way we do.

The truth is, men and women are different in their emotionality—and all individuals are different. There is no normal brain-wiring diagram. Researchers have discovered many different patterns of nerve networks in the brain. There is wide variability in brain chemistry and metabolism, as well. We are wired differently. Some people are much less emotional than others. That's not necessarily a bad thing—it doesn't mean they can't love, be loyal, feel intimate. But they often envy more passionate people; they feel they're missing out on intense feeling. I reassure them that there's nothing wrong with them: they're *naturally* less emotional than others.

And, too, standards of what's considered "normal" emotionality are not absolute but relative to the *zeitgeist*—the prevailing philosophy of the times. Like all social trends, what seems "hip" today may appear excessive or foolish years from now. As the feminist movement took hold in the early 1970s, the sensitive and emotional male was one ideal. In the greed-driven 1980s, Donald Trump was considered a role model by millions of men. In the 1990s, two best-selling books by Robert Bly urged men to rediscover the primitive male inside them. "Normal" is never an absolute.

Let's reconsider the myth of uniformity. You will find that people have a rich variation in temperaments. It is possible to let go of judgments and comparisons and celebrate the richness.

THE MYTH OF GOOD AND BAD

Feelings are either good or bad; unpleasant feelings are bad and should be eliminated. It's good to be happy and confident; it's bad to be melancholy or anxious. Insecurity, depression, and fearfulness are weak. Anger and rage are negative. Contentment, serenity, and enthusiasm are admirable. Shame is toxic. The value myth about emotions is so pervasive, such a fundamental belief, that you may be only dimly aware that you're making such black and white judgments about how you feel.

Take a moment. What is your *immediate* response to remorse, sympathy, admiration, confidence, guilt, shame, dread, despondency? Chances are, you have definite value judgments about these emotions. We make harsh character and moral judgments about emotions, for example:

"I shouldn't get so angry at Barbara about this—it's beneath me." (Anger is bad.)

"I'm silly for feeling so rejected when Ken hasn't phoned me again." (Hurt is bad.)

"I feel guilty about not stopping to talk with that older woman,

Melanie, who lives down the hall. Oh, who needs guilt trips? I'm late as it is." (Guilt is bad.)

We've learned that emotions are either good or bad, and so we move quickly to deny or push away the painful or sad emotions that could make us feel weak or vulnerable. Let's look at this from a different angle. The existentialists believe that to be alive is to suffer as well as to feel joy. Taking on life's challenges, living life to the fullest, inevitably results in failure, betrayal, and loss as well as victory, grand alliances, and abiding achievement. Birth, death, marriage, divorce, success, failure, young love, growing old—with these rich experiences come hundreds of emotions.

From early childhood, we learn to be intolerant of "bad" emotions. We become alarmed when we feel too intensely: we hasten to calm down and pull back into the safe middle ground. The dictum seems to be, "If I don't feel good, there's something wrong with me!"

Instead of pushing away certain emotions, I advocate honoring them as teachers. Emotions are guideposts that make it possible to reframe the reactions above as follows:

"I'm right to be angry at Barbara. Next time we have an interaction, I'm going to set clear ground rules so she knows it's not okay to take advantage of my time."

"I'm *sad* that Ken hasn't called me again. I'm disappointed; I really like him. Why don't I call him and be warm and friendly and let him know I like him?"

"I feel remorseful about rebuffing Melanie's efforts to be friendly. I was rude and probably hurt her feelings. That's one of the things I hate most about the city—how nobody knows their neighbors. I'll get a loaf of fresh bread from the bakery and take it to her when I get home from work. Maybe she'll turn out to be wonderful new friend."

We begin to adopt the myth of good and bad in early childhood. As young children, we're praised for happy behavior, and are often pushed away or chided for showing "bad" or "negative" emotions. We're not reassured that feeling anxiety, sadness, or anger are as acceptable as feeling joy or contentment.

Like bonsai trees, our natural selves begin to become distorted when we're little more than seedlings.

Part of this myth, surprisingly, results from well intentioned but misdirected attempts to nurture our self-esteem. Self-esteem is one of the touchstones of modern popular psychology. It's my view that genuine self-esteem arises from confidence in one's accomplishments and good character, which unfortunately has been widely misconstrued to mean that kids should feel good about themselves regardless of their achievements (or lack of them) or their good character (or lack of it.) When we wrongly emphasize good feelings as the source of self-esteem, the flip side of the message is that kids should rid themselves of negative feelings as quickly as they can. The child who feels anxious (bad feeling) before he confronts a bully, and then feels proud and powerful (good feelings) after he stands the bully down, is earning true self-esteem. The child or adult who only wants to have good feelings and excludes negative feelings owns only fool's gold.

In terms of temperament, it's unfortunate but very common to hear a naturally shy or introverted child being judged as having less self-esteem than a more popular, extraverted child. The aware parent will acknowledge and validate the shy child's temperament, while encouraging him or her to take more social risks—to broaden the child's emotional comfort zone. Children should get the positive message from early childhood that it's not better to be bubbly and social than to be reserved, and quieter: all people are different.

Like adults, children need to be told that it's okay to feel the way we feel. One of the smartest and most loving things a parent can do for a child is to acknowledge and honor the child's range of feelings. The parent who unwittingly imposes the myth of good and bad feelings on a child is distorting the child's natural, honest responses. Teasing or criticizing a child for expressing sad, anxious, or "negative" emotions derails the important role emotions play in our lives. The boy who is taunted for "sissyness" when he mourns the death of a beloved dog, and the girl who is told, "Don't worry, just have fun" before a regional spelling bee, will be adrift and confused. Let's consider how these two examples might be handled:

1. "You really loved Prince. You'll miss him a lot. You've lost your best friend and you're feeling so sad. You're a very loving boy. I'm so glad you're my son."
2. "You're nervous about being in front of so many people. I'm sure the other kids are nervous, too. Most people, even famous actors and actresses, get nervous before they go onstage, no matter how long they've been doing it. It is part of the experience, part of the fun. Wait and see: I bet it'll go right away once you're out there and you answer a couple of questions."

Misconceptions about self-esteem follow children into high school. Current textbooks from courses such as *Senior Problems* or *Health Psychology* stress feeling good about yourself. Some say it's okay to feel sad or tormented when a boyfriend/girlfriend relationship breaks up, but they go on to say you should "get over these emotions as quickly as possible." Kids who show "negative" emotions are identified as kids with problems. Their parents are urged to send them to therapy or counseling where the focus is on working through and getting over these undesirable emotions. With this emphasis on feeling good, it's no wonder many kids take the short cut of substance abuse.

By adulthood, the myth of good and bad feelings has done considerable damage to the average person's natural responses. The most powerful and pervasive driving force my patients talk about is shame. They not only feel anger, fear, or depression but they're also ashamed of feeling these "bad" emotions associated with "bad" character traits. Shame is a learned response to natural emotional states. It can come from parents, teachers, or religious teachings that praise "good" emotions such as love and compassion, and condemn "bad" ones such as envy and anger.

Anger can be genuine, justified, and cathartic. Without question, there's a lot to be angry about in the world. Often anger drives people to see me for help. Sam came to see me with his wife, Sandy. She was threatening divorce if he didn't cease his angry outbursts. In exploring his emotionality, I discovered that Sam had been a somewhat explosive personality since childhood. He was not abusive or vicious toward others when he exploded. He simply had a short fuse, a low tolerance, and he would blow when he got frustrated or impatient.

In other areas of his life, his temperament was accepted. His coworkers and his secretary always knew where they stood with him and, because Sam was warm and good-hearted most of the time, they didn't take his outbursts personally. "That's the way Sam is," they'd say. But he wasn't getting the promotions his work product deserved; his temperament was holding him back.

His wife Sandy had decided after three years of marriage that his anger was an embarrassment and a sign that there was something seriously wrong with him. She wanted it "fixed," changed his wardrobe, scolded him into toning down his Boston accent, and made him lose forty pounds.

It turned out that Sam was, in fact, angrier with Sandy than he was with anyone else—because she made such an issue of it! He anticipated that she'd be disgusted with him if he got angry, so he got twice as angry!

I described the workings of Sam's underlying temperament to him and how to orchestrate it more effectively. Sandy's task was to stop trying to remodel her husband and to focus instead on creating a more challenging and rewarding life for herself.

Honoring your temperament and your emotions can lead to a richer, more compassionate, more genuine style of moving through your world. As we'll see, emotions have a biological basis. It's in your genetic code to be quick-tempered or spirited or impulsive or prone to the blues.

Let's consider the myth of good and bad. For now, try to suspend your ingrained value judgments of emotions and moods. Think of them not as good or bad, but as guideposts.

THE MYTH OF CONTROL

We can and should strive to control our emotions. This myth patronizes your emotions; it treats emotions like unruly children who must learn self-discipline, circus tigers that must be caged. We're taught that life should be on the emotional middle ground: calm, poised, in control.

The message that we can and should control our emotions

starts pounding us from infancy: "That's a good baby, don't cry." And we're not more than three feet tall when the message gets tough: "Stop acting like a baby. You're too old for that kind of behavior." "If you can't control yourself, you can go to your room." "Don't make a scene." "If you don't stop crying, I'll give you something to cry about."

By adulthood, if we haven't learned to project a controlled public image, if we wear our emotions on our sleeves, we're likely to be branded difficult, overemotional, unstable, even crazy. We're warned, "Pull yourself together," if we wander from the middle ground of emotional expression in any direction.

So-called lack of emotional self-control can jeopardize our careers, friendships, and marriages. And nowhere are emotions less welcome than in the corporate world. When a man or woman is praised for behaving in a professional manner, what that means is an emotional demeanor that is contained, inscrutable, smooth. We live in an era in which science and technology create an illusion of mastery over the environment.

But what's truly normal and what's out of control? There's no absolute standard. "Normal" changes depending on social context, class, culture, role, and gender. Generally, the more public and formal the context, the more educated and upper-class the players, the more contained and controlled is the emotional expression. Rational, reasonable, sane, enlightened, and civilized behavior are code words for emotional containment. The higher the players on the social scale, the more they disdain the uncivilized, noisy flow of emotional expression.

1. The Japanese corporate executive probably would be disgraced permanently if he burst into tears at a board meeting. But the Sicilian fisherman who sobs at his youngest daughter's wedding is admired for his deep feeling, his soul, his humanity.
2. The popular BBC television series "Upstairs, Downstairs," contrasts the lives of restrained upper-crust British family with the noisier lives of their servants.
3. In Tennessee Williams's play *A Streetcar Named Desire* the central conflict is Blanche Dubois' "refined Old Southern

gentility" and Stanley Kowalski's "savage, lower-class" emotionalism.

In the United States, as in most countries, women are allowed a wider range of emotional expression than men. They can get more excited; they can express more joy than men. They can cry and be seen as warm, feeling, expressive, alive. Why do American men keep such a tight rein on their emotions? Because the social consequences can be brutal. We fear being judged as unmanly. The myth of control wreaks incredible havoc on men. This myth is likely the leading reason men enter therapy. The initial revelation I often hear from my male clients is, "I feel like I'm going to blow up." Women hope counseling will help their men show their feelings more. One patient's wife told me, "Sam is a powderkeg. He terrifies me with this radiating tension, but when I ask him what's wrong, he says, 'Nothing, I'm fine.' "

Eventually, this tight containment stops working. Emotions are like air in a balloon: if the pressure builds too high, the balloon will pop. These strong emotions often leak out in physical illnesses or distorted expression such as sarcasm, passive-aggressive behavior, numbness, withdrawal—the list is long. Although we may succeed in not revealing strong emotions, we still feel them.

Not a week goes by in my practice without a patient coming in with a book or magazine article proclaiming some breakthrough new therapy or pill that will "cure" anxiety, depression, the explosive personality. It's my view that temperament needs no cure. Stuffing, denying, or trying to dominate every unpleasant nuance is a prescription for violating who we are, and often for adding a layer of frustration over the inability to change. My prescription is acceptance, respect, and appreciation for an expressive emotional life.

The sitcom "Roseanne" starring Roseanne Arnold touched a nerve in America and garnered top ratings with its emotionally expressive portrayal of a working-class family with three children. Although some people slammed the show for holding up "fat, loud-mouthed, uneducated slobs" as role models, many therapists, including myself, found them a welcome relief. Every character in the family is moody, imperfect, dimensional. It's wonderful to watch Roseanne and Dan Conner acknowledge and honor their three childrens' disparate personalities and temperaments. The parents continually recognize, validate, then guide their children. Roseanne makes frequent references to her (TV character's) childhood "dysfunctional family" and vows that her family (on the show) "is going to be a functional family if it kills all of us." If functional means honoring your kids' emotional uniqueness, "Roseanne" deserves the hit ratings she's drawing from family therapists.

Let's reconsider the myth of control. Embracing your emotions rather than subduing them is the only way you will learn to orchestrate and thereby master them.

THE MYTH OF PERFECTABILITY

We can and should strive for psychological perfection. Therapeutic ideology and techniques have promoted the perfectability of men and women—setting even higher standards of personal growth leading inevitably to an enlightened, self-actualized man or woman who is characterized by openness, kindness, spontaniety, and emotional expressiveness.

Beginning in the 1950s, Carl Rogers, the "father of client-centered therapy," championed the concept (now being repopularized by John Bradshaw) of the wounded inner child who can be "reparented," or brought back to his "open self" through the unconditional acceptance of the therapist. Rogers termed the therapeutic community "basically subversive" because it promoted a more loving, less competitive model of humanity than is generally accepted in most societies—the poet (or therapist!) replacing the general as the ideal man. Rogers readily conceded that the "closed self," with more rigid, traditional values, may have more survival traits in the real world. And he said he doubted that most people would feel secure with the "open self." Rogers continued to promote his antitraditional stance; he said he hoped people would bring new openness and flexibility to all areas of their lives.

High standards and ideals can be wonderfully motivating: to

seek challenges, to take risks, to push ourselves to do our best; to choose the harder, right path instead of the easier, wrong path. But the myth of perfectability sets up unattainable standards. It sets us up for failure and discontent.

Who among us is operating at peak performance, using all our talent, all our intelligence, being as kind and compassionate as we can be—at all times? The myth of perfectability—that therapy can unleash your full potential—creates an unlimited market for therapy. And *more* therapy! The relentless striving for perfectability inevitably makes you disenchanted with your own fallibility.

Endless self-improvement can be a frustrating treadmill, generating relentless discontent and living in the future: "I'm not okay now, but I'll be okay when I change this, learn this, etc." There are limits to personal change. It's like the horse who pines because he's not a bird—why not be the happiest horse he can be?

Let's consider the myth of perfectability. Accept as a working hypothesis that you can honor your natural temperament and let go of trying to become a "better person." Instead, you can try to become more genuinely who you are.

THE MYTH OF EMOTIONAL ILLNESS

Emotional distress is a sign of emotional or mental illness. This myth began to surface in the 1930s, when well-intentioned health professionals attempted to remove the stigma from mental illness. People who before had been "insane" (an incurable state) now were "mentally ill" (they had a disease that could be cured). Even with the new label, there was such a social stigma surrounding mental illness that only severely dysfunctional men and women with clear-cut psychoses, phobias, or neuroses were likely to seek help from mental health professionals.

It wasn't until the 1960s in the United States, with the rise and popularity of the human potential movement and its adoration of personal growth, that men and women with everyday dilemmas began to seek help. Their problems were not debilitating enough to qualify them as ill. Instead, they had emotional problems, character disorders, or personality problems. These were labeled "problems in living" that required *counseling* rather than *treatment*.

Since the 1970s, the pendulum has swung back to an illness model, largely for financial reasons! Simply put, medical insurance will not cover psychotherapy that is not considered medical treatment. Most people cannot afford to pay the entire cost of psychotherapy out of their own pockets. If insurance won't pay, people who are not severely troubled won't schedule appointments—therapists won't have patients.

So, what happened? Did the mental health profession meekly scale down its operations? No. Not surprisingly, the definition of illness broadened. Psychiatrists and psychologists simply changed their criteria for normal/abnormal and health/illness. What previously was considered normal human anxiety now became an affective disorder. A personality trait became a personality disorder. Disorders require treatment. And insurers reimburse *treatment*.

The mental health profession, together with the burgeoning industry of addiction and dependency clinics and twenty-eight-day programs for every marketable problem, have acted in total self-interest. They have created a huge market for their services by peddling new definitions of mental health that are so encompassing that nobody's left who's well! It's impossible to overlook the obvious economic gains from the ever-widening number of commonplace emotional dilemmas that now are deemed illnesses. By subtly convincing people they are disordered and in need of treatment, we produced rampant therapeutic consumerism. Just look at the balance sheets of psychiatric hospitals that specialize in substance abuse. Thankfully, many of these programs are coming under increasing scrutiny. In the more cost-conscious 1990s, many insurance companies and physician review boards are coming to the conclusion that it needn't cost $30,000 per month for treatment, when one of the most important things these hospital programs do is introduce patients to free, ongoing twelve-step groups.

Most of the distresses now labeled illness are, in truth, within the normal range of human emotions and experiences. There are many of us in the therapeutic profession who agree that most of the conditions that lead to suffering are not illnesses, not disorders, not medical problems that require treatment. Anxiety is a normal state, not an illness. So is sadness. Of course, when anxiety or depression becomes so debilitating that one can no longer function at home or on the job, these feelings can appropriately fall under the rubric of disorder. However, as any therapist knows, there are many variations of human misery that are equally disabling and yet we don't even label them disorders. A good example is the anguish of divorce.

You may ask, what about the new field of biopsychiatry and the synthetic drugs that mimic brain chemicals to correct chemical imbalances? Aren't they conclusive scientific proof of emotional disorders or illnesses? Not at all. While severe disorders such as schizophrenia and major depression may rightly be classified as illnesses, vast numbers of those who take tranquilizers and antidepressants are not ill or abnormal.

Recently, I had a patient, Eugene, who had been on various antidepressants over the years on an episodic basis. This treatment helped him get over serious slumps. When I commented that he seemed to have the blues quite often, he became indignant. "Look, I have an affective disorder—that's just a fact of my life."

I asked him how he knew that, and he responded that each psychiatrist who prescribed medication had told him that. My response was that, yes, he appeared to have a temperament that led him to periods of melancholy or sadness more often than any of us would find comfortable. But that didn't mean he was ill or had a disorder—unless that label made him feel more comfortable. He brightened. "Yes, I don't feel as responsible for feeling so gloomy." "Fine," I said, "I'm not saying your black moods are your fault. But merely resigning yourself to having a disorder isn't helping you. In fact, it seems to condemn you to never finding a nondrug way [such as brief counseling] to cope with your natural temperament. You take medication, the depression dissipates, you feel better for a few months, then the blues return."

I suggested to Eugene that there was a different perspective on his emotions that might be more helpful, even if he chose to take medication again. "Right now," I said, "you're a victim of the myth of emotional illness. A victim because you feel totally out of control over your own nature."

The myth of emotional illness is doing us all a disservice. Normal human feelings and moods are wrongly being defined as illnesses. We're already suffering; the illness label compounds the suffering. It feeds into our sense of shame and deficiency. More destructively, labeling ourselves ill (we need to be treated by a doctor) takes away our sense of responsibility concerning our emotions and moods. My purpose is to help you learn ways to identify your unique emotionality and how to work with it.

Let's reconsider the myth of emotional illness from a new perspective. We will find that our innate temperaments have a normal and broad range of emotions that keeps life interesting. Illness is a label with self-defeating consequences.

THE MYTH OF POSITIVE THINKING

We create what we feel by what we think. We believe "it's all in our mind" and willpower can change our emotions. The sophisticated version of the myth says that if you have a painful or uncomfortable feeling, it has been generated by a negative or irrational belief about yourself or your world. When you uncover and rid yourself of negative emotional beliefs, you will rid yourself of painful feelings. The unsophisticated version is critical: "Don't you realize it's all in your head, stupid? Why don't you just get over it? Use your brain! Exert some willpower!" The implication here is that we're holding onto feelings out of pig-headed perversity, yet we know better—we should use our heads!

Traditional insight or talking therapy focuses on the process of gaining new insight, new perspective. Talking about painful experiences, understanding and forgiving, for example, our parents' failure to give us unconditional love, and working through and letting go of painful emotions will lead to new ways of thinking about ourselves and our lives. A new, more positive perspective will lead to different, more positive feelings. How does this theory explain why so many people who have had years of psychoanalysis, years of group therapy, say in great frustration, "I have great insight into my childhood. But I'm still prone to depression [or anxiety, or being quick tempered or overemotional]"?

The myth of positive thinking derives its power because it is partly true. How we *think* about something does affect the way we *feel* about it. Understanding the connection between our thoughts and feelings is a pivotal element of self-knowledge. The falsity in this myth stems from the assertion that our feelings are generated entirely by our thoughts.

Since the 1960s, American psychology has been dominated by the cognitive school of thought: the way a person thinks about or perceives his environment determines what he feels. If you're sad, and you examine the helplessness it conjures up, you will realize these thoughts are irrational and your sadness will lift; new thoughts will create new emotions. However, as we'll see, the emerging discoveries about brain chemistry suggest a radically different theory—that emotions are biologically (not environmentally) triggered. And that our brain's interpreter experiences an emotion, *then* associates this emotion with a set of facts from the environment to explain the emotion. In other words, *emotions can create thoughts.*

Many of my patients are in the business world and they find motivational audiotapes quite helpful. They find that positive thoughts, positive self-talk ("You're a winner!") and visualizing themselves, for example, closing that sale, keep them focused. These tapes help them cope with rejection and help them bounce back from setbacks. However, positive thinking doesn't work for everyone.

Christina, an advertising account representative, came to see me, tearful and frustrated. Unlike other salespeople in her company, motivational tapes and seminars were not working for her. Moreover, she felt deficient because she just couldn't "think right." She was quite anxious when she went on sales calls. The more she tried to think positive and pump herself up, the more aware she was of her anxiety. She was closing sales and doing quite well, but she wanted to get rid of the anxiety. She thought she could do much better. "It's really holding me back," she said.

I suggested that she stop disowning her anxiety and, instead, embrace it as a familiar companion. I suggested that, in fact, it may have been contributing to her success—that maybe her contacts found it more appealing than the usual salesperson's pushy confidence. They probably saw Christina as more human, sensitive, and accessible. I suggested that what she might focus on was *what she did with the anxiety* when she initially felt it. Her attempt to stifle the anxiety made her feel worse. So now, when she went on a call, as she felt the physical signs of anxiety, as she accepted its presence and inevitability, a disconnection occurred between her tension and her conscious embarrassment and self-doubting. As she stopped trying to suppress her anxiety, it gradually diminished rather than overwhelmed her.

Fighting our emotions, using brainpower or willpower to overpower them, is not the answer to combatting unsettling feelings. Often, this only makes them more intense. However, I hasten to add that, as you read on, you can use your intelligence and will to understand your temperament and, ultimately, to find desired emotional relief. Believing strongly in yourself will help you feel better.

Let's reconsider the myth of positive thinking. Positive thinking, self-talk, and visualization can be powerful and helpful. But acknowledging instead of denying human feelings such as doubt, sadness, or anxiety can lead to genuine confidence rather than wishful thinking.

These are the six most common self-defeating myths you may have about your emotions. As we've seen, they have taught us to judge, deny, and suppress our natural feelings. They have fostered misunderstanding and made our emotional life mysterious and confusing. In so doing, they have blocked us from possible solutions to emotional distress. They are based on false understandings of the true source of our emotions. It's important to set aside these old ideas in order to open the way for a new understanding of your emotional life.

Chapter 3

PSYCHOBIOLOGY: AN EMOTIONAL THERMOSTAT

UNDERSTANDING some of the basics of your brain biochemistry is the next step in solving the mystery of why you feel the way you do. The key new findings we will explore in this chapter are:

- That emotions are largely biological in origin, not learned.
- How the unique mix of neurotransmitters or chemical messengers in your "brain soup" at any given time dictates whether you're feeling cheerful, depressed, focused, angry, or wonderfully intuitive.
- How the typical level of excitement or arousal in your brain dictates the most pivotal personality trait of all: whether you're introverted or extroverted.

In the not-so-distant past, we knew so little about the biology of human behavior that we assumed all human behavior was learned. But, since the 1980s, so much has been discovered about how the brain works and, more specifically, about the brain chemistry and structures that govern our emotions. A new field has emerged from this work called *psychobiology*. It seeks to:

- Study how brain chemistry (biology) affects the way we think, feel, and behave (psyche).

- Understand how the brain and the mind interact to cause behavior.
- Learn how brain states (metabolism and chemistry) create mind states—everything from phobias to falling in love to memory functions.

Psychobiologists are finding that our underlying biology functions like an internal thermostat, regulating our emotional life, and that emotions have a more biological, more simple origin than the more complex, conscious, interpretive origin we've been assigning to them. The new findings point to biology rather than learned responses as the true causes of our emotions.

Consider the emotion we call anxiety. Traditional psychologists believe it is a learned response caused by childhood trauma or faulty thinking and, thus, can be unlearned through psychotherapy. Biopsychiatrists, on the other hand, who are committed to a medical and illness model, assert that anxiety has a clear biochemical basis, and therefore it is an illness that should be treated with medication.

Each school is half right and half wrong. What is left out of these two professional camps is what I see as a new emerging reality: our emotions are primarily biological and instinctive, and are secondarily influenced by our thoughts, judgments, and interpretations. It is the integrated approach that respects both the biochemical dimension and the psychological dimension that is going to revolutionize the psychotherapy of the near future.

THE BRAIN-MIND SPLIT

The human brain has been called the most complex organ on the planet. It's estimated there are 100 billion neurons in the average human brain, and most of them are hard at work at any given time.

Before the 1970s, brain scientists and mind scientists were in opposing corners. The brain researchers tried to figure out the "hardware": the functioning and organization of brain cells, nerve networks, chemical neurotransmitters, and so on. They also studied how the brain processes sensory input and stores information (short- and long-term memory). The mind scientists focused on mental behavior: how the mind takes raw data, interprets the data, and then acts on that information—the processes that shape our own internal personal reality and the behavior that results.

The mind scientists and the brain scientists were speaking two different languages. For example, Amelia, a young legal secretary, acquired a sudden phobia of tall buildings. The brain scientists would suggest her problem was biochemical. The mind scientists—the psychiatrist or psychologist—would start probing for the traumatic incident in Amelia's childhood. They would both miss the target. Psychobiology brings the two disciplines together.

UNDERSTANDING AN EMOTIONAL TRAUMA

One lunch hour, Amelia is strolling downtown near her office when she suddenly feels terrified. No scary external event is occurring. It's an internal event in her brain chemistry. Her brain is experiencing a sudden dump of a chemical. These variations in brain biochemistry are known to happen to all of us. Perhaps a variation occurs as a reaction to a stimulus in the outside world, or a sudden reaction in our internal brain chemistry, or maybe for no perceivable reason at all.

In Amelia's case, the sudden activity of a stress-released chemical creates a feeling that her interpretive mind doesn't just register as a biochemical "burp." It rushes to find a set of facts around which to weave a story: I'm feeling this way because . . . It sees the tall buildings and decides to pin the strong feeling on them—the buildings are causing this feeling and it's *fear!*

Amelia's brain stores the memory. The next time she's downtown, she gets to the same spot. Her memory sparks to life and triggers the fear she felt the first time. She feels terrified again, and *this* experience gets stored in her memory. After she suffers her third attack of terror downtown, Amelia quits her job and consults her internist. She tells Amelia it was probably just a biochemical fluctuation and she gives her a prescription for a tranquilizer. Amelia's anxiety subsides, which confirms the internist's diagnosis that the phobia was caused by a biochemical fluctuation.

The problem is, Amelia is still frightened of going downtown. Her attacks of fear are firmly stored in her memory. The experience now has a psychological dimension as well as a biochemical dimension. She remembers how frightened she became and she'll do anything to avoid feeling like that again. Like a pebble thrown on a lake, her terror of tall buildings ripples outward to now include crowds, traffic jams, any sort of human congestion.

This formerly independent (although somewhat anxious) young woman begins to hide inside her apartment. She becomes depressed and puts on fifteen pounds from junk food munched in front of the TV. Her boyfriend breaks up with her. Her friends and family worry about her. Because she is a legal secretary and the big law firms are all downtown, she quickly gets into financial trouble because she is unable to work!

Amelia's chemistry produced a change in her mental outlook. Now, her fearful memory, when triggered, in turn creates fearful feelings. That one "burp" in her biochemistry started a chain reaction of events and responses that undermined her confidence and had enormous consequences in her life.

In reality, Amelia suffered from a panic disorder—an unexplained shift in brain neurotransmitters that created an acute moment of anxiety. If she had entered psychotherapy, she might have spent years exploring the symbolic meaning of tall buildings and gotten nowhere. Many unexplained panic attacks are best treated by antidepressants (not tranquilizers), which modulate neurotransmitters and prevent the panic.

Incidentally, there are phobias and vague fears that may be related to past experiences, including childhood. I'm certainly not trying to imply that all emotions are simply expressions of chemical variations. But I can assure you that right now there are millions of people in counseling searching for the childhood roots of emotional distress that in reality had nothing to do with their childhood.

It's foolish to be simplistic or reductionist in our thinking. The conventional doctor who gave Amelia antianxiety medication did nothing to address the way the way the phobia had altered her general outlook and confidence. Conversely, the conventional therapist probing Amelia's early childhood would have been driving down a blind alley and would have been inadvertently training Amelia to view herself as someone with a disordered personality. The integrated approach that acknowledges both the biochemical dimension and the psychological dimension of Amelia's distress leads to real help.

Had I been treating Amelia, I would have strongly endorsed the need for medication for a relatively short time until her panic attacks were less frequent. Then I would have helped her to understand why she had the attacks (her underlying biological temperament), how these inexplicable biological states had created her apprehension, and how they had caused her apprehension to spread into other areas of her life. Amelia could gradually overcome the fear that had now been learned in response to her original anxiety attack. For people like Amelia, overcoming the fear becomes rather easy when they shed their secret belief that they have a defective personality.

Amelia's experience demonstrates that these complex mind-brain interactions have enormous implications about how we perceive the world, how we feel and think, and how we behave. Let's look at the biochemical origins of these processes.

BIOLOGICAL COMMUNICATIONS: NEUROTRANSMITTERS

The basic structure of the human nervous system (this includes the brain) is the neuron. Neurons differ in size and shape, but the basic model is the same. The neuron's purpose is to transmit information. Dendrites and axons are part of a neuron. Messages are received through the dendrites and are transmitted along the axons. The neurons lie close to each other, but they don't overlap. The axon of neuron 1 almost makes contact with the dendrite of its neighbor, neuron 2. How does information get through the gap, or synapse?

When the axon of neuron 1 is stimulated enough, chemical messengers, or neurotransmitters, are released from tiny ports at the ends of the axon (or transmitter). The neurotransmitters sail across the synaptic "sea" to the dendrite (or receptor) of neuron 2. When the neurotransmitter docks at the receptor site of neuron 2, the chemical information turns into electric energy, and the information is fed to neuron 2 in tiny wavelike pulses. Although we've discovered much about these electrical-chemical processes, we have yet to break the code of how these billions of chemical and electrical pulses translate into ideas, memories, and reminders like, "Buy a carton of low-fat milk on the way home."

Think about the molecular level of activity that begins when your finger touches a hot stove. The message then travels through billions of neurons to your brain, where the information is processed, and the message then goes back through the same billions of neurons to tell your finger to retract. No wonder we're bushed at the end of the day! The ebbing and flowing of neurotransmitters is an ongoing process, creating a chemical soup in the brain with an infinite variety of flavors.

THE BIOCHEMISTRY OF MOODS

For the past century, the study of mental illness has focused on the psychological history of patients. The problem is that establishing cause and effect relations in psychology is very difficult. The schizophrenic who thinks he's Napoleon may have the same childhood history as his brother, who's leading a happy, normal life. This puzzle as to what causes mental illness led to the search for a biological trigger—that is, something beyond learned experiences and family dynamics.

Many of the discoveries about drugs that treat mental illness came about by accident, decades before we had the technical means to probe the brain. It was just a blind process of trial and error. Doctors simply tried every substance they could obtain on mental patients and kept a log of the results.

One example is chlorpromazine (Thorazine), which emptied the mental hospitals in the 1950s and 1960s. It was originally synthesized in Germany in 1900, by dye chemists who were trying to invent more vivid colors for fabrics. In 1949, a French surgeon noted that it seemed to have a tranquilizing effect on patients going under the knife. Doctors started trying it on mental patients to see what would happen. In the next few years, Thorazine allowed millions of schizophrenics to go home from the hospital. It wasn't a cure, but they were more rational more of the time. The hallucinations and voices stopped.

Another accidental discovery was the use of lithium, a common salt, to treat manic depression, or bipolar disorder—the tendency to cycle between extreme elated moods and depressive moods. An Australian physician, J. F. J. Cade, in the late 1940s hypothesized that deficient bodily fluids might be the cause of this disorder. In experimenting with different fluids, he administered lithium carbonate to some patients and found their manic states were reduced thus calming them. While not knowing exactly how it works, scientists speculate that lithium alters the calcium-sodium balance between brain neurons. Regardless, giving just the right dosage seems to dramatically "even out" the moods of manic depressives.

The successes with lithium and Thorazine set off an explosion of experimentation. Thus, the biologically oriented revolution in the treatment of mental illness began. The effectiveness of these drugs also revealed much about our brain chemistry and the range of emotions we experience.

Anxiety

Anxiety is thought to be caused by an overproduction of certain stress-related chemicals. The autonomic nervous system generates adrenaline and other chemicals leading to heavy breathing, shakiness, sweating, and other responses. A class of antianxiety drugs or tranquilizers called "benzodiazepines" reduces anxiety by stimulating the neurotransmitter, GABA (gamma-aminobutyric acid). GABA apparently acts as an inhibitory agent affecting the autonomic nervous system.

Depression

Modern antidepressants work by increasing the amount of norepinephrine or serotonin to the nervous system. Depression is associated with diminished activity of these two chemicals. The most common biological theory of depression is called the

"monoamine hypothesis." Neurotransmitters like norepinephrine and serotonin are both called monoamines. Today, because
antidepressant drugs that stimulate or facilitate the "flow" or
transmission of these chemicals seem to "lift" people from depressive moods, it is hypothesized that a deficiency in these
chemicals must be the "cause" of depression.

Addictions

There is increasing biological evidence that certain people truly
are addictive personalities. They regulate their emotions with
substances whose need soon dominates their life. Substance
abusers are, in effect, desperately trying to regulate their moods
and emotions. New theories suggest they may instinctively be
taking drugs or other substances to make up for deficiencies or
overproduction of certain brain chemicals. For example, cocaine may be especially addictive to those prone to depression
because it is known to stimulate the neurotransmitter, norepinephrine, whose deficiency is thought to be one of the biological
"causes" of depression.

THRESHOLDS OF AROUSAL: EMOTIONAL
THERMOSTATS

Why do people differ in their emotional intensity? Along with
most psychologists, I have been impressed with the new findings
in psychobiology. It is obvious that the effectiveness of mood-
altering drugs such as tranquilizers and antidepressants forces
us to take a new look at emotions and their origins. If these
chemical drugs alter emotions, it follows, of course, that they
must be affecting basic, innate biological processes in the brain.
Each of us is born with varying amounts of these chemicals;
therefore, we are inherently prone to certain emotions. The
biochemistry of arousal offers some provocative answers. The
concept of arousal has been around for a century. It is loosely
defined as a generalized and diffuse activation of the central
nervous system—how awake or alive we feel, from a coma state
to extreme excitement.

We are all familiar with the physical sensations that accompany our emotions. These sensations are examples of arousal: the sweating and rapid heartbeat of fear, the sense of nonfeeling or deadness when we reject or lose something we cherished, the rapid heartbeat of excitement. Obviously, if you have ever been "turned on" by the opposite sex, you are familiar with sexual arousal. It's not just one body structure that is involved in arousal. In the brain, cortical arousal or activity can be measured by an EEG (electroencephalogram). Arousal can also be expressed in peripheral autonomic activity including heart rate, blood pressure, sweating, and muscle tension. Arousal is not necessarily conscious; you may not even be aware of this physiobiological process as it is occurring. Awake or asleep, we are always in some state of physiological arousal.

Arousal can be triggered either internally, by spontaneous activity in our brain, or externally, by experiences in our environment, including interactions with other people. Most of us are familiar with the arousal that is triggered by external situations. We are aroused by frightening situations—the body's fight or flight response wherein stress hormones prepare us to either run from danger or to confront it.

LEVELS OF AROUSAL AND COMFORT ZONES

Each of us has a predictable threshold of emotional arousal. Some people are more intense in their emotional response than others. This is true whether the intensity is externally triggered (such as a clear-cut danger), or internally triggered (such as feeling anxious for no discernable reason). It follows that there is a range of arousal or comfort zone that is typical or customary for each person, a range determined by basic biology.

I believe that each of us has a degree of emotional arousal we find comfortable or tolerable. When we drift out of this comfort zone to a level of arousal that is so high or so low (so unpleasant or unfamiliar) that we become uncomfortable, like many biological processes, we instinctively obey homeostatic laws. We will do something, instinctively, to return ourselves to our comfort zone.

Our biological or natural self functions like an inner thermostat. If we have a low threshold, our arousal is easily activated and our emotions are easily triggered. If it is set high, our arousal is less easily activated and our emotions may not be triggered enough—we may be numb, rigid, bored.

Our inner thermostat is on automatic—we don't have to think about it. It is a self-regulator. Typically it is busy, making constant adjustments trying to keep within our comfort zone. This self-regulation is going on all the time, whether you're aware of it or not; there is a perpetual ebbing and flowing of brain chemicals. Arousal and its typical level or range of variability is the source of normal emotions. We all have a wide range of chemical activity, and to say "imbalance" is abnormal is like saying only men who are between 5 feet 7 inches tall and 5 feet 10 inches tall are normal. Chemical variabilities are *not* indications of emotional illness but the normal ebbing and flowing of healthy neurotransmitters or chemical messengers.

WHY A PARTICULAR EMOTION?

What causes arousal to be expressed as a particular emotion? Why, when two people are threatened, does one react with angered confrontation, and the other with fear and retreat? Obviously people differ not only in arousal levels but also in their biological choice of emotions. Why are some people prone to sensitivity and fear, some to moodiness or sadness, some to outward expressiveness like anger, and still others to seeking danger, challenge, and adventure? The final step in my understanding was developing the theory that each of us has an underlying emotional temperament, and these might even be a finite number of basic emotional types.

Chapter 4

TEMPERAMENT: THE MOOD FORECASTER

Two thousand years ago, Hippocrates and the physician Galen divided people into four temperament types. They had no understanding of science as we know it today, that is, no behavioral or psychological science. Their humoral theory said each person had a preponderance of bodily fluids or humors that determined his or her emotional temperament. If blood was the major fluid, the person was said to have a sanguine or optimistic temperament. If yellow bile was the major fluid, that person was said to be choleric or prone to anger. If phlegm predominated, the person was likely to be unexcitable, calm. And if black bile was the dominant fluid, the person was melancholic or depressed. This theory and variations of it survived until the nineteenth century. Although the actual physiology was dead wrong, the theory lasted because the personality types they described were so familiar.

In the 1920s, Ernst Kretschmer, a Swiss psychiatrist, decided that physique was linked to temperament. He believed there was a connection between body type and the likelihood of mental disorders. He took photographs of thousands of people and speculated about their personalities. He coined the terms *ectomorph* for the thin nervous type, *mesomorph* for the athletic and aggressive type, and *endomorph* for the heavy and jolly type. His theories have remained part of popular thought.

Concurrently, the Viennese psychiatrist Carl Jung was developing his famous personality theory of introversion and extroversion. Jung characterized introverts as inwardly focused. They were shy, reserved in demeanor, and rational minded. The extrovert was a person of action—gregarious, ambitious, and romantic. In 1929, Jung's theory inspired a fascinating paper that foresaw discoveries in brain science fifty years later. "A Chemical Theory of Temperament" by William McDougall, a prominent American psychologist, hypothesized that a fluid in the brain causes extroversion; when its flow is obstructed or blocked, inhibition or introversion results.

In the 1950s, the American psychologists Stella Chess and Alexander Thomas did long-term studies on children and theorized about inherited, innate temperament traits that seemed to be genetically dominant. They identified traits such as activity level, approach or withdrawal tendencies, threshold of responsiveness, and distractibility. Chess and Thomas braved the wrath of the psychological establishment of that time by daring to state that their research indicated that at least some of what and who we are is not the result of environment but of inborn characteristics that interact with environmental forces to shape our personalities.

Since the 1960s, Hans Eysenck, an English psychologist, has done an enormous amount of research on introversion and extroversion and their connection to arousal. Introversion is a turning inward of your energy and attention—to introspection and self-focusing. Extroversion is a turning outward, attending to objects, people, and goals. Eysenck believes the introvert has overly high levels of internal cortical or brain arousal; therefore, she typically avoids external stimulation and turns inward. The extrovert has a typically low level of arousal. He craves stimuli that excite him, that is, increase his arousal, so he is attuned to external goals and stimuli. Eysenck, not surprisingly, finds that too much arousal is related to anxiety; too little is related to depression. He and his colleagues have done hundreds of studies on this introvert/extrovert dimension (a combination of activity level and emotionality) and find it to be a key factor in determining personality.

Arnold Buss, a psychologist at the University of Texas, divided temperament into traits such as emotionality, activity, sociability, and impulsivity, which seem intuitively accurate. Jerome Kagen at Harvard is another researcher who became convinced of the innate and inborn nature of certain traits that we see in childhood. He has studied the ways in which some children, from birth on, seem much more active and aggressive than others who seem to have an innate shyness and reserve.

TEMPERAMENT AND GENETICS

Each of us has a genetic blueprint made up of some 100,000 genes. For a long time, we have accepted the fact that predispositions to many physical illnesses such as diabetes, heart disease, and breast cancer are genetic or inherited. We also have known from simple observation that traits such as intelligence, musical ability, and even mental illness tend to run in the family. But until recently, we neglected to explore the inherited basis of personality, what is now called behavior genetics—the study of how genes determine our behavior, that is, how we feel, think, and act.

Modern psychological ideology emphasized the influence of early childhood experience on shaping personality: "Billy is shy because his parents isolated him." Billy was thought to be a blank slate, and what he learned as a child wrote his story. If Billy has a problem, the thinking went, it is probably his parents' fault. Yet we sensed there may be another answer.

Every parent has had the experience of watching a child evolve from infancy in ways that seem miraculous and unique. As if by some hidden set of imperatives, the child takes on a personality almost as though we have no impact on him. As soon as we bring this little person home from the hospital, he starts to reveal his embryonic personality. Some babies are on the shy side, a little passive, and we may rejoice for this peaceful personality. Others seem feisty and active; we're a little concerned and a lot worn out, but we interpret this behavior as tough—we have a survivor on our hands. Much of who and what we want our child to be seems outside our control.

Research is confirming our suspicions that much of our temperament is innate. In a recent survey of the research on the role of inherited characteristics of behavior, Robert Plomin, a psychologist working in behavior genetics, estimated that as much as 50 percent of the style of our personality characteristics is inherited. (In identical twins, it may be as high as 70 percent.) This finding supports the work of other investigators who study basic traits such as emotionality, activity level, impulsivity, and sociability using twin and family studies. Employing complex analyses of the data, they conclude that many of our basic predispositions are genetically based and innate.

IDENTICAL TWIN STUDIES

Identical twins who were raised apart are the dream subjects of researchers into almost any aspect of human behavior. Identical (monozygotic) twins develop from the same fertilized egg and therefore share the *exact* genetic blueprint. It follows that any differences are a result of nurture (environment) rather than nature (inherited).

Thomas Bouchard, a noted University of Minnesota researcher in behavior genetics, has located 100 pairs of such twins and, since the 1970s, has flown many of them to Minneapolis for extensive testing. The similarities are almost unbelievable. One pair were twin brothers who met for the first time at age thirty. They were shocked to find each other sporting similar moustaches, hairstyles, aviator glasses, big belt buckles, and big key rings. They discovered they both drank the same brand of beer and even shared the habit of crushing the cans when they were finished. Astonishingly, they were both volunteer firefighters and both made their living installing safety equipment. As bizarre as this may seem, Bouchard's research indicates such surprising similarities are common.

Another famous case made newspaper headlines around the world. This was the case of the two Jims, identical twin boys who had been adopted into different families when they were a few weeks old. Their adoptive parents coincidentally named each baby Jim. When they were thirty-nine, they found each other through court records and met for the first time in Dayton, Ohio, in 1979.

- Both had nervous tendencies, bit their nails, and were chain smokers.

- Both had married women named Linda, divorced, and had remarried women named Betty.
- When they were boys, both had owned a dog named "Toy."
- One of the Jims had named his first son James Alan; the other had named his first child James Allan.
- They both lived in Ohio, and spent their annual vacations at the same 300-yard-long beach near St. Petersburg, Florida.
- Both were good at math and bad at spelling.
- Both have had two heart attacks.
- Both have hemorrhoids.
- Both have tension headaches.
- Both have the same sleeping problems.

The subjects were raised in entirely different environments, by parents of different income levels, different educational attainment, and with disparate styles of child rearing. Despite radically different environmental opportunities and expectations, innate temperament traits proved to be so dominant that the twins ended up leading almost parallel lives!

We see that genetically based patterns of brain functioning and brain chemistry dramatically shape our temperament and thus our personality. Behavior genetics is the first body of research that tells us that in addition to our conscious identity, we have a physical or biological natural self that is innate and inherited.

I am not suggesting that biology is destiny. Environmental influence, the moral choices that define our characters, and the serendipity of opportunities that life presents to us all work to make us who we are. When I underscore the biological or genetic determinants of our emotions, and state their primacy, I want you to know there is still vast room for conscious and deliberate modification and orchestration of emotions—but only when your efforts are based on the new truths about your emotions.

AROUSAL PLUS ACTION TENDENCY

As I discussed in chapter 3, we know that the intensity of our emotions is biologically based; we differ in the amount of arousal we feel. But, as I indicated, temperament is comprised of two parts: arousal, plus something instinctive that determines how the arousal is expressed. The missing piece is what I call action tendency, the innate, instinctive predisposition to express arousal in a particular way. For me, action tendency is best understood in terms of the most researched and most intuitively compelling temperament dimension—introversion/extroversion, that is, whether you are either inward oriented or outward oriented.

As is true of many biological processes, there is an instinctive movement toward homeostasis or balance. If we become unusually underaroused or overaroused, something takes place in our brain chemistry to bring us back into our usual level of arousal. I believe that action tendency is what returns us to our comfort zone or our characteristic level of arousal.

Please look at the chart. You will see the relationship between emotionality (level of arousal) and action tendency (expressed here as introverted/extroverted). As you will notice, the four temperament types correspond to the four primary emotional predispositions: anxiety, sadness, anger, and craving or impulsivity.

YOUR TEMPERAMENT TYPE

As my observations crystallized over the years, I eventually identified distinct similarities and differences between my clients. Four emotional types emerged. These are broad groups, and there are individual differences within each group, but the similarities outweigh the differences.

As you can see in the chart, arousal plus action tendency determine your temperament type. First, there is the characteristic level of inner arousal, that is, high or low. Second, there is action tendency, that is, the instinctive direction of one's emotional expression: inward or outward, introverted or extroverted. By combining arousal and direction, four possible types emerge. Each of the four quadrants represents a type. The farther out you go in the quadrant (i.e., away from the center where the two lines meet) the more distinctly you are that type.

Please do not try to guess your type yet. Keep an open mind until you've read chapters 5 through 8. My purpose here is to introduce the concept. As you read each description, be aware that each type has a particular level of arousal and a particular action tendency. As you read, you can refer back to the chart.

TEMPERAMENT TYPES

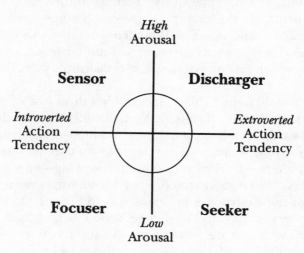

High
Arousal

Sensor   **Discharger**

Introverted   *Extroverted*
Action   Action
Tendency   Tendency

Focuser   **Seeker**

Low
Arousal

Sensor: You have a low threshold of arousal; in other words, you are easily aroused. Typically, you feel arousal most of the time. You may have been called an introvert. You tend to be shy, cautious. You avoid as much external stimuli as you can in order to not become more aroused. You're prone to feeling nervous or anxious. Your emotional thermostat is usually trying to lower your level of arousal, that is, raise your threshold. You're very sensitive to other people, to all kinds of external stimuli such as noise, color, and movement. Sensors are inclined to be compassionate, emotionally vibrant, and intuitive.

Focuser: You have a high threshold of arousal that causes you to be in a state of underarousal. You tend to turn inward and ruminate on your feelings and what you can do about them. This self-focusing is intended to arouse your feelings. You are prone to melancholy and worry. Focusers can become depressed or markedly obsessional. But when they're within their comfort zone, they are focused in the positive sense—attentive, connected, conscientious.

Discharger: You have a low threshold of arousal and feel over-aroused much of the time. Your instinct is to discharge this tension outwardly, expressively. You are somewhat similar to the extrovert. At the extreme, you can become irritable and prone to anger and hostility. When comfortable, this same predisposition leads to expressiveness of a more passionate nature. Dischargers can be quite dynamic, especially in a work situation.

Seeker: You, like the focuser, have a high threshold of arousal. You're typically underaroused. Your instinct dictates that you turn outward, to seek out sensations and high-risk activities that will arouse you. When your cravings for arousal get the best of you, you are blindly drawn to sensation seeking—either in love or in work. When misdirected, your seeking may result in impulsive or self-destructive behavior and addictions. On the plus side, the seeker may find challenge, action, drama, and adventure from which he derives enormous satisfaction.

Those on the border of two quadrants may be mixed types, although usually one is dominant. Those who fall close to the center (where the two lines intersect and are contained within the circle) fall into a category that I would characterize as emotionally at ease or rarely emotionally distressed.

Obviously, the farther out one gets, the more likely one is to become psychologically impaired or disordered. Thus, a sensor with a high level of arousal who is very introverted might end up having to take tranquilizers for any anxiety disorder. Based on my own clinical experience and research, 30 percent of the population falls into the at-ease category. However, because you have some concerns about your emotions, enough to buy this book, most of you probably do not! (And, that's okay—neither do I!)

Another 20 percent of the population falls into one quadrant or another, but near borders. They have a predominant temperament, but there are times when they could actually feel like another temperament. Their task is to be honest with themselves about the intensity and nature of their emotional responses. They may be a disguised type—they appear one way but are actually another. However, even when they cannot distinguish between the two types, they can learn to modulate and successfully master their emotions simply by following the advice in this book according to which type they feel like at a particular time.

I should note that there are certain border types whose emotional makeup corresponds to the clinical phenomena therapists see frequently. For example, the focuser/seeker (very low level of arousal and without a clear-cut action tendency) corresponds to the highly emotional manic-depressive type, shifting between highly active sensation-seeking states and sad or despondent states. The sensor/discharger is another border type with a high level of arousal, shifting between anxious withdrawal and bouts of angry expressiveness. The sensor/focuser's arousal level is moderate. This person is typically quite introverted, prone to shifts between moodiness and anxiety.

THE KEY TO COMFORT ZONES

Each temperament type has emotional predispositions that may lead to difficulties. Each has positive qualities and a very specific task or strategy that enables people to deal with the difficult aspects of their temperament—a task, you will see, that also serves to expand their comfort zone.

As you read part two, if you refer to the chart on page 65, you will see that a person's task moves him away from the extremes of his type and closer to the center of the chart, to the at-ease area. The task not only relates to the person's action tendency, but also involves shifting his arousal level. For instance, the task of the sensor moves him away from being oversensitive and socially fearful to being more confident and less aroused. For the seeker, her task moves her from sensation seeking to being more serene and reflective.

TEMPERAMENT AND RELATIONSHIPS

ROMANCE AND LOVE

What creates chemistry between two people? Why do two strangers at a big party find each other in the crowd? You may believe attraction is elusive, mysterious, even inexplicable. But you surely know what chemistry feels like, when you explain, "I feel terrific being with him!" or "It's wonderful being with her."

We sense that some types of people are drawn to each other and other types tend to repel each other. We love the romantic advice in horoscope columns. It's not surprising that temperament plays an important role in love relationships. We have acquired a lot of folk wisdom in this area. Everyone is familiar with the theory that opposites attract. What you may not know is why this is true. The primary purpose of attraction may well be emotional self-regulation. I know this doesn't sound romantic, but it feels wonderful when it happens!

In my work with couples, the most powerful predictor of compatibility or conflict is how they make each other feel. I urge my single clients to ask themselves only two questions about someone they're dating: How do you feel when you're with that person? And how does he or she make you feel about yourself? If people honored this intuitive sense, they would make much wiser choices.

I believe that temperament solves the mystery of romantic chemistry. Physical attraction alone can be fleeting—it can evaporate in the first few minutes of conversation if you find you have nothing in common. Lasting chemistry goes deeper: it's a feeling of ease coupled with promise. You feel terrific because you feel accepted *and* excited.

In my clinical practice with men, women, and couples, and in my lectures and discussions with singles groups, I've determined that men and women connect with each other on the basis of a meeting of their emotions and comfort zones. We are drawn to people who don't drive us out of our emotional comfort zone. But that's only half of the equation. If a man makes a woman feel too comfortable, he's likely to become a friend, not a lover, because the other part of the chemical equation is excitement. He must add something new; he must expand her comfort zone.

The distinctions I'm talking about underscore one of the first laws of relationships. We don't necessarily gravitate to those who just soothe us, or who fit nicely into our emotional comfort zone. We connect with people who bring out behaviors and emotions for which we hunger.

MARRIAGE

There is an old saying, "When a woman marries a man, she hopes he will change. When a man marries a woman, he hopes she won't. They're both disappointed." I present this quote not as a way to illustrate the folly of trying to change the person we love but to underscore both the folly of trying to change a person into someone he is not and the folly of denying our own temperament in order to accommodate someone's expectations.

A key insight that evolves from a knowledge of temperament types is what I call emotional osmosis. Other people's emotions get "into" us—we absorb them. Our boundaries are permeable, meaning that just as outside events can trigger emotions in us, so, too, can the emotions of other people. Consider the "contact high"—a person is smoking marijuana and laughing and a sober person "catches" the high. As laughter is infectious, so are bad moods such as depression.

This concept speaks directly to the codependency issue. Certain types may connect with other types in a very extreme form as a way to regulate their own moods. Unfortunately, "using" other people's emotions, though natural and commonplace, has its own set of risks. When we get into the habit of using others' emotions, we may lose sight of our natural selves. In time, we no longer can discriminate between what is triggered internally and what is triggered externally—our emotional boundaries have crumbled. The seeker, for example, can be so lost in attachment hunger and so fearful of abandonment that she can lose sight of herself.

Couples run aground when they ignore each other's temperament. A woman may be surprised when her teasing over breakfast sparks anger in her husband. A man may feel irritated when his girlfriend won't snap out of a blue mood on a weekend away. Clashing moods are a big reason why intimacy is so difficult. But your mate's moods are likely to have nothing to do with you—she's just being herself, cycling through emotions that are triggered internally. You have to learn that her emotions have nothing to do with you!

For example, the husband who is a discharger may not intend to be abusive toward you. His temperament is partly why you are with him in the first place—he provides a level of intensity and passion that drew you to him. When a couple comes in to see me to explore ways to resolve their fighting, I stay away from simplistic explanations like, "You need to communicate more." Instead, I focus on identifying their true temperaments. When they have a genuine understanding of who they are and who their mate is, we focus on accommodations that will enrich rather than make each person feel compromised. Most husbands and wives find this reassuring. They know that real hope and progress in a marriage is based on mutual acceptance.

Even affairs can be understood by looking at temperament. If we use other people to regulate our emotional states, we will tend to look elsewhere when our mate cannot supply that emotional catalytic force. The seeker husband is the most likely to play around—he craves the thrill of a new romance, even the danger of getting caught. A woman who is a focuser may have an affair as a way to get out of a depression. She is self-medicating herself by distracting herself. These unfortunate solutions are not likely to be employed by people who are aware of the options available to find a comfort zone without being destructive.

Sexuality is another common area of clash and disappointment. Making love is not just an expression of caring and intimacy. Nor is it merely a tension reliever (as so many disgruntled mates declare!). Sex is one of the primary ways we regulate our emotional states. It is an arousal activator. Sex can be threatening (overstimulating) at times, or welcome (arousing, discharging, releasing). When you are in tune with your inner thermostat, you know what effect sex will have on you. When you are comfortable with your emotional rhythms and understand your mate's, it is much less likely that sex will be a battleground or a source of disappointment.

TEMPERAMENT IN THE WORKPLACE

We are just as passionate about work as about love—some of us more so. I am convinced that temperament is a major determinant of comfort, success, and failure in the work arena. Indeed, I believe the key to understanding the phenomenon of work stress and burnout is temperament. I can point out two individuals who work side by side, doing the same job, putting in the same number of hours, with identical stresses and hassles. But one man is a wreck and the other is enjoying himself. The difference usually is their awareness of emotional temperament and how well they accept this factor in themselves and others.

We've spent so much time dealing with stress that we have failed to realize we know little more today than we knew twenty years ago. *Stress* is a catchall term on the front covers of news magazines and included in warnings about heart disease. However, some people, such as seekers, thrive on stress. Others, such as sensors and focusers, may become overwhelmed by too much stress.

In today's working world, we increasingly see signs of emotional deadening. People appear exhausted, emotionally overloaded, and emotionally detached. Burnout, when the emotional cost of our efforts is greater than the rewards, leads to emotional meltdown. At its core, burnout is a result of overloaded brain chemistry. It is a direct result of self-deception or the denial of one's temperament.

Awareness of your emotional makeup is essential to choosing the right career. Down the line, it dictates your work style, including how you delegate responsibility and how you manage others. Show me a boss who can manage his own moods and I will show you someone who understands his subordinates' moods as well.

Unfortunately, when I conduct seminars for executives and managers, I find that the vast majority have a rather anemic understanding of their own temperament. They also treat their subordinates as though they were all the same. They rarely ask themselves, "What is the emotional makeup of my subordinates? Why am I having such difficulty with them?"

They are unaware of the ways in which temperaments mesh or clash with each other. Yet blending is probably the most essential facet of a successful organization. Managing a group or a company is not simply about leadership skills but more specifically about a leader's obligation to acknowledge the nature of each individual and bring out the best in each person. For example, the discharger boss can help her sensor assistant feel less intimidated by saying, "Hey, that's just me. When I get upset, don't take it personally."

Temperament is also pivotal in ambition. When we talk about drive or motivation in a career, we usually think in terms of a mindset, a way of thinking that conscious resolve is what determines ambition. But there's an emotional dimension as well. Our emotions influence both our mental and physical energy. When we speak of drive and motivation at work, we are actually making a statement about the intensity and direction of our emotions.

Every group, organization, even army, has vulnerabilities that prevent them from doing their best. It is the identification and understanding of vulnerabilities that make for success whether it's identifying them in your employees or in yourself. To bring out the best in someone means to also understand what *limits* the best from taking place. A chain is only as strong as its weakest link. Vulnerabilities can be understood by learning about temperament, both yours and those around you. My promise in this book is that by identifying your temperament, you will learn to work around your emotional vulnerabilities, maximize your strengths, and live life at work in a new and broader comfort zone.

OUR GOAL: HONORING OUR TEMPERAMENT

Our temperament is ultimately a mood forecaster—it predicts how our emotions reveal themselves over time. It not only tells us why we feel the way we do but it can predict how we will feel in all of life's critical arenas including work and love relationships. Temperament predicts life's pains as well as its joys. It tells us where and how to find emotional relief and inner peace. Our personality naturally does evolve as we go through life's experiences, but the choices we make, the reactions we have, are all shaped by innate factors. We still have freedom of choice, but greater freedom comes from a vivid awareness of our natural self, and the courage to accept and honor our temperament.

Honoring our temperament creates an honest self-image; this honesty forms the foundation for confidence. It's one thing to glibly speak about self-esteem builders to momentarily feel more confident, but our emotions don't lie and they don't allow themselves to fall prey to mental sleight of hand—they are too powerful for that. I promise you that whichever type you are, you will be embarking on a journey of self-discovery that will be liberating.

AS YOU READ ON

As I mentioned earlier, many of us think we are one temperament type and are actually another beneath our learned "disguise." For example, the person who is shy and sensitive may have learned to overcome (i.e., deny) her shyness and may truly believe she is a different temperament type. Read each chapter not only to discover more about yourself but to discover more about those in your personal and work life.

At the conclusion of each chapter, take the quiz. Do this even if you are convinced you are a particular type. By taking all the quizzes, you may discover that while dominant in one temperament type, you also possess many traits of another temperament. This information is essential in learning to modulate your emotions.

PART TWO

RECOGNIZING YOUR
INNATE EMOTIONAL TYPE

Chapter 5

SENSORS: FROM ANXIETY TO COURAGE

SHERRY IS A MARKETING EXECUTIVE in the competitive, fast-changing computer software industry. She heads a department of sixteen people, meets daily with other hard-driving department heads, and invariably holds her own. She loves and hates her work at the same time. Her career takes a heavy toll on her.

I met Sherry when she came to see me for what she described as a premature midlife crisis. At thirty-three, she already felt burned out. She was crying and mentally exhausted, fearful that she would fall behind and no longer be considered a player in her industry.

She told me about her childhood and adolescence—her shyness, hypersensitivity, timidity in new situations—all telltale signs of the sensor. Her parents had pushed her to be more outgoing, chiding her and teasing her when she was fearful. Consequently, Sherry had forced herself to be outgoing and to act confident in spite of her inner feelings, which were quite the opposite.

As an adult, she still feels nervous in groups, although she plunges ahead into the crowd. When asked how she feels in stressful situations, Sherry listed the sensor's signs of physiological overarousal: flushing, blushing, sweating, and difficulty in breathing. She confessed she secretly viewed herself as scared rather than courageous.

When I first saw Sherry, she had been taking Prozac, the antidepressant, for three months. It was no wonder her internist had prescribed it: when she saw him, she had all the classic signs of an agitated depression including early waking, loss of appetite, forgetfulness, a growing disinterest in activities that once had been exciting and stimulating. I told Sherry the Prozac was prescribed because she had pushed herself into a seeming depressive state because of her exhaustion. That's why it appeared to help her for a brief time. But I also suggested to her that what she called depression was really a by-product or *secondary* reaction to a more basic dilemma—anxiety. I explained that unrelenting anxiety can cause a kind of pseudodepression, making her feel dispirited and exhausted.

"I'm not exhausted—I'm depressed," she insisted. "How can I be exhausted when I'm in bed by ten almost every night?" I explained that she was exhausted by an entire lifetime spent denying who she was and fighting her temperament. When I described what I felt was her real or underlying temperament—that of a sensor—Sherry grudgingly recognized the inner qualities, but quickly added that she was getting over these traits. She really was an achiever. "I'm very aggressive, and I'm challenged by risks. I don't run from them!" she protested.

Those qualities were also part of her identity, but I explained that she was denying more basic predispositions. She had created a life characterized by grinding ambition and pressure to perform. Her refusal to respect her genuine emotions had thrown her into a chronic state of overarousal that was revealing itself, finally, in exhaustion. If she were to set aside her denial, Sherry would see that being a sensor did not preclude assertion, ambition, and drive, but that these traits must be integrated with her more basic emotional style. It is not her temperament that is exhausting her but her denial. As she gradually came to understand her temperament, she found that acknowledging it would in no way hinder her ambitions; rather it enhanced her ability to get what she wanted.

My patient Alan is a shy and reserved man who generally feels comfortable with himself. At times, he secretly regrets he isn't tougher, but he wisely has made his natural tendency to avoid social confrontations work for him rather than against him.

Attracted to the movie industry, after being a film buff in college, Alan decided to become an entertainment attorney. He does not bring in new business through social hustling. Alan excels in working out the incredibly complex contracts his firm arranges between actors and movie studios. His role requires little social involvement beyond working with his immediate staff, which exactly suits his temperament.

I met Alan when he entered marital counseling with his wife, Elana. She was unhappy because she felt that, "With all his brains and talent, he's not living up to his potential." What Elana meant was, he should be more successful and, frankly, should make more money. Dynamic and vivacious, Elana had seemed to be the perfect counterpoint to Alan. He had sensed that she would bring social involvement into his life and compensate for his natural reserve. Whereas he was slow to make friends, she connected right away. Whereas he had difficulty being aggressive and political in his firm, she was the power behind the throne, counseling him on when and how to make power plays and get the credit (and profit share) he deserved. She was savvy and her advice worked, as Alan readily conceded.

But three years into their marriage, Alan became increasingly frustrated with, and resistant to, Elana's attempts to mold him and shape him into someone else. "I have to do it at my own pace," he kept insisting. Over dinner at a restaurant, he had suddenly hissed, "You should have married Ted Turner!" in response to Elana pointedly telling him her friend's husband had just made partner at a competing law firm.

Alan felt inadequate in the face of her criticism. His anxiety and undermined self-confidence made him withdraw from his wife, both emotionally and physically. They were in crisis, snapping at each other, making constant digs, agreeing on truces only to argue again hours later. In public, they were going through the motions of playing the happy couple while privately they worried about divorce.

During the course of therapy, Elana recognized she was urging her husband to deny who he was. She acknowledged his natural temperament and how his emotional comfort zone differed from hers. I suggested to Elana that she refocus on accepting her husband, on loving him and meeting his needs for support and reassurance. Elana said she would move heaven and earth to save her marriage. She admitted that the disruption in her marriage was starting to frighten her.

Relationships as well as self-esteem must be built on a foundation of honesty and acceptance. You must accept who you are, accept who the other person is, know what you cannot change about yourselves, and perhaps most importantly, know what you *should not* change!

THE SENSITIVE TEMPERAMENT

To be sensitive, or easily aroused and highly reactive, is a mixed blessing. On the positive side, the sensor temperament type is perceptive, empathetic, even soulful and sensual. Sensors are aware of every nuance of mood in people around them. The sensitive person is more emotionally intense than others without such fine-tuned antennae.

Sensors often feel too much and become overwhelmed. They are predisposed to anxiety. Life can be too intense, too painful—there are far too many ups and downs. People inclined to emotional sensitivity often feel touchy, high strung, tense, nervous, anxious.

The sensor is the most common temperament type. Many of you are sensors, yet you may not recognize yourself. It is not only the most common emotional type but also the type with the most self-loathing and denial. Who wants to admit they are prone to feeling anxious and scared?

As a sensor, when you deny or even despise your nature, you are a boon to the mental health profession and the drug industry—legal and illegal. When too uncomfortable with your emotionality, you will drink, take drugs, or attend endless therapy and recovery groups. You will spend your entire life in search of relief from anxiety, which to you, means trying to fashion another personality, acting as if you're more socially confident, as if you don't feel as deeply as you do. Some of what you do may help you, but sensors pay an enormous toll in pain along the way.

Of all the patients who walk into my office, the ones who need to be there the least are sensors. Every therapist sees the sensor

and really wants to say, "You're okay just the way you are."
Sensors are not defective or dysfunctional; they are simply more
emotional than most other people. The sensor nature might be
viewed as a plus. Don't people want to be more feeling, more
aware? However, the sensor would probably trade his thin skin
for a thick hide in the wink of an eye.

Because you are so vulnerable to other people's opinions if
you are a sensor, your worst fear is rejection. You care deeply
about what other people think of you, and you're likely to try to
be what you think other people want you to be, and to say what
you think they want to hear. In situations such as cocktail parties, you feel uncomfortable because there are too many people
to impress. Your need to be liked and accepted powerfully
shapes all that you do. You can be emotionally devastated by
romantic rejection, divorce, or getting fired from a job.

Because you're prone to becoming embarrassed by blushing,
sweating, or getting nervous in front of others, you tend to
avoid calling attention to yourself. You're a security-driven temperament; you're most comfortable with what's familiar. When
you're on your own turf, you're more relaxed and more open to
other people. You tend to stick close to home and build your life
around a few close friends and your family. When you feel
criticized or insecure, you can be overly needy, dependent, thin-
skinned, moody. Conversely, when you're sure of someone's
love and respect, you're a kind-hearted friend, a devoted mate,
a terrific employee or boss.

Your infant and early childhood behavior supplies important
clues to your innate temperament type; it can be quite helpful to
ask your mother and father what you were like. As an infant,
you were probably highly reactive to your physical environment. Sensors are not the easiest babies. Your mother will likely
recall that you demanded a lot of attention and love, abundant
physical soothing. Sensors usually exhibit an exaggerated need
for attachment. You are biochemically wired to be high strung
and fearful, and you may have needed lots of comforting to feel
secure.

You may have been a polite, obedient child, timid and shy,
preferring to stay close to home. You may recall having one best
friend at a time rather than a group of playmates. When you

were a teenager, you may remember feeling awkwardly self-conscious; you may have drifted into a group of disaffected, alienated teens. You may have experimented with drugs—they're a big temptation to the sensitive sensor teen who wants to blunt her feelings. As a child, if your needs for security and attachment were not met, you may, as an adult, be struggling with emotional neediness and insecurity. If your needs for reassurance were met, you're more fortunate—you're more likely to be a caring and resilient adult.

MISLEADING MESSAGES

From early childhood, you were likely distanced from your true feelings by misleading messages and advice you got from your parents, teachers, and other children. If you're a sensor, you were probably told: "There's nothing to be afraid of—look—Kathy's not scared." "Stop acting shy." As you got older, you were probably told to "toughen up." You may have been teased or taunted for your sensitivity; thus, you learned to hate it and hide it.

It's important to understand that the misleading advice virtually all of us have received about our emotions leads to deep self-loathing. As an adult, you may have sought some form of assertion training to overcome your social anxieties. Assertion training—confidence building, affirmations, role playing, confrontation practice, ways to stick up for yourself—is based on the idea that you learned maladaptive ways of behaving and all you need to do is learn more successful ones. But when you find you still feel the same inner distress and nervousness even after you "graduate" from assertion training, your failure to change your feelings becomes a confirmation of your worst fears. There is something wrong with you: you must be deficient, cowardly, inept.

Suppose you sought therapy. You and your therapist could have spent a year, or years, exploring the childhood causes of your sensitivity or predisposition to anxiety. All this didn't make a dent in the way you still respond to life, but now you have a false reality. You may resent your parents causing your dysfunctional behavior and wounds to your inner child. And you may bring these linkages, which in terms of causing your emotional responses may be false, into your life today: "I'm intimidated by my wife because she's so like my overbearing mother." Or, "I'm nervous around my boss because he reminds me of my disapproving and domineering father."

It's true that you may have learned from early experiences and may be transferring these learned reactions onto contemporary figures in your life. But it's more likely that you may have responded to both childhood and current personalities because your temperament is biologically programmed to respond in a particular way! Again, it's not your fault and it's not your parents' fault—it's just the way you're wired! Rediscovering our true emotional character requires cutting through lifelong denial and learned disguises. What's your reward for peeling off these layers and masks? Genuine self-acceptance.

THE SENSOR'S NATURAL SELF

LOW THRESHOLD OF AROUSAL

Sensors have a low threshold of arousal. If you're a sensor, you are easily aroused and highly reactive to external stimulation. On the positive side, you're sensitive, emotionally alive, and able to empathize with others. Unfortunately, your easily triggered arousal is often internally interpreted or labeled as anxiety with all of its negative connotations. When mild, this arousal is experienced as a vague uneasiness. When moderate, as tension or anxiety. When intense, as distress, even terror.

ACTION TENDENCY: INTROVERTED/HARM AVOIDANCE

The physiological arousal (interpreted as threat) predictably causes the sensor to back away from the arousal trigger, to avoid the perceived threat. As you withdraw from the perceived threat, your arousal diminishes, and you feel relieved. This sequence of reactions—arousal plus avoidance—characterizes the temperament of the sensor.

We all have a harm avoidance mechanism in us—it's adaptive; it protects us from danger. It's called the fight or flight mechanism. In the face of perceived danger, our body gets prepared to either run like hell or stand and fight like hell. But if you're a sensor, flight, or harm avoidance, is the dominant action tendency toward behavior dynamic, coloring your everyday life choices, experiences, and responses.

There are many studies on children that identify them as sensors by their earliest responses. When they are overaroused by other people, or by new situations, they instinctively pull away. They are shy and reticent children. In one study by Alexander Thomas and Stella Chess where they observed children at play and relating to adults, they identified 15 percent of the children as "slow to warm up." These children were emotionally and physically more guarded than other children.

In many ways the sensor is the classic introvert. In studies of the brain activity of introverts, researchers found that these seemingly tranquil and reserved people typically are in a state of high cortical or brain arousal—they are anything but placid inside. Their normal inner arousal is high. Not surprisingly, external stimuli that would not phase another temperament type push the introvert over the edge. Because of his typically high level of arousal and his low threshold, he is easily overloaded and overwhelmed.

We see that the sensor's instinctive action tendency is withdrawal from, or avoidance of, whatever triggers arousal. However, the solution to this distress is the opposite of the instinct to run away.

THE BIOCHEMISTRY OF THE SENSOR

I suggested that the brain chemistry of each temperament type is typically governed or dominated by a particular neurotransmitter. And the primary emotional dilemma of the sensor is anxiety. The more we learn about antianxiety drugs and how they work, the more we can work backward and speculate about the biochemistry of anxiety and the biochemistry of the sensor. For sensors, research points to the importance of the neurotransmitter or chemical messenger GABA (gamma-aminobutyric acid).

Antianxiety drugs are effective because they copy or mimic the receptors for GABA. The group of tranquilizers called benzodiazepines inhibits the receptors for GABA. By making these receptors less reactive, less likely to "soak up" GABA, more GABA flows through our neurons. Tranquilizers open the floodgates for GABA to flow.

The more GABA is flowing, the less likely it is that our autonomic nervous system will be triggered, that is, we don't get anxious. Conversely, the less GABA is flowing, the more anxiety we experience. When we're in a state of too little GABA, first our central nervous system is aroused, then our autonomic nervous system, which triggers familiar signals such as sweating, heavier breathing, and physical tension. These are the telltale signs of the sensor. It follows, then, that the anxiety-prone sensor has lower-than-average levels of GABA.

Like all antianxiety drugs, alcohol is a central nervous system depressant, or sedative. Like antianxiety drugs, alcohol increases the amount of GABA in the brain—that's why it feels so good initially. Research on alcoholism parallels the GABA link to the sensor's biochemistry. Alcoholism studies indicate that the sons of alcoholics are born with lower levels of GABA. *They're biologically predisposed to feeling tense.* They are prone to drinking as a way to *increase* the amount of GABA in the brain, to ease their tension and feel better, happier, at least initially. Whether they're aware of it or not, these alcoholics who are born with low levels of GABA are medicating themselves, using alcohol to compensate for inherited factors in their brain biochemistry.

Similarly, if you're a sensor, you are likely to turn to alcohol to take that rough edge off of life. In biochemical terms, you're adding alcohol to your "brain soup" to compensate for deficiencies of GABA.

THE GIFT OF SENSITIVITY

Alison writes children's books. She works in a studio in the middle of her garden. She is deeply happy with her husband and their two young daughters. Alison is grateful for her flourishing career and family, especially when she thinks about her own painful and fearful childhood.

Alison would have you believe that her success comes from her ability to capture a child's sense of wonderment and innocence. While that may be how she explains her mental state during the creative act, something else is fueling her generous talent. Alison is able to draw on the positive aspects of her temperament, especially her empathy.

As a child and teenager, she was highly emotional. When happy events occurred, she was more than happy—she was ecstatic. When she was fearful or nervous in the face of novel situations, such as the first day of school or giving an oral book report in front of her classmates, Alison would break down in tears or throw up. When she was eight, her worried parents took the advice of a child psychologist and vigilantly monitored her moods. They tried to teach her "appropriate" responses, and would tell her, "Calm down," "Don't get upset," "Be brave— I'm right here with you." This did help Alison. And by not allowing her to stay home from school with nervous stomach, by firmly insisting that she go to parties and take dance classes, Alison did become desensitized to, and ultimately comfortable in, situations that had terrified her.

Alison's parents helped to expand the range of experience she could handle: they helped their daughter to expand her emotional comfort zone. Of equal importance, they gave her consistent love and acceptance. Their message was: "You're nervous. Let's learn how to cope with it." Alison always knew she could go to them for solace and reassurance.

As a result, Alison acknowledged and respected her emotionality from childhood. She accepted that she was different from other kids. As an adult, she chose a career she could do in the security and familiarity of her own home, one requiring little interaction with strangers. She consciously married a more outgoing man. They have a terrific marriage because they cherish their differences.

If Alison had had different parents, she might have been pushed to blunt her gift—her fine-tuned and high-strung nature. She would, in essence, have destroyed the very qualities that make her an imaginative author. If Alison's parents had discouraged her from being autonomous and independent, if they had given in to her tendency to withdraw, she may have become a fearful, indecisive, uncertain adult. Luckily, Alison got the balance of reassurance and prodding the sensor needs.

The sensor who feels secure and appreciated can utilize his or her special gifts of perception, empathy, and emotionality to be successful in almost any field—from the shop owner who builds a loyal clientele through her warmth and caring, to the middle manager who brings out the best in his staff through listening and encouraging his people, to the writer, engineer, inventor, or artist who draws on his intuitive creativity to find new solutions, new connections, new ways of seeing and expressing. The key to drawing on your ample sensor gifts is understanding the requirements of your temperament.

THE DARK SIDE OF THE SENSOR: ANXIETY

When too much arousal is experienced, the sensor is often diagnosed as having an anxiety condition: apprehension or fearfulness as a chronic emotional state. In varying degrees, anxiety is revealed by shakiness, muscle tension, restlessness, sweating, dry mouth, flushed feelings, breathing difficulty, and keyed-up feelings. Other symptoms are concentrating difficulties, hypervigilance to one's surroundings, and sleeping difficulties. The umbrella term is *nervousness*.

But I hasten to add that calling the sensor an anxious personality doesn't do him justice. Yet this is how many sensors describe themselves. Whenever they feel too much, they are urged by doctors, mental health people, and others to take a tranquilizer. Or they are told, "You're too nervous, too uptight, too emotional." People may be sympathetic, but also hope they'll get a grip on themselves or toughen up.

The sensor is ill served by patronizing suggestions such as, "Don't be so nervous." The myth that we can be free of anxiety is false and does a lot of damage. We are becoming increasingly sophisticated about anxiety and how commonplace it is, yet we're told that it can and should be overcome. Suggestions to relax may help break the anxiety circuit for other temperament types, but when they fail the sensor, he ends up feeling worse. He feels bad about feeling bad.

Anxiety without a good reason is seen as maladaptive. The myths of normalcy and uniformity tell the anxious sensor that something is wrong with him. For too many men and women, being a sensor means a lifetime of feeling slightly defective. If we succeed, we think we did in spite of having something wrong with us.

The intensity of being a sensor can be terribly taxing. I remember speaking to Joan, a young patient of mine who is a warm and insightful grade-school teacher. She was unhappy because she is often nervous around men. When I asked her if she would prefer feeling nothing, she actually considered the possibility for a long, long moment. I was amazed!

"How could you even consider not feeling anything?" I asked. She explained that her emotions cost too much, she was in too much pain, and she was fed up with being a "nervous Nellie." I told her I thought she was forgetting all the good things that come out of her temperament, and that she was comparing herself to others whether she recognized it or not.

"What would it be like if everyone felt as intensely as you do?" I asked. She thought a while and said, "Maybe that would be easier." She understood what I was getting at. Most of our emotions take on their positive or negative coloring not because of their physiological qualities but because of the value judgments we learn to make about them.

Panic Attacks and Phobias

Even when their outer environment is nonthreatening, sensors are prone to inner restlessness. In the extreme, they feel panic attacks that seem to come out of nowhere. This free-floating anxiety can attach to nothing. Sensors can be sitting, reading a good book, or watching television, and suddenly, a vague and gnawing discomfort creeps into their conscious awareness. Idly, or fearfully, they begin to wonder what triggered it. By doing this, they compound and prolong their discomfort—we can always find something to worry about.

The cause of this distress is simply that there is a precipitous drop in the threshold of arousal. This is purely biological and can't be accounted for. It won't kill you, and it won't cause a heart attack, but nonetheless it is scary. Without warning, sensors suddenly feel an increase in arousal: heavy breathing, sweating, dizziness. They focus on these signs, thus magnifying them. Anything associated with the panic attack's onset now becomes scary. The sensor feels driven to avoid that situation. For example, a woman who experiences a panic attack on the freeway can become freeway phobic. Tranquilizers will soothe her, but she still won't want to drive on the freeway.

THE DISGUISED SENSOR

I've described a rather predictable picture of sensors. You prefer quiet evenings at home with your family to loud parties or nightclubs. You're loyal rather than ruthless, followers rather than leaders, loners rather than joiners of social groups. You prefer a job that is stable and secure. You don't job hop or fight your way to the top at the expense of other people. And you certainly don't become salespeople . . . or do you?

The point is that you can throw out the rules. Many sensors ignore their fears and lead, risk, socialize, and compete with the most thick-skinned and outgoing of the pack. The sensor is very likely to be found behaving in what therapists call a *counterphobic* manner, rushing into that which they fear.

Ambition can be perfectly natural for the sensor. Your temperament does not dictate a life spent in the shadows or being timid. If you begin from a foundation of self-acceptance, you can be dynamic leaders. The unaware counterphobic sensor, however, diverts untold creative energy into masking secret fears, self-loathing, and denial.

I would like to have a dime for every sensor who becomes a power in her profession by virtue of her ambitions and dreams, yet is still prey to hypersensitivity and emotional upheavals. When sensors come in for counseling for stress, burnout, depression, or midlife confusion, I sometimes ask them, "Why don't you consider changing professions, or dropping out, scaling down, cashing it all in and moving to the country?" Invariably, they answer, "Not on your life! I just want to be more comfortable doing what I'm doing."

Nine times out of ten, what these ambitious sensors want from therapy is for me to show them how to toss out the negatives of their temperament and keep the positives. They're operating on the myth of control; they want to simply pick and choose their emotions. And they're used to getting much of what they want. I often meet stubborn resistance when I tell them that I can help them learn to master their emotional life, but only if they're willing to understand, accept, and integrate the bad with the good.

I explain that, as sensors, if they learn how their temperament actually functions—what triggers their emotions—they can become more comfortable in their pressured careers, and probably can achieve more success with less straining and distress. They can break through the barriers that puzzle them and realize their full potential

THE GENDER CHASM

The woman sensor can be loved and admired for her tenderness. The male sensor can be disparaged as a wimp. The woman is demure; the man is unassuming. The woman is devoted; the man is dependent. The woman is feminine; the man is weak. Depending on the gender politics of who's doing the judging, there can be a brutal double standard when it comes to sensors. With this temperament type, it's more than a gender gap—it's a gender chasm.

Thus, the male sensor is likely to feel chronic low self-esteem. He's much more likely than the woman sensor to buy into the myths of good and bad and control. Chances are, he'll start from an early age to disguise his true temperament. Although it may be true that we criticize the man who is seemingly without feelings as being cut off or too macho, the man who is sensitive and emotional is often seen as soft. Even those who value the sensitive male may, deep down, judge him as weak, especially if he's sensitive without a cause—his art, his writing, his social cause, his recovery group. The word that haunts the male sensor is *wimp*.

The sensitive woman, in contrast, is understood, forgiven,

even admired for her compassion, her emotional nature. It's okay for a woman to talk about being scared or emotional. Women are not only socially conditioned to accept their more emotional nature but biochemistry research shows they are hormonally more emotional than men.

This cultural acceptance allows the female sensor to be more accepting of herself than the male sensor. She does not judge herself as harshly for being anxious or vulnerable. But it's no secret that women, as well as men, have to compete and fend for themselves in an increasingly aggressive world. The numbers of women now in the work force are finally resulting in some "feminization" of the rules of the game, that is, in some contexts there is more approval for an expressive emotional style. But no matter what the context or the challenge, the sensor's task, male or female, is to learn to expand his or her emotional comfort zone so the innate withdrawal tendency does not interfere with the sensor's dreams.

THE SENSOR IN RELATIONSHIPS

ROMANTIC CHEMISTRY

As we discussed in chapter 4, romantic chemistry is a two-part equation. We are drawn to people who don't drive us out of our emotional comfort zone; we feel comfortable with them. The other part of the chemical equation is a promise that a partner will help us expand our comfort zone. Sensors are drawn to people who make them feel not only comfortable but also excited. For example, for the sensitive, anxious sensor, a desirable romantic partner is one who makes the sensor not just nonthreatened but more courageous and spontaneous. If you're a sensor, your deep desire is for a mate who will enhance your life, complement your nature, and bring you confidence.

You might think you would choose someone reassuring, unassuming, reserved. Someone safe. Maybe someone just like yourself—another sensor. However, that's rarely the kind of person with whom sensors fall in love! Most sensors choose best friends, lovers, and spouses who are outgoing, social, easygoing, and lively. Being with other sensors only compounds your own fears. Worse, if you're a sensor who secretly dislikes the way you are, you certainly won't admire your emotional twin.

Two sensors—like two of any temperament—can bring out the worst in each other. You exacerbate the worst of each other's temperaments. When a sensor feels anxious, the partner sensor, aware of every emotional cue, will pick up on it right away. Dueling anxieties are the result. Thus, there is truth in saying opposites attract. In fact, a sensor may prefer a seeker who will be stimulating and will enliven things. If you are a sensor, you may want to find someone courageous who will bring out that same quality in yourself. For this reason, the ideal chemistry for the sensor is a combination of a comforter and a catalyst for courage.

To the sensor, every affair is serious. You cannot stand the insecurity of dating. You are slow to warm up to someone. You behave in a courteous, reserved manner until you're sure of your potential partner's interest. You need affection and acceptance in order to open up. Once you open up, you will be attentive—sometimes too intensely, too soon. Your fear of rejection and need for security and certainty may make you push too fast toward a commitment. You may feel that you have scared away potential partners in the past by moving too fast.

As a sensor, with your need for home, family, and stability, you can be an ideal mate. The married sensor who feels accepted and secure is faithful and devoted. You feel most comfortable close to home with your family and a few close friends. You may rely on your mate to take the lead in your social life.

CONFLICT IN RELATIONSHIPS

Your emotional sensitivity and ability to empathize can cause serious problems in a marriage. The sensor is very susceptible to codependency, that is, losing yourself in your partner. You "feel into" your mate and lose touch with your own boundaries. The danger is that you can be so afraid to displease your mate that you compromise your own goals and values. Your own needs go unvoiced while you anticipate your partner's every need. Sensors work hard to keep a marriage together, often at their own expense; it is easy to take advantage of a sensor mate.

In the absence of acceptance, you can become quite unhappy with almost any partner. Life becomes an ongoing dangerous situation. You become impossible to live with. Everything your partner does or says sparks an overreaction. You're hurt, sullen, touchy, and moody. You may invite nagging with your passivity and resistance. All you need is reassurance.

Sadly, as with any emotional type, there are sensors who have given up on love. Perhaps you've been betrayed, walked on, abandoned, and you feel you lack the resilience to try again. You are now your only trusted companion. You are no longer looking for any comfort from others; you just want to be left alone. You can no longer trust a lover's devotion. Being with someone is not soothing—it's threatening. All that relationships mean to you is conflict, discordance, and disruption. No matter how kind or reassuring someone is, you can't bring yourself to trust his commitment. The sensor is more at risk to these feelings than any of the other three temperament types. I promise that when you gain a working knowledge of your temperament and how to orchestrate your emotional highs and lows, you'll gain the emotional self-confidence to risk loving someone again.

FRIENDSHIPS

The sensor typically establishes friendships in a slower and more cautious manner than others. Wary of possible threats, she implicitly requires that others prove their trustworthiness. When trust is established, the sensor may be more steadfast and loyal than others are. When a companionship bond has been established, there is often no real evidence that one is a sensor; such emotions are not aroused because of the sense of safety.

THE SENSOR PARENT

As a sensor, you're likely to be a caring, attentive parent; you build your life around home and family. You may, however, find that you're oversensitive to your children's needs. You need to encourage autonomy and independence in your children, who, given their genetic inheritance, are likely to be sensors as well. You need to be constantly vigilant not to overprotect your children because of your own anxious concerns, and not to scare your children with your own fears. A balance of reassurance and prodding is the parental style that should work best for you.

THE SENSOR AT WORK

Sensors often feel they succeed in spite of their nature. Because aggressiveness is so highly touted as a pivotal trait of success, you often secretly believe you succeed in spite of your inner fears. Remember, left to your own devices, you're a turtle— your visceral impulse is to withdraw into your shell. Job interviews, cold sales calls, and asking for a raise put you through torment.

In the work arena, the ambitious counterphobic sensor can be as successful as anyone else, but you are the most vulnerable of the four types to the demands and pressures of a striving career. Your low threshold of arousal is repeatedly battered except in the most menial or undemanding jobs. What's more, when you settle into a comfortable routine, you're likely to bounce yourself right out of it, because, typically, you have learned to equate stress with progress, which explains why sensors are often driven into chronic tension and anxiety.

THE SENSOR EMPLOYEE

The employee sensor works best in a secure atmosphere where there is little turnover in staff. You maintain a polite reserve until you know people and feel secure of their respect. You are most comfortable with a defined work role and routine. Sensitive to the emotions of your coworkers, you help to build a family atmosphere and staff loyalty by sympathizing and counseling coworkers on their personal problems and aspirations.

Fearful of negative evaluation by others, you may put in long hours to meet deadlines and quotas. Again, your fear of confrontation and your tendency to be unassuming can make you take a backseat to other employees. When you're criticized in an overall context of respect and appreciation, you're open to criticism and will work hard to improve. But you will suffer emotional stress, even physical problems, if you're saddled with a boss who criticizes you harshly or unfairly; you're liable to quit abruptly to escape from such a work environment. But if you are teamed up with a boss or manager who gives you the right combination of reassurance and prodding, you work creatively and confidently.

THE SENSOR BOSS

If you're a sensor boss, you've likely gotten where you are by pushing yourself out of your comfort zone—through aggressive behavior that goes against your innate tendencies. Or you may have attached yourself to a mentor who has brought you up the ladder behind him or her. In either case, once you are in a position where you can make some of the rules, you'll surround yourself with a loyal team of people you know and trust. You'll likely have on your team at least one or two more outgoing subordinates to whom you can delegate the more socially demanding tasks. Consciously or unconsciously, the sensor boss almost without exception has a right-hand assistant who is warm, good with strangers, vivacious, even aggressive—someone who feels comfortable doing what makes the sensor boss uncomfortable.

You're most comfortable on your own turf, in your office. In meetings you'll set the agenda ahead of time, but leave the presentations and debating to others. You avoid public speaking when you can; when it's unavoidable, you write, rehearse thoroughly, dread the speech for days beforehand, and stick closely to your notes. Of course, like any other anxiety-producing situation, the sensor who is required to give frequent talks to groups will become desensitized, and eventually will do well at public speaking.

THE DISGUISED SENSOR AT WORK

Barbara is a department head in a state government bureau. Outwardly, she is cool and calm to the point that her associates had dubbed her the "ice queen." No one ever would have believed she was so emotionally reactive under that exterior, but she was. Barbara is one of the millions of sensors who disguise their sensitivity, and carefully mimic a cool professional demeanor.

She entered therapy because of relationship conflicts. I was aware that she was overworked and somewhat burned out. Her exhaustion and agitated depression, not surprisingly, were putting a damper on dating. Barbara either became impatient if she didn't feel immediate chemistry, or she became overly anxious when she liked the man and feared her interest would not be reciprocated. She was going through hellish days and nights waiting for men to phone: "Men I've only been out with once— I'm driving myself nuts over sheer strangers!" she confided.

My prescription for her was to work on displaying her vulnerability and fears both on dates and at her office—behaving in a more genuine manner. I suggested that she begin to communicate a sense of self-acceptance. I reassured her that it would be contagious and would not undermine her authority. She did, at first anxiously and fearfully, and she was delighted to find that, as her frosty demeanor melted, her colleagues melted as well. She felt she managed her staff better and experienced less stress during her workday.

Previously she had always declined her colleagues' invitations to go to a local watering hole for happy hour after work. She was afraid her associates would discover how vulnerable and anxious she was underneath her professional mask. Now she started going. She became friends with a group of her peers and her social life blossomed. The important message is that Barbara did not change inside. What changed was that she began behaving in a more genuine manner.

FALSE PATHS TO EMOTIONAL RELIEF

In their search for emotional relief, sensors are prone to particular false paths, including avoiding all anxiety-provoking situations, substance abuse, and becoming emotionally numb. I believe that the worst thing a sensor can do is establish too narrow a comfort zone, limiting life to a range of interests, activities, and endeavors that are so safe you never really feel overaroused. If this rings true to you, you're cheating yourself of some of life's more rewarding complexities. I am aware that this is a value judgment. Everyone doesn't have to become a great psychological navigator, always exploring new territories, always probing into the unknown. But I am saying that choosing safety and comfort should be your choice and not your only perceived solution to your emotional sensitivity.

Too often there are sensors who, very early in their lives, decide that their temperament has sentenced them to a particular choice. The shy person, for example, my conclude, "I'm just not a people person." If you are like this, you need to realize that it's not people who scare you but the newness of people and their potential power to hurt you by criticism and rejection. You may have decided you're not a social person solely on the basis of feeling overaroused in new situations. So you learn the behavior pattern of retreat. That's a bad situation—you protect yourself, but you are isolated.

ALCOHOL AND DRUGS

Perhaps the most common method of self-regulation for the sensor is to ingest some substance that momentarily raises your threshold or blunts some of the pain of a lowered threshold. Alcohol is probably the most common of all soothing agents for the sensor. Because of its effect on the neurotransmitter GABA, it slightly raises your threshold of arousal, and softens the negative tone of that arousal. It smoothes you out . . . or seems to. All it really does is tone down your anxiety. The initial effect on the sensor is quite positive—you become more social and outgoing. Yet, ultimately, alcohol can render you depressed, out of touch with yourself, even remorseful and ashamed the morning after you were the life of the party. That initial glow of well-being and social confidence can be quite seductive to the sensor. It follows that, as a direct consequence of temperament, sensors run a higher-than-average risk of alcoholism.

The soothing effect of alcohol comes in the form of prescription pills, as well—a rainbow assortment. However, antianxiety drugs don't work as effectively as their proponents would have you believe. They may momentarily raise your threshold, but they can also freeze your threshold, that is, you can become dependent on the pills' effect to make you feel better—or feel less—and you can lose your ability to manage your threshold on your own. When people are on long-term, daily tranquilizers, they often come to feel that they're defective, mentally or emotionally ill, unable to cope with life without their chemical crutch. They are disempowered and the damage to their self-esteem should be recognized.

And, too, perhaps, being dependent on a particular drug wouldn't be so detrimental if drugs were more advanced—that is, without the side effects—but many of them are more toxic and more addictive than drug companies or doctors let you know. I am not against drugs in all cases, but I do believe you should know why and how drugs work. You should realize you are using chemicals to alter internal chemical activity that is probably okay; you don't have an illness that needs medication to cure it.

Of course, there are exceptions. Some sensors have thresholds of arousal that are so low they suffer from chronic, unrelenting anxiety on a daily basis. For these people, short-term courses of antianxiety drugs can be valid and appropriate. The medication subdues their painful emotional reactivity to a tolerable level at which they can then benefit from psychotherapy.

In sum, very little learning comes with drug use. I will explore drugs more in chapter 12. At this point, I can only say they are about as benign as alcohol was thought to be many decades ago. There are many serious side effects from chronic tranquilizer use, not the least of which is a strong potential for addiction. I believe it can be helpful to use them for a few weeks to relieve acute distress. Beyond that time, the dangers usually outweigh the benefits. I issue this warning especially to sensors, since your oversensitivity problem is dramatically but illusorily affected by alcohol and drugs.

NUMBNESS

What happens when you behave in a blindly counterphobic manner, rushing into experiences that overwhelm you? What happens when you ignore the signals of your natural self's threshold of arousal, and act as if you can, by force of will, become someone else? You may find yourself living in a state of chronic and exhausting overarousal, never finding comfort, living in a state of inner chaos. Or you may become emotionally numb.

Sensors who keep subjecting themselves to too much stimulus habituate themselves to overarousal. Over time, you become increasingly numb to your inner feelings. Your emotions become blunted. Whereas you used to feel too much, you now feel nothing; you feel anesthetized. You appear depressed, but it goes beyond depression. You no longer have access to your feelings.

Numbing explains the extreme cases of the turned-off people we all have known. Clinically, they are known as *alexithymic* people, which means they have difficulty labeling their emotions. They are no longer aware of what they feel.

Recently, a couple in their late twenties, Greg and Liz, came to see me. Married for six years, with one son, Liz constantly badgered Greg to be more expressive in his language and emotions. She felt lonely and bored with his stoic, flat behavior. "He's a lump; he's a total thud," Liz complained. Greg said he wasn't being uncooperative. He was trying to be more lively and share his inner life with his wife, but he found it difficult and confusing. It became clear to me, over the course of several sessions, that Greg was a sensor who had totally lost any sense of his inner life.

From high school graduation on, he had bulldozed his way into more and more career challenges that required (he believed) a tough exterior. At twenty-eight, he was a sales manager in a large electronics company—an unusual job for a sensor. He was doing quite well. But his denial of his temperament was exacting an enormous emotional price. He was faking an outgoing personality ten hours a day on the job. By the time he got home, he was so exhausted that he had nothing to give to his wife or son. He had turned off his insides and wasn't available, even to himself.

EXPANDING YOUR COMFORT ZONE: DESENSITIZATION

You can live more comfortably as a sensor. Notice I say *live more comfortably*, because trying to eliminate disturbing emotions is what gets us in trouble and is the reason so many sensors who seek help fail. The key to enlarging your comfort zone as a sensor is to modify your action tendency, which is to withdraw from potential harm. By utilizing *desensitization*, in which you experience the scary thought or situation and defuse it of its power, you can condition yourself to have a higher threshold of arousal. The more you face threatening situations, the more you will raise your threshold and have an enlarged comfort zone. This must be done in a conscious, systematic, and carefully orchestrated way.

We'll explore this process in detail in chapter 10.

SENSORS: LIBERATION FROM TOXIC MYTHS

Let's reframe the toxic psychological myths specific to the sensor's temperament dilemmas:

1. The myth of uniformity: We are not all alike. Some of us respond with more anxiety than others, and that's okay. People whose confidence you envy probably feel unpleasant emotions now and again just as you do.

2. The myth of good and bad: Fear and anxiety are neither good nor bad. Accepting the presence of varying degrees of anxiety will release you from the shame of bad emotions.

3. The myth of control: Conquering or eliminating nervousness or anxiety is a futile task; anxiety is a normal response to life situations. To master anxiety is to rid yourself of a valuable biological and psychological signal of threat to your well-being. Instead of subjugating anxiety, make it an occasional acquaintance with whom you are on speaking terms.

4. The myth of perfectability: No one is courageous all of the time. Courage is not about living without fear but what each of us does in the face of fear. To wish for anything, to take risks, is to subject yourself to the possibility of nervousness and anxiety. Give yourself a break and embrace the inevitability of nervousness as you go through life.

5. The myth of emotional illness: Nervousness is not a sign of emotional illness. It is a normal accompaniment to life's challenges. Even those who decide to take medication to banish or sedate unwanted nervousness are not necessarily ill. A chemical supplement may offer relief, but as you will learn in chapter 12, it may cost you more than you think.

6. The myth of positive thinking: No matter how much you think you can talk away nervousness, it won't disappear. You cannot use willpower to rid yourself of anxiety in the face of triggers that simply make you nervous.

THE SENSOR IDENTIFICATION CHECKLIST

Rate the following statements by marking an "X" on the blank line next to the response that best describes you:

1. When I meet new people, it takes me a while to feel comfortable talking with them.

   _____ 1 Not at all true
   _____ 2 Rarely true
   _____ 3 Somewhat true
   _____ 4 Always true

2. I often push myself to do things and then feel over-whelmed.

   _____ 1 Not at all true
   _____ 2 Rarely true
   _____ 3 Somewhat true
   _____ 4 Always true

3. I am shy.

   _____ 1 Not at all true
   _____ 2 Rarely true
   _____ 3 Somewhat true
   _____ 4 Always true

4. I worry about the future and frequently anticipate the worst.

   _____ 1 Not at all true
   _____ 2 Rarely true
   _____ 3 Somewhat true
   _____ 4 Always true

5. I feel upset and sometimes even sick in new situations.

_____ 1 Not at all true
_____ 2 Rarely true
_____ 3 Somewhat true
_____ 4 Always true

6. I have difficulty accepting criticism and usually withdraw from its source.

_____ 1 Not at all true
_____ 2 Rarely true
_____ 3 Somewhat true
_____ 4 Always true

7. I cry during movies (happy and/or sad ones).

_____ 1 Not at all true
_____ 2 Rarely true
_____ 3 Somewhat true
_____ 4 Always true

8. I try to avoid confrontations.

_____ 1 Not at all true
_____ 2 Rarely true
_____ 3 Somewhat true
_____ 4 Always true

9. I can easily understand how others feel when they describe their experiences to me.

_____ 1 Not at all true
_____ 2 Rarely true
_____ 3 Somewhat true
_____ 4 Always true

10. I have difficulty controlling and managing my emotions.

_____ 1 Not at all true
_____ 2 Rarely true
_____ 3 Somewhat true
_____ 4 Always true

11. I startle easily.

_____ 1 Not at all true
_____ 2 Rarely true

_____ 2 Somewhat true
_____ 3 Always true

12. I find it difficult to relax.

    _____ 1 Not at all true
    _____ 2 Rarely true
    _____ 3 Somewhat true
    _____ 4 Always true

13. I often feel apprehensive and cannot identify the cause of my worries.

    _____ 1 Not at all true
    _____ 2 Rarely true
    _____ 3 Somewhat true
    _____ 4 Always true

14. My emotions tend to be intense and extreme.

    _____ 1 Not at all true
    _____ 2 Rarely true
    _____ 3 Somewhat true
    _____ 4 Always true

15. I feel uneasy in situations where I am the focus of attention.

    _____ 1 Not at all true
    _____ 2 Rarely true
    _____ 3 Somewhat true
    _____ 4 Always true

16. I have used alcohol or tranquilizers to help me relax.

    _____ 1 Not at all true
    _____ 2 Rarely true
    _____ 3 Somewhat true
    _____ 4 Always true

17. I crave constant reassurance in my relationships.

    _____ 1 Not at all true
    _____ 2 Rarely true

_____ 3 Somewhat true

_____ 4 Always true

18. Security (in relationships, jobs, etc.) is very important to me.

_____ 1 Not at all true

_____ 2 Rarely true

_____ 3 Somewhat true

_____ 4 Always true

19. I often deny when I feel anxious about something.

_____ 1 Not at all true

_____ 2 Rarely true

_____ 3 Somewhat true

_____ 4 Always true

20. People have told me that I am overly sensitive.

_____ 1 Not at all true

_____ 2 Rarely true

_____ 3 Somewhat true

_____ 4 Always true

21. I am sometimes ashamed of my sensitivity.

_____ 1 Not at all true

_____ 2 Rarely true

_____ 3 Somewhat true

_____ 4 Always true

22. I feel the most comfortable when I am with longtime friends and acquaintances.

_____ 1 Not at all true

_____ 2 Rarely true

_____ 3 Somewhat true

_____ 4 Always true

23. I am very aware of my bodily sensations.

_____ 1 Not at all true

_____ 2 Rarely true

_____ 3 Somewhat true

_____ 4 Always true

24. When facing new or unusual circumstances, I often sweat, get a dry mouth, feel my heart beat fast, and experience shakiness.

_____ 1 Not at all true
_____ 2 Rarely true
_____ 3 Somewhat true
_____ 4 Always true

25. I depend on my friends more that they seem to need me.

_____ 1 Not at all true
_____ 2 Rarely true
_____ 3 Somewhat true
_____ 4 Always true

26. When I get upset, the bad feelings tend to last for a long time.

_____ 1 Not at all true
_____ 2 Rarely true
_____ 3 Somewhat true
_____ 4 Always true

27. I often focus on small events or details that others would consider unimportant.

_____ 1 Not at all true
_____ 2 Rarely true
_____ 3 Somewhat true
_____ 4 Always true

28. Dealing with problems exhausts all my energy.

_____ 1 Not at all true
_____ 2 Rarely true
_____ 3 Somewhat true
_____ 4 Always true

29. When I run into obstacles, I often change my original strategy or intentions.

_____ 1 Not at all true
_____ 2 Rarely true
_____ 3 Somewhat true
_____ 4 Always true

30. Even when I am with friends, I often feel lonely or unimportant.

_____ 1 Not at all true
_____ 2 Rarely true
_____ 3 Somewhat true
_____ 4 Always true

Be sure that you have responded to each of the items. Calculate your score by adding the numbers next to the responses you have marked. Record the sum here:_____.

90 and above: a definite sensor
80–89: many sensor characteristics
70–79: some sensor characteristics
70 and below: few of these characteristics play an important role in your temperament.

Chapter 6

DISCHARGERS: FROM ANGER TO RELEASE

KEN, AGE THIRTY-FOUR, is the editor of a small but influential business journal. His most recent staff meeting was almost his last. When he heard that the word in the business community was that he had botched a feature series by misreading a corporation's annual report, Ken exploded. He hurled some files across the conference table, narrowly missing a reporter. Then he began shouting. "I can't believe you didn't follow up on this!" he snarled to his female assistant. After he had chewed out three other people in a screaming and abusive manner, Ken began to pace around the conference table, agitated and angry.

Two minutes later, though it seemed like an eternity to his staff, he shrugged his shoulders, laughed, and said, "Well, we'll just have to get cracking on the next series and make it a whole lot better." He then tried to motivate his staff with some pep talk. It fell on stunned, shocked ears.

Late that afternoon, the owner of the magazine called Ken into the conference room. Without mincing words, he said he'd be fired if he kept up those kinds of tirades. Ken protested: "Yeah, I did overreact today, but my staff knows that's just my style. They weren't that upset, anyway." "You're wrong," the owner told him. "Three of your associates told me that they've had it with your temper and they're ready to quit."

When Ken left work that day, he met Charlene, the woman he had been dating for the past year. At the restaurant, he launched right into the story, though this time with the wit he was famous for. Ken was quite startled when, instead of joining him in his bemused recounting, or trying to soothe him as she usually did, Charlene held up her hand to stop his reenactment of the drama. "You've got a serious problem with anger and you had better see somebody about it. You pull the same stuff with me. You think because you're so talented, all will be forgiven—well, it won't."

When Ken and Charlene came to see me, Ken was no longer remorseful. He painted a flattering picture of himself. "Look, doc, I'm a gunslinger. That's why they pay me a lot; that's how I turned that magazine around. My people know I'm tough, and they respond to toughness because I'm also a guy who praises them and goes to bat for them. I was the same kind of guy in college; I was the captain of the basketball team, and my personality hasn't changed one bit."

Charlene turned to me with a knowing look. "That's exactly what I'm afraid of—he's always been that way and he'll never change." Ken softened: "I really do apologize. You don't think I'm abusive, do you?" Charlene nodded. "Yes, sometimes you really do push me, and other people. But most of the time, you're more exhausting than abusive, like a child with his temper tantrums. And I'm not sure I can handle it."

For the first time, Ken looked worried, even frightened. The possibility that he would lose Charlene was the motivation he needed to take an open-minded look at his temper and his personality. Ken is a discharger, prone to ventilating emotional frustrations and anger.

Like Ken, Ellen also has a troublesome personality. As her best friend says, "You either love Ellen, or you can't stand her." Ellen's friends see her as vivacious, charming and fiery. As one friend put it, "She's the most loyal person I know, but at the same time, she gets hurt and angry at the drop of a hat."

Ellen was in the audience at one of my lectures. She was, indisputably, the most outspoken person in attendance, and she asked the most challenging questions. It was a lecture on marriage and conflict resolution. Not surprisingly, Ellen was arguing in favor of the appropriateness of anger in marriage. Weeks afterward, she made an appointment to see me for a private consultation.

Her emotional dynamic quickly became apparent to me. Ellen had been excitable and temperamental since she was a child; it was clearly her nature. Although she had been to a number of therapists over the years in hopes of becoming "more mellow," her emotional manner had never changed.

Like so many dischargers, Ellen secretly felt uncomfortable with her emotional reactivity. She always thought that if she could only be more gentle and reserved, she would be a better person. Not that her outbursts weren't justified. Her hurts were real: a close friend let her down; her husband didn't fulfill his end of the marital bargain; her kids became unruly and oppositional; a doctor made her wait over an hour in his waiting room. Yet she was aware that, "No one I know flies off the handle as much as I do." Her volatility was, in fact, self-defeating at times. Many friendships and projects had unraveled because, as Ellen put it, "I just don't have the presence of mind sometimes to count to ten and curb my tongue."

Whenever she had these outbursts, she felt ashamed afterward. She believed that somehow she hadn't achieved the level of maturity she should have. "After all," she asked, "isn't one aspect of maturity the ability to contain your emotions? Why don't I have more presence of mind, so I can cool off before I speak?" she asked.

THE EXPRESSIVE TEMPERAMENT

Dischargers are complicated and intriguing. They can fascinate us or wear us out with their emotionality. If you're a discharger, you are demonstrative, quick to react to others. You're not afraid of interpersonal clash or give-and-take. Containing your emotions is foreign to you—it's almost a biological imperative that your intense feelings be discharged or expressed.

Like the sensor, the discharger feels too much. But the discharger is extroverted. His expression of emotional energy can range from moments of irritability to face-to-face confrontation. But to characterize him simply as angry doesn't do him justice: the discharger is not one-dimensional. It's more fair to say she is prone to varying intensities of emotional expressiveness—joy to anger, soup to nuts. Dischargers are easily frustrated, and they are likely to vent impulsively on anyone or anything that happens to be handy. Because anger is so scary to others, dischargers often feel ashamed and are filled with self-loathing after they express anger. They vow to count to ten the next time, but they may find this promise impossible to keep. It's not always anger that finds expression; obviously their explosive energy can be manifested as spontaneity and passion.

As a child, your parents may remember that you were prone to temper tantrums, that you were combative, confrontational, and you rarely let minor annoyances pass without reacting to them. As one of my patient's mothers recalled, "She didn't take anything in stride. She was always in a huff, or yelling at somebody, or in tears." You likely required a lot of attention and disciplining; you may have been labeled hyperactive, or perhaps just spirited, rambunctious, and full of life.

ETHICS AND THE DISCHARGER

I've described two dischargers, Ken and Ellen, who are essentially kind and caring, even though their quick tempers might at times suggest otherwise. But there is another type of discharger who seems to accept his temperament yet fails to take responsibility for it.

Raymond is a film executive. He came to see me because his wife, Stephanie, wanted a divorce. She had hired an attorney and had locked Raymond out of their condo. Stephanie said he verbally abused her and she felt emotionally neglected. When she described his behavior, I agreed it was abusive and sexist. He had married her because she was younger, gorgeous, and looked up to him. Yet in the year they'd been married, he constantly put her down, in private and in front of other people, for her lack of education and sophistication.

Raymond was hoping I would convince his wife to "come to her senses" and stop the divorce proceedings. I found Raymond to be bright, open, and expressive. I also found his air of superiority offensive. I told him this in the first session and it really set him off. "Wait a minute, pal," he shouted. "You're supposed to be supportive and . . ." I cut him off. "No, *you* wait. I'm supposed to tell the truth as I see it." I told him I found his behavior understandable, from a biochemical perspective, but this did not justify bullying his wife. I also told him that I suspected he had some residual hyperactivity or attention-deficit disorder left from when he was a child; this happens for one-third of all hyperactive children.

He seemed surprised. "Yeah, I was hyperactive as a child. But that's not the point here. I'm in a creative industry, and this is how we act." He saw himself as an "enfant terrible," a gifted but tormented artist whose temper tantrums should be forgiven. I responded that I found his behavior indefensible. Raymond became enraged by my statements and walked out on the session.

Three months later, he telephoned me. His wife had gone through with the divorce, and he had been fired in a studio shake-up. "Okay, I'm whipped," he said over the phone. "Will you see me?" I agreed to see him, on the condition that he leave his arrogance at the door. To his credit, he was able to do so, and we began to work.

Raymond had been a difficult child, diagnosed as hyperactive but very bright. His parents foolishly let him get away with screaming fits and bullying younger children. In my opinion, they failed him in a huge way. They always excused his behavior: "He's hyperactive. He can't help it." I suspect that, secretly, they thought their son's intelligence and their social prominence put him above the rules of simple, decent, considerate behavior. Their spoiling of Raymond continued into his years at a top Ivy League university.

Unlike Ken and Ellen, who felt genuine remorse over their excesses, Raymond felt too little remorse. He would explode at people, put them down, and humiliate them whenever he felt like it. And, like so many other bullies, he made sure he surrounded himself with subordinates who couldn't hit back. With his peers or superiors in the entertainment industry, he admitted that he did use restraint.

My diagnosis was that Raymond was lacking in compassion. I told him that he was open to therapy, at the moment, because he had lost his wife and his job, but that he was likely to revert to old behavior when he got another fast-track job and another pretty woman sitting next to him in his expensive sports car. My prescription was that he stay in therapy and learn to modulate his temperament. My other suggestion was that he volunteer a minimum of ten hours a week with a local agency that sends people into the homes of dying AIDS patients to keep them company. If Raymond couldn't learn compassion from this volunteer work, he wasn't going to learn it at all. It's only been three months, but Raymond is hanging in there with the assignment, and his heart is opening.

Ellen, Ken, and Raymond illustrate the propensity of the discharger to anger, impulsiveness, and the need to vent what they feel inside. Ellen and Ken were brought up well, but Raymond's parents were neglectful of him, in my opinion. These angry people are not markedly dysfunctional or self-destructive. Their lives seem to be working, although not in all areas. They are all successful in various ways, but their inability to manage their temperament is diminishing their lives.

MISLEADING MESSAGES

If you are a discharger, it's likely that, as far back as you can remember, you've heard a lot of guilt-inducing messages that never really helped you understand your emotions. In one way or another, you heard you were bad because you were prone to anger, prone to confrontation, or exercised insufficient self-control. As an adult, if you sought traditional counseling, you may have inadvertently found people to blame for your problems. You may have been told that someone abused you as a child, or that parental love was never forthcoming and you had to make a scene in order to get noticed. Then therapeutic advice told you to confront those who disappointed you; it was important to get your feelings out to validate them.

Unfortunately, these messages are based on the notion that if you confront those who hurt you, you will be healed, and you will never be angry again. Therapists may foolishly provide targets for you as they help you to understand your history. You may now begin to believe that your mate is similar to a parent with whom you were angry, or that a boss is similar to a hurtful person in your past. These theories will lead you astray if you are a discharger. They are based on a model of learned conflict that very likely has nothing to do with why you're prone to irritability.

Much advice about anger is based on a hydraulic model of emotions—that you have a finite amount of anger that needs to be discharged once and for all. The advice is based on misunderstanding as a cause of your temperament, and if you only clear it up, you'll be fine. These false messages give you circumstances and people to blame, and they serve to reinforce anger as a habit. However, the anger is not your parents' fault, or society's fault, or your own fault. The way you're wired is to blame.

THE DISCHARGER'S NATURAL SELF

Low Threshold of Arousal

The discharger has a low threshold of arousal; he is chronically overaroused. Consequently, like the sensor, he feels too much. Things get to him that other people don't even notice. He has a short fuse. He is highly reactive.

Action Tendency: Extroverted/Confrontation

Unlike the introverted sensor, whose action tendency is harm avoidance and withdrawal, the discharger is an extrovert. When his arousal is activated, it takes the form of immediate outward expressiveness. When he feels too much, his action tendency is to express the emotion toward a target. Anger or aggressiveness is what results from the combination of high arousal plus this extroverted action tendency.

In my view, there is ample scientific evidence that the behavior I described when we looked at Ken, Ellen, and Raymond is not totally under their control, is not their fault, and is not caused by early childhood experiences—it's innate, biological, and biochemical. In fact, it's fundamental and instinctive. You're familiar with the very basic physiological fight or flight response to perceived dangers. This is the elemental survival mechanism of most living species. It explains not only the sensor's action tendency to withdraw but also the discharger's tendency to confront.

Keep in mind that I'm describing an instinctive response. Obviously, given sufficient provocation, any temperament type can feel angry. But the people I am discussing are those for whom irritability and anger are their predominant emotions when they go over the edge. If someone cuts us off in traffic, we can all feel angry, but the discharger feels it more intently and gets angrier than the person who isn't a discharger.

Internal and External Triggers

The discharger is triggered in two ways: by an external event, like the jerk behind you honking his horn; or by an internal biochemical event, a biochemical "burp." When aroused internally, discharges often don't know why they feel aroused. They just feel aroused and then, as if automatically, they tune in to a particular target. In the absence of an obvious, immediate provocation, they will start to search for a target—it's the interpretive function of the mind at work, looking for some external event to justify their internal feelings, "I'm cranky because . . ." Oftentimes, it becomes the last irritating event or person on their minds; they actually find themselves mentally dredging up old hurts.

Perhaps you've had this sensation. If so, you may be a discharger. For example, you wake up cranky and you don't know why. For most people the crankiness will subside to a neutral position. For the discharger, something else happens. Reflexively, he is driven to sort through his memory for some recent hurt or frustration. He finds a convenient target, and pretty soon he's consciously preoccupied with that target. He focuses in and the anger builds. When he wears out that target, maybe he reads the paper and he finds another target. He turns on the news. Another tax hike! And he gets going again. Each time he focuses outward, his threshold rises for a moment and he feels better because of the momentary release, then it drifts lower again until the next provocation.

In theoretical terms, the discharger's instinctive expression of the energy of high arousal leads to release attainment. As soon as she fixates on the external target, the arousal momentarily decreases. The problem for the discharger is that by continuing to focus on the target, she restimulates herself. Her satisfaction quickly evaporates. Her threshold falls again and she continues to feel angry, sometimes even more intensely. Now she has the feeling, "I can't let go of my anger."

THE BIOCHEMISTRY OF THE DISCHARGER

There is increasing evidence confirming the biological basis of the discharger's emotional predispositions. This evidence is coming from a variety of areas of research, from behavior genetics to psychopharmacology.

Anger is aggression, of course, and we know that certain tendencies toward aggression are inherited. For example, studies find higher levels of the male hormone testosterone in aggressive men than in more easygoing men. And testosterone levels, high or low, seem to run in families. Other research that is providing telling clues to the biochemistry of the discharger focuses on activity level, hyperactivity, and the enzyme MAO (monoamine oxidase).

Separate studies done by Chess and Kagen on the nature of the child indicate that some children are more active and aggressive than others. I believe there is a high correlation between a high activity level and the discharger's temperament. In a subgroup of active children, labeled cranky children, researchers found lower levels of MAO in their blood. MAO is an enzyme that regulates emotion-linked neurotransmitters including serotonin. Lower levels of MAO lead to lower levels of serotonin, and low levels of serotonin are associated with impulsivity, a trait related to anger.

Other studies of cranky and irritable babies also point to low levels of MAO. Moreover, MAO levels are inherited. Studies of aggressive and criminal personalities also show low levels of MAO. I'm not suggesting that the cranky baby is going to become a criminal, but that there is a clear chain of evidence that anger is partly determined by inheritance, and highly correlated with low levels of MAO.

Recent research findings also point to low levels of MAO in

the biochemistry of attention deficit disorder (ADD), also called hyperactivity, in children. These children are easily frustrated, easily distracted, and prone to impulsivity and anger. One theory of anger holds that any frustration or interruption of a person's behavior leads to anger or aggression. In the past, it was thought that children outgrow hyperactivity by the time they're in their teens. Newer research shows that one-third or more of all children who are diagnosed as ADD carry their emotional and behavioral predispositions into adulthood. Even as adults they may be prone to irritability (for example, Raymond), have a low tolerance for frustration, have difficulty concentrating, and be easily angered. They're not bad people filled with anger; they are easily distracted and emotionally overloaded. Their frustration is expressed as irritability.

Tranquilizers don't work with hyperactive children. Instead, the only drugs found to be effective are stimulants, such as Ritalin. The use of a stimulant to calm a "hyper" kid has always been confusing to parents. Intuitively, it doesn't make sense to use a stimulant to calm someone. Today, researchers are finding that the parts of the brain that control attention and distractibility or impulsiveness are governed by MAO. If the levels of MAO are too low, then the person is hyperactive; if MAO is boosted, the person will be more able to focus and will be calmer. Some scientists believe that stimulants such as Ritalin calm hyperactive children by stimulating MAO activity, which then allows the child to slow down, cool off, and concentrate more. And Ritalin stimulates areas in the brain that (via MAO) control attention, resulting in a calmer, less frustrated and distracted child.

THE DISCHARGER'S SPECIAL GIFT: PASSIONATE EXPRESSION

Although I may seem to be emphasizing anger as the dominant emotion of dischargers, their feelings are also passionate. Dischargers respond to life with energy free from the inhibitions and constraints that most of us have. Their proclivity for emotional reactivity makes them lively and energetic.

Whereas others may be dull, boring, and predictable, dischargers are never that way. They present the possibility of the unexpected. Thus, dischargers are likely to be sought out socially. They are seen as "real" in comparison to men and women who are masked and are in so much control of their emotions that you rarely know what is going on inside them. Many dischargers see their temperament as an asset, even though they probably spend more time apologizing than others! They view themselves as engaging life rather than being beaten down by it.

Sara owns and runs a neighborhood restaurant. Like many dischargers, Sara is a big personality. Sara creates the noise, the activity, the emotional energy of three average people. She's in perpetual motion, chatting to customers, directing employees, ringing up tickets, bringing out special dishes from the kitchen. She seems to be a near-total extrovert, in constant interaction with other people. If she's not talking, she's laughing or shouting!

And Sara has the discharger's quick temper. More than once, her customers have heard her blowing up at the chef (who happens to be her husband) from the kitchen, or giving a supplier a tongue lashing for delivering produce or meat that she considers inferior. But her outbursts are quickly followed by equally intense apologies and hugs. Although the food at her restaurant is terrific, it is Sara's passion and emotional generosity that have created a loyal following of customers. She makes you feel alive, cared for. She's glad you came and she wants you to have a great time. Her emotional expressiveness encourages you to come alive, too. Her passionate engagement with life rubs off on everyone around her.

THE DISCHARGER'S DARK SIDE: ANGER

A number of fine books describe anger and explore ways to diffuse it. But none attempts to define a distinct temperament for which anger is the most predictable response to inner arousal. In the majority of studies on anger, researchers do not separate people into emotional types in order to determine whether catharsis (expression) or containment of anger is a better strategy for each distinct emotional type. I think my theory begins where these studies leave off. People who are better off expressing their anger are what I call dischargers. For them, catharsis is not just beneficial but necessary. It's my conviction that their brain chemistry has given them an innate biochemical predisposition to high arousal. And their inherited behavior genetics dictate an action tendency to focus on a target outside themselves. My years of clinical experience and observation have demonstrated to me, in patient after patient, that dischargers who do not express their emotional energy, who contain it or suppress it, wind up emotionally numb, hostile, self-defeatingly passive-aggressive, or chronically exhausted and depressed.

Cultural and social attitudes toward anger and what we should do with it have shifted enormously in the past few decades. In the 1960s and 1970s, people who openly expressed their feelings got some approval in popular psychology magazines and journals. People were urged to get in touch with their feelings and to express them. The expression of anger was sanctioned as long as you didn't hurt anyone which, of course, depends on who's making the call. Discharging and expressiveness were seen as positive and we embraced a hydraulic theory of emotions—the belief that there is a finite amount of emotional stuff, and if it's repressed, it will kill us, physically or psychologically.

In the 1990s, an opposing theory predominates. Newer research indicates that expressing certain emotions reinforces them and we develop the habit of that emotion. If we're talking about a "negative" emotion such as anger, then it's regarded as a bad habit. For example, if you explode with anger over a flat tire or losing your keys, you thereby increase the likelihood of such outbursts in any frustrating situation, no matter how trivial. This current ideology encourages the containment of "negative" emotions as the path toward the good and healthy life.

Almost twenty years ago, Ray Rosenman explored the effects of anger and hostility on heart trouble: the famous study on the type A, type B personalities. The type A personality was said to be prone to stress-induced heart disease because of emotionally intense, driven, impatient, easily frustrated behavior. The type B person was more easygoing, patient, placid, calm, and nonaggressive. Type A's were encouraged to become more like type B's.

In the intervening years, updates on that study pointed out that, for the type A's, it isn't anger, as such, that is the problem. Rather it is hostility (chronic and overly controlled anger). Anger is to hostility as an outburst is to gritted teeth. Importantly, these follow-up studies found that rigid containment of angry feelings not only led to hostility but a panoply of physical problems, including heart attacks. They also noted that the type A personality who is chronically hostile also suffers inner self-loathing—he hates himself for being dominated by such an "ugly" emotion. Clearly, the myth of mastery and the myth of good and bad emotions—"I must contain these shameful feelings"—can have deadly consequences for the discharger.

My belief is that temperament obeys no social context. To ignore the truth of a particular temperament is tantamount to telling people to hide it, hate it, deny it, and suppress who they are. I'm not suggesting a blanket license for expressing anything you wish. Dischargers have a moral responsibility to modulate their emotional expression. I'm emphatically not urging you to blindly seek catharsis as the only way you can be true to your temperament. While brain chemistry and behavior genetics predispose you to certain emotions, how, where, and when you choose to act on your emotions is a moral and behavioral issue, not a biological one. Happily, there are fairly simple techniques to discharge this emotional energy without doing harm to yourself or to others. We'll discuss them at the end of this chapter and in part three of this book.

THE GENDER GAP

Dischargers are treated quite differently in our society depending on their gender. Anger is often seen as an indicator of strength by others. The male discharger is accepted much more readily than the female. His energy level, when it takes the form of anger, is traditionally sanctioned as gender appropriate. From the time of "boys will be boys," even troublesome behavior is seen as understandable (except when criminal) and as part of testosterone-influenced psychology. Even now, in the era of the more sensitive male, the discharger is viewed as exhibiting reasonable behavior . . . for a man.

The female discharger is superficially seen as lacking in femininity when the latter is defined as softness and receptivity. The discharger certainly doesn't seem soft and is aggressive in nature. She is much more apt to be viewed negatively, especially by men. The woman with high energy and a lot of passion has traditionally been controlled by men because they may fear her strength. As a result, even when the female discharger is more passionate than angry, more vivacious than irritable, there still may be negative repercussions. Thankfully, every year we are growing closer to gender-free ideals of behavior and conduct.

THE DISCHARGER IN RELATIONSHIPS

ROMANTIC CHEMISTRY

Keeping in mind the idea that romantic chemistry happens when someone not only makes us feel comfortable but also holds the promise of expanding our comfort zone, dischargers are likely to feel attracted to someone who can tolerate their emotional expressiveness and volatility, yet also serve as a calming, soothing influence. Because the discharger is likely to feel ashamed of his quick temper, he needs a partner who does not make him feel loud, or out of control, and who accepts and respects his passionate nature.

Oddly enough, dischargers do better in the single world than one might think. Because they are seen as alive and even exciting, they are more magnetic than people who are wary and guarded. Moreover, dischargers typically have enough self-control that their bouts of irritability or temper can be suppressed during courtship, a period of being on one's best behavior. If you are a discharger, when you begin dating someone new, you feel best when the person you're seeing is accepting of your nature and forgiving of any untoward expressions of anger.

Few dischargers are simply angry or quarrelsome people. While their mates may be seen as the victims of their expressiveness, they are just as likely to see themselves as recipients of an exciting relationship. This is a fact that is neglected in most marriage counseling sessions; by focusing on anger, we forget the passion and intensity that may form some of the adhesive in the relationship.

The dynamic individual who speaks his mind stands out. Those who tend to be timid or lack intensity will be drawn to this energetic personality. A kind of modeling or imitation occurs. As Charlene remarked to me about Ken, her boyfriend, "I like him even when he explodes. I admire his courage and his willingness to throw caution to the winds. He's not afraid of life or taking challenges head-on. It makes life more exciting for me to know that it is possible to live that way." Taking spontaneous vacations or just grabbing a quick bite and rushing off to take in a movie were qualities she loved in Ken. When she was bothered by something, he sensed it and responded. He would say, "Let's go and talk about it at a restaurant."

Charlene feels she is more spontaneous and less inhibited as a result of being with Ken. I understand Charlene's appreciation for Ken, but I also understand that the way she views him is why so many dischargers feel they don't have to play by the rules. They sense they are admired and the rest of us will put up with almost anything they do. That's not always such a good idea. There's a point where the line between dynamism and dictatorial behavior becomes very thin.

The important thing for the mate of a discharger to accept is that what you've signed on for is a ride that will be stormy as well as enlivening. While I have focused on some of the more problematic areas that interfere with good relationships, I want the reader to know that the discharger can learn to master his comfort zones just as any other temperament type can. Relationships can actually be more alive, more vibrant and intense as the discharger learns to master his expressiveness.

CONFLICT IN RELATIONSHIPS

Often, dischargers will find passive partners who admire them and won't challenge their authority: a classic dominant-submissive role split. This kind of relationship diminishes both partners. But it is a common pairing for the discharger. She can have the satisfaction of venting her feelings without being suppressed or punished for doing so.

One of the common problem relationships in marital therapy occurs when a sensor has linked with a discharger. For example, Diana, a nurse and a sensor, was married to Bart, a computer salesman and a discharger. Diana was attracted by the excitement of being with someone who was so emotionally courageous. She loved his social aggressiveness and outgoing nature. Initially, Diana could tolerate all of his emotional exuberance, even occasional angry outbursts, because she felt secure in his love. "I thought we'd be together forever, and that I had to learn to accept for better, for worse," she remembers. When he got angry, she felt emotionally aroused in an almost sexual way. But as their marriage progressed, Bart's expressions of love were, too often, replaced by moments of anger or irritation. In time, these expressions occurred without being balanced by expressions of love or appreciation.

A discharger like Bart may come to take his wife for granted, which is when the relationship sours. When the spouse is a sensor, it is too much for her to endure feeling unloved and insecure. Diana said she was feeling overwhelmed, anxious, and fearful much of the time. What at first seemed like passion and excitement had evolved into tedious disruption at best and abusive emotional squalor at worst.

When I work with a couple that includes a discharger, I take great pains to cut short the recitation of all the accusations; I go directly to temperament issues. I tell the spouse that she is living with someone whose nature mandates that he blow off some feelings every now and again. And that dischargers instinctively seek out targets for their excitable behavior. This passionate nature is partly what attracted the spouse in the first place.

"But I didn't bargain for *this!*" many partners object. I inform them that as a marriage progresses it is only natural for negative expressions to come out more often, partly as a result of feeling safe and accepted by one's mate. This is similar to not teasing a friend until you know him well—you don't feel safe enough in the friendship to risk disapproval, so you're on your most gracious behavior at first.

"He used to be fun—stimulating to be around. Now all he

does is complain and put me down." That's usually the way it goes. My strategy is to focus on the temperaments involved rather than the content of what the fighting is about. I have found that if you focus on the content of conflicts in marriage, the couple could see a therapist for years without really getting better. The therapist becomes a paid negotiator for them. Instead, I believe it's more productive for the couple to understand themselves and to accept each other's temperament. The husband of the discharger needs first of all to see that his wife doesn't mean to be mean. Her husband is just a convenient target. Recognize that old saying, "What drives you crazy, keeps them sane." In other words, the discharger is simply using arguments as a way to regulate her emotional state.

The next step is to swiftly and immediately get the discharger to find other options for his behavior. He must change his focus or target. Dischargers are good at finding excuses not because they are liars but because their interpretive mind has been finding targets and reasons for their biological anger all their lives— it's an ingrained habit as automatic as breathing in and out. I cut rationalizations short. Excuses can't continue if a discharger wants to find different dimensions for his emotions.

As I explained to Diana, Bart will be extra expressive for the duration of their marriage. Her task, if she wants to stay happy and comfortable, will be to detach herself and not personalize his outbursts. The secret of every good relationship is based on understanding and accepting your mate's underlying temperament. This is especially difficult for the mate of a discharger, because outbursts are hard to take. But understanding does make it easier.

FRIENDSHIPS

Eric was constantly frustrated with the people around him. He was either disappointed and enraged, hurt and enraged, or ignored and enraged. He would come in to see me and want to find some way of telling people off, or putting them in their place, or sharing his feelings in the hope of making them act "right." I would say to him, "Suppose you did nothing? Suppose you just accepted how they are, and let it be?"

Well, of course, he couldn't do that: it sounded cowardly. I then said, "Let's assume your nature is such that your irritation is easily triggered. Why don't we talk about ways to vent that steam and not overly complicate your friendships with confrontations, scenes, blame, accusations, etc.?" As soon as he contemplated letting go of the triggers to his anger, the focus shifted to himself. He was left with his arousal, his low threshold, and the task of managing them. At first, he protested. After trying it, he was motivated to do so; he found that he was breaking a pattern that made him miserable.

Some of the complications that arise in the discharger's relationships with others can be altered by the discharger taking responsibility for his nature. As he does this, he begins to feel more hopeful, because emotional relief is now under his control, and he becomes less volatile.

Sure, sometimes it is important to share a complaint with a spouse or friend, to let someone know you feel angry or hurt or frustrated by something she has done. But, in my professional experience, I have found there are lots of relationships that flourish, endure, and get along just fine without encounters, without resorting to that thinly veiled excuse for venting (or "dumping").

THE DISCHARGER PARENT

The discharger parent may be seen as overbearing, but not as frequently as one might think. Dischargers are not mean or bad. They are expressive, and their children may be fearful at times, but will still feel loved. Indeed, one might argue that children always know where they stand. The discharger parent is not masked or given to sterile talk rather than emotions.

THE DISCHARGER AT WORK

AMBITION AND CAREER

In the tough economy of the 1990s, increased levels of tension, anxiety, and anger are epidemic. It's imperative for anyone who wants to stay employed, who wants to retain clients or customers, to understand his own temperament, and the temperaments of clients and coworkers. No other factor is so critical to success or failure than getting along with people, being likable, being worthy of trust. Because we're now seeing the tail end of corporate loyalty and job security, your reputation and your relationships with people in your field are your only true job security. The discharger employee has even more motivation than a boss to tune into her natural self; her irritability may not be tolerated.

It's important to remember that the most common temperament is the sensor. The temperament type that can cause the sensor the most emotional distress is the discharger. If you are a discharger, I would estimate that more than 50 percent of your conflicts at work come from this combustible combination.

In the work world, the discharger often becomes one of two people: a dynamic leader, or a source of problems for himself and those around him. When dischargers get into emotional difficulty, it is usually because they have not harnessed their energy in adaptive and positive ways. Because of their emotional makeup, dischargers have a lot of energy available to them. But when they get sidetracked and caught up in provocations or frustration, they typically waste their time, feel victimized by perceived injustices, and destabilize their work team. The common denominator between the two paths they take is, of course, their aggressiveness. Being aggressive is a virtue in any competitive society, but being aggressive in a resistant and passive way only gets you into trouble.

THE PASSIVE-AGGRESSIVE DISCHARGER EMPLOYEE

When I do management consulting, I frequently encounter the discharger passive-aggressive employee, who is subtly resistant, obstinate, and infuriating to his colleagues. Typically, as a child, he learned to disavow his temperament. He learned to view anger as bad, something to be suppressed. It's the suppression that gets him in trouble, not the anger. As an adult, every time he feels inner arousal, he is so controlled in its expression that all he does is become resistant rather than expressive. The remedy is for him to reconnect more fully with his natural self, to appreciate his aggressiveness, and to learn to express it constructively and assertively.

THE DISCHARGER BOSS

The discharger who is comfortable being dominant and becoming a leader can also create his own trouble, but not nearly as much as the passive-aggressive discharger. As the saying goes, dischargers don't get ulcers; they give them. They are seen as leaders because they are outspoken, and their expressiveness stands out like a beacon. The discharger's problem at work is that he can fall into the habit of criticizing and complaining about coworkers without balancing those expressions with something constructive. He gets into the anger habit and soon discharges like a loose cannon, with repeated outbursts of anger and impatience. These emotional outbursts confuse the people who work with him. "When should I take him seriously, and when should I ignore him?" they wonder. If you are a discharger, don't ignore your effect on your coworkers or employees.

Repressed anger emerges later as hostility. It is the most difficult emotion a subordinate can sense in a boss. Hostility is so pervasive and unfocused it can mean almost anything to an employee. Usually the worker concludes the boss doesn't like him and becomes paranoid about his job. The discharger who is unaware of his temperament and how it appears gets all his subordinates upset. It is a lot better to discharge anger openly and directly—but not abusively—then reassure your staff, and go on. Jimmy, a supervisor at a company with which I consulted, told me he went out of his way to tell his subordinates, "Don't take my anger personally. That's just me; it's not about you. When I'm done, I'll tell you, or you ask me, 'What's the message I should take away from this exchange? What's really the issue here?'" This directness takes the pressure off everyone.

The discharger at work is best served when he looks at targets of his anger as problems to be solved. Unlike relationships, where you cannot, or should not, attempt to change your mate, in a work environment you have a different task: solve the problem. You need to change the way you target your anger in order to enhance productivity. This constructive focus redirects your energy to problem solving, which requires compassion, sensitivity, and tact.

Jason is a junior executive with an advertising agency. He, too, is a discharger, given to explosiveness, prone to anger with his subordinates. Because he was so ashamed of his impulsiveness and lack of control, he worked extra hard to contain it. At work, he contained his anger by saying nothing, but the anger would stay with him. When he and his wife came to see me, Jason was a physical and emotional wreck. He was trying so hard to be someone other than who he was that he was becoming exhausted and depressed. There's nothing wrong with trying to modulate your emotions, but when you try to behave like someone with a different personality, it will take a terrible toll on you.

Jason's wife and son were getting the worst of this false solution. Pent up with emotions, he would come home and dump all of his feelings on them. He was snappish and sarcastic. Jason was unhappy with his behavior and he wanted help. He and his wife came into therapy at her urging. She said, "Everyone loves him at work, but at home he's a monster. Why can't he be calm when he sees Danny and me?" Certainly a reasonable request. The problem was that he was denying his temperament at work, and he ended up building a head of steam that finally erupted at home where he felt safe.

After doing an exhaustive diagnostic session with Jason alone, I realized that he had always had a predisposition to erupt, that he was easily frustrated. He had never worried about his personality because it never had gotten in his way before. In college, he was seen as aggressive and dynamic, the envy of his fraternity brothers. It was only when Jason started his career that his emotional style got in his way. On his first job after graduate school, he got some poor performance appraisals because of his anger. His subordinates were scared of him. They felt intimidated. They perceived his angry outbursts as preludes to their being terminated. At first, he protested to his boss. "I like the people on my team. I don't mean to hurt their feelings or undermine their morale." Secretly he fancied himself as a General Patton–type leader. Nevertheless, the head of the agency told Jason he wanted to see him behave in a more supportive and caring manner with his staff. Through enormous attempts at emotional containment and suppression, Jason seemingly turned into another leader, kinder and more sensitive.

I told Jason about the executives I've worked with who had similar temperaments, and how they worked out this dilemma. Many of them had tried to change as Jason did, and with the same dubious results. Either they couldn't pull it off, or they found themselves taking out their frustrations on their families. Or, like so many people in high-pressure jobs, they developed the happy hour habit. They started stopping off at the local bar after work to soothe their aggravated feelings with booze. Unfortunately, this often led to even greater eruptions at home because the alcohol undermined their self-restraint.

I began to reveal to Jason the slow and steady educational process of understanding and honoring his temperament rather than starving or suffocating it into submission. Jason could learn to harness his passionate nature. He would be liked and appreciated (and employed), but he would not be wearing the mask of Mr. Placid.

Dischargers can make excellent spouses, workers, and bosses, as long as those around them understand their emotionality and the dischargers learn to modulate what they do. Dischargers make it easier for themselves and their coworkers when they explain their personality and ask their subordinates not to take their outbursts personally.

FALSE PATHS TO EMOTIONAL RELIEF

RATIONALIZING

When they are frustrated with themselves and don't know what is going on, dischargers would prefer to keep part of their temperament and dump the rest. They want to remain spontaneous, alive, expressive; they don't want their expressiveness to erupt in the form of anger. Well, you *can* have it both ways. The discharger ultimately can become comfortable with his temperament, and can learn to expand his comfort zones. But many dischargers cannot stand their emotionality and they look for relief in the wrong places.

One strategy for relief is to create a set of attitudes excusing their behaviors. Raymond is a good example. He created a rationalization for himself that he was a gifted tormented artist, which justified his outbursts. For him, the choice was to feel badly about his temperament (which he couldn't stand to do), or to create a self-image that made expressiveness of any kind a virtue. Obviously, there is a middle ground, but due to his parents' excuses for him during his childhood, he never searched for it. He just concluded, "The hell with it. This is who I am, and if people don't like it, that's tough." And he got away with it, for a while.

ALCOHOL AND SUBSTANCE ABUSE

Dischargers are looking for internal calm to replace the internal heat or fire they feel—they look for sedation as a way to regulate their emotions. Some theorists believe people prone to anger, like dischargers, have a lack of natural, calming opiates in their brain chemistry. The person who jogs and stimulates endorphins is, in effect, modulating her emotions with a self-stimulated neurotransmitter that works like an opiate.

Some dischargers take tranquilizers for their anger, not realizing sedatives don't help, since anxiety is not the issue. If a discharger feels anxious over his lack of control, a tranquilizer will reduce that anxiety, but he still needs to discharge his arousal.

Another common source of relief is drinking. Alcohol clearly softens the edge for the discharger and can be a real problem. There are many dischargers who become alcoholics, not realizing that alcohol aggravates their predisposition. Alcohol relieves our inhibitions, as well as soothes us. We've all seen the nasty drunk who starts out boisterous and seemingly full of goodwill, but in a relatively short time, as the inhibition drops, the good cheer becomes poisonous and bitter. With alcohol, there is almost no ability for self-focusing—all your energy is directed outward.

NUMBNESS

An equally destructive false solution dischargers employ is numbing their emotions. Imagine setting your thermostat so high your emotions never come on. People turn off their awareness, but not the biochemical processes. Pressure builds. While the numbed sensor becomes a containment dome packed tight with dread, the numbed discharger becomes a containment dome stuffed full of anger. Both types experience pressure building within their containment domes. The sensor feels like he'll have a nervous breakdown. The discharger feels as though he will explode.

Lenny was a discharger, although only his wife was aware of it. A sales representative in the clothing business, Lenny was seen by fellow workers as intense and driven, though likeable. No one ever saw him get angry. He had a strict, religious up-bringing; he was severely punished as a child for any expression of anger. He grew up thinking that angry people were bad and inherently unlikeable. He never labeled himself as angry—he saw himself as overworked, underpaid, and therefore justifiably cranky.

But his wife Elaine knew his real temperament. She described some incidents in which he smoldered until he exploded and then knocked his fist through a wall, and one time when he actually ran someone off the road during a freeway altercation. Mostly she saw Lenny as cold, unexpressive, and rigid. When he was at work he tried to be likeable; at home he turned every-thing off, most of the time.

What Elaine was seeing was a man who was trying so hard to deny his nature and to suppress it that he was a walking time bomb—like the people you read about who snap one day and shoot down five strangers. Lenny was from the school of force of will. The myth of good and bad had certainly convinced him that anger was undesirable. The control myth had taught him that a man controls his emotions. The myth of uniformity had taught him that other people didn't appear to be as angry as he felt, so he shouldn't be feeling that way either.

When he felt inner arousal, he would clench his fists, grind his teeth, and not allow a breath of this energy to escape. He never achieved release, so he just built up a storehouse of re-sentments and fantasied enemies in his head, enough to keep him very angry most of his waking hours. But his threshold got cranked up so high that he was no longer aware of arousal. He felt a chronic kind of numbness, punctuated every now and again with an outburst. Yet Lenny was actually proud of his self-control.

Since Lenny struggled so hard to be good, his dilemma was tragic. He had one of the most lifeless existences I have ever encountered. Because he never really experienced any release, he lost sight of what it means to feel inner peace or happiness. His wife initially thought he was depressed, but he was far beyond depression. He was at war with himself, bent on killing his emotional self.

THERAPY

In therapy, you can explore the origins of your anger and irritability from now until doomsday and often not experience any change or relief at all. I don't mean to say this exploration is not important. You can create a useful chronology of events in your life that shaped the ways you express your emotions. This is helpful because it provides clues to current triggers. But such an exploration can usually be accomplished in a few sessions rather than months or years. An astute therapist can quickly determine when he or she is treating a discharger. The discharger will have an easily recognized pattern of responding to many situations with anger or irritability.

EXPANDING YOUR COMFORT ZONE: BENIGN RELEASE

Catharsis has an inherent appeal for dischargers, for release is partly what they need. But they don't realize that simple expression or discharge of the emotion will do the job. You can stop there—you don't have to go on to find a target and lash out at it. In other words, venting anger briefly while you are alone is sufficient to vent the arousal. There is an explosive component in temperament that needs to be satisfied, but there are many safe and ethical ways to do this. Beyond a brief catharsis, all the recent research suggests that chronic expression of anger leads to the probability that anger will become a habit. Children who learn to strike out when frustrated will strike out with greater frequency.

The task for the discharger is benign (not destructive) release or catharsis: shifting attention away from the target and back onto your arousal. By benign catharsis, I mean the expression of emotion in a way that does no harm to others or yourself. You don't hit people or things, you don't insult others, and you don't tell off your boss or your best friend. Those are all self-defeating strategies. This does not imply that you can never get angry again. You may say, "Okay, but can I get to the point where I don't get angry so often?" No, you may still get angry with the same frequency as you do now, but it can last seconds rather than minutes, hours, or days.

In chapter 10, we will explore in detail how dischargers can reset their thermostat and expand their comfort zone.

LIBERATING YOURSELF FROM MYTHS

Let's review what you must do to clear your mind for change:

1. The myth of uniformity: Most people don't get as frustrated as you do, but they have their own unpleasant emotional states to deal with. Your emotions are just more obvious and revealing.

2. The myth of good and bad: While I don't want to romanticize anger, it is certainly an instinctive and normal emotion, and sometimes it is highly adaptive and indicative of a healthy sense of indignation.

3. The myth of control: Dischargers who attempt to master their anger find themselves becoming less outwardly obnoxious and more subtly hostile. You cannot bludgeon anger into submission; it will get the best of you.

4. The myth of perfectibility: As someone who is angry, and given how anger is viewed, you certainly won't feel perfect. Your task is to know that perfection is not about being in neutral all the time.

5. The myth of emotional illness: Fortunately, even though dischargers can be criticized for their behavior, it is rarely diagnosed as a mental disorder. Don't label yourself.

6. The myth of positive thinking: No matter how much you try to talk yourself out of your feelings, it won't work. Your temperament demands expression, but how you do it is your ethical responsibility.

THE DISCHARGER IDENTIFICATION CHECKLIST

Rate the following statements by marking an "X" on the blank line next to the response that best describes you:

1. I react quickly to others when they say or do something that bothers me.

   _____ 1 Not at all true
   _____ 2 Rarely true
   _____ 3 Somewhat true
   _____ 4 Always true

2. I tend to experience both positive and negative feelings with much intensity.

   _____ 1 Not at all true
   _____ 2 Rarely true
   _____ 3 Somewhat true
   _____ 4 Always true

3. When I am angry, I need to express my feelings immediately.

   _____ 1 Not at all true
   _____ 2 Rarely true
   _____ 3 Somewhat true
   _____ 4 Always true

4. People view me as aggressive and dynamic.

   _____ 1 Not at all true
   _____ 2 Rarely true
   _____ 3 Somewhat true
   _____ 4 Always true

5. I have used alcohol or drugs to calm myself when I felt angry.

   _____ 1 Not at all true
   _____ 2 Rarely true

_____ 3 Somewhat true

_____ 4 Always true

6. I get easily irritated.

_____ 1 Not at all true

_____ 2 Rarely true

_____ 3 Somewhat true

_____ 4 Always true

7. When I try to suppress my anger, I end up feeling tired and/or depressed.

_____ 1 Not at all true

_____ 2 Rarely true

_____ 3 Somewhat true

_____ 4 Always true

8. I hate myself for feeling hostility so frequently.

_____ 1 Not at all true

_____ 2 Rarely true

_____ 3 Somewhat true

_____ 4 Always true

9. People feel intimidated by me.

_____ 1 Not at all true

_____ 2 Rarely true

_____ 3 Somewhat true

_____ 4 Always true

10. I wish that I were not so emotionally reactive.

_____ 1 Not at all true

_____ 2 Rarely true

_____ 3 Somewhat true

_____ 4 Always true

11. People draw away from me when they think I am getting angry.

_____ 1 Not at all true

_____ 2 Rarely true

_____ 3 Somewhat true

_____ 4 Always true

12. My approach to most matters is very passionate.

    _____ 1 Not at all true
    _____ 2 Rarely true
    _____ 3 Somewhat true
    _____ 4 Always true

13. When I express anger, I often feel ashamed afterward.

    _____ 1 Not at all true
    _____ 2 Rarely true
    _____ 3 Somewhat true
    _____ 4 Always true

14. I am an impatient person.

    _____ 1 Not at all true
    _____ 2 Rarely true
    _____ 3 Somewhat true
    _____ 4 Always true

15. It doesn't take much to make me angry.

    _____ 1 Not at all true
    _____ 2 Rarely true
    _____ 3 Somewhat true
    _____ 4 Always true

16. I find that I often take out my feelings on my loved ones after having a rough day.

    _____ 1 Not at all true
    _____ 2 Rarely true
    _____ 3 Somewhat true
    _____ 4 Always true

17. Sometimes I cannot label the cause of my anger.

    _____ 1 Not at all true
    _____ 2 Rarely true
    _____ 3 Somewhat true
    _____ 4 Always true

18. I am easily frustrated when things do not go my way.

    _____ 1 Not at all true
    _____ 2 Rarely true

_____ 3 Somewhat true
_____ 4 Always true

19. I have difficulty in controlling my temper.

_____ 1 Not at all true
_____ 2 Rarely true
_____ 3 Somewhat true
_____ 4 Always true

20. I make up excuses to legitimize my anger to others.

_____ 1 Not at all true
_____ 2 Rarely true
_____ 3 Somewhat true
_____ 4 Always true

21. I do not feel sorry after I have expressed my anger to others.

_____ 1 Not at all true
_____ 2 Rarely true
_____ 3 Somewhat true
_____ 4 Always true

22. I find myself frequently complaining.

_____ 1 Not at all true
_____ 2 Rarely true
_____ 3 Somewhat true
_____ 4 Always true

23. I am easily distracted from what I am doing.

_____ 1 Not at all true
_____ 2 Rarely true
_____ 3 Somewhat true
_____ 4 Always true

24. I am very critical of others.

_____ 1 Not at all true
_____ 2 Rarely true
_____ 3 Somewhat true
_____ 4 Always true

25. I usually feel that if I try to hold in my anger, I'll explode.

    _____ 1 Not at all true
    _____ 2 Rarely true
    _____ 3 Somewhat true
    _____ 4 Always true

26. I am an energetic person.

    _____ 1 Not at all true
    _____ 2 Rarely true
    _____ 3 Somewhat true
    _____ 4 Always true

27. I frequently get involved in confrontations.

    _____ 1 Not at all true
    _____ 2 Rarely true
    _____ 3 Somewhat true
    _____ 4 Always true

28. Once I get angry, it takes me a long time to feel calm again.

    _____ 1 Not at all true
    _____ 2 Rarely true
    _____ 3 Somewhat true
    _____ 4 Always true

29. People see me as rigid and cold.

    _____ 1 Not at all true
    _____ 2 Rarely true
    _____ 3 Somewhat true
    _____ 4 Always true

30. I often get angry about small events or items that others would consider unimportant.

    _____ 1 Not at all true
    _____ 2 Rarely true
    _____ 3 Somewhat true
    _____ 4 Always true

Be sure that you have responded to each of the items. Calculate your score by adding the numbers next to the responses you have marked. Record the sum here:_____.

80 and above: a definite discharger
70–79: many discharger characteristics
60–69: some discharger characteristics
60 and below: few of these characteristics play an important role in your temperament.

Chapter 7

FOCUSERS: FROM MOODY
TO ALIVE

WILLIS is chief financial officer at a large company, and for years he had worked long hours. But during the previous twelve months, his hard-driving work style had crossed the line into workaholism. Both his wife and his cardiologist were concerned. His cardiologist referred Willis to me for evaluation. Willis was suffering from angina. He suggested to Willis that he think about changing jobs to lower his stress level. He also prescribed an antidepressant.

Willis's symptoms ranged from a sense of agitation, to exhaustion, to an inner "hollowness" as Willis characterized it. His doctor diagnosed depression. What worried Willis most were the increasing hours in which he felt that life was meaningless. In session, Willis described a grueling work life, dealing with cut-throat investment bankers and a rather tyrannical boss. That was the *content* of what he said. But it was obvious to me in every session that whenever he spoke about his work, he came alive. He was animated and even showed a sense of humor as he recounted run-ins with his boss. It was at home that he most often found himself feeling blue. "These rotten moods come over me and I don't want to get my wife depressed, too, so I just go in my study after dinner and start on the pile of work I've brought home from the office."

"Am I exhausted and depressed because I'm a workaholic?" he asked. "No, it's probably the other way around," I replied.

"You are inclined to seemingly workaholic behavior partly because you wish to avoid feelings that you might label as depressive, that is, feeling dead, bored, flat. In fact, without the work you probably would always be clinically depressed." He didn't comprehend at first. "Work is the only distraction and activity that makes you feel alive," I told Willis.

Willis had no real awareness of his natural self—his innate emotional temperament—or that he was a focuser. When not busy, he was susceptible to focusing attention on his lack of inner feelings. He wasn't a workaholic in the sense of work being an addiction; in truth, it was saving his life. And he wasn't depressed; he was simply exhausted from focusing on his lack of emotional arousal at home. He needed to learn what to do with his underarousal—the central task of the focuser.

Bettina, another patient, came to see me because of bad moods. She had recently mentioned to her internist that her husband was becoming fed up with her craziness at home: obsessive concerns about her children, how well they were doing in school, whether they were in the right class, whether they had enough friends, and so on and so on and so on!

These are normal concerns that every parent will understand, but Bettina's endless and ruminative thinking was dominating her life. Whenever she and her husband were together, she invariably would steer the subject to talk about the children and her latest anxieties. Tearfully, she described this process, declaring that she would give anything to let go of these obsessions. "It's gotten out of control." She was exhausted and afraid, and she could no longer rationalize her behavior as that of a concerned parent.

Bettina had been an accomplished actuary for an insurance company before she quit work to stay home while her children were young. She was proud of her analytical skills, her ability to sit with a mathematical problem and steadily work her way through to a solution. She possessed all the positive attributes of a focuser: attentiveness, concentration, and analytical skills. But at home with two toddlers and little adult interaction, it seemed these abilities had turned on her. Bettina had gradually fallen prey to ruminative behavior that was getting out of hand.

Her internist correctly identified her problem as obsessional behavior: endless and repetitive worries or concerns. He believed her condition was serious enough to consider treatment for OCD (obsessive-compulsive disorder). He knew of a new drug, Anafranil, that was having marvelous success for this ailment. I asked Bettina to hold off starting the medication. While the medication could diffuse her worrying temporarily, she would not learn to cope with her temperament on her own. What's more, she would be likely to relapse if she discontinued it, and she would be back to square one.

As you can surmise, I certainly didn't agree with their doctors that either Willis or Bettina were suffering from disorders or illnesses that required medication. It might be argued that their symptoms were diminishing their lives, but the remedies, in my mind, need not be as radical as had been suggested. Depression and obsessionalism may have been technically appropriate labels, but they were negative and simplistic. They pointed to illness more than to solutions. My approach is reempowering the patient by teaching him how to use his own nature and insights into himself to rebuild his emotional vibrancy. My take on psychiatric medication is like the Peace Corps's credo: Give a man a fish and he'll eat for a day. Teach him how to fish, and he'll feed himself the rest of his life.

Willis and Bettina were struggling with moods that were different only in degree from what most of us cope with on a daily basis. Like other focusers, they are temperamentally predisposed to occasional bouts of inner emptiness, which only in the extreme become depression or obsessionalism.

THE MOODY TEMPERAMENT

If moodiness—sadness, worry, melancholy—overcomes you more often than you'd like (or if you're living with someone who's like this), you may want to read this chapter quite carefully. You might be biologically predisposed to such occasional moods. You might have the temperament I call the focuser.

If you're a focuser, your strengths include a gift for introspection and a heightened ability to concentrate on, analyze, and devise solutions to intricate issues or projects. You probably owe much of your success in life to your ability to research an opportunity or project comprehensively. You analyze its strong and weak points, and show your attention to detail in following any project through, whether it's making a purchase, organizing an event, or shepherding a work project to completion.

Like warp and woof, your strengths are woven with your vulnerabilities. The focuser's vulnerabilities are boredom, sadness, worry, and malaise. These are normal and inevitable moods states for all of us. But if you're a focuser, you're prone to letting these feelings get out of control.

You're especially vulnerable when you're not busy—in solitude, when you can't sleep, when you go on vacation. When you're left with literally nothing to do, your inner thoughts may emerge to disturb you. Your mind starts free associating; random thoughts pop up from nowhere. Your thoughts may give rise to brooding, the recalling of old resentments, opportunities blown, trust betrayed, should-haves, would-haves, could-haves. And you end up feeling the hurt feelings all over again. Or, in such times of quiet, you may be prone to worrying about current problems, and working yourself into an anxious, unsettled mood, imagining worst-case scenarios.

If you're a focuser, you're all too aware that free time or time spent by yourself can be problematic for you. What's at work is the key dynamic of the focuser: introspectively creating unpleasant emotions or bad moods when there's nothing going on in the real world around you to trigger such emotions. Remember that temperament is a private experience; only you know how you genuinely feel inside. Behind the upbeat, composed public face you show to others, you're likely to hide your down moods. You don't want to be a dark cloud and alienate people, and you don't want to make the people around you miserable as well. You probably hide your downs from everyone but your closest friends and confidantes.

Usually your spouse bears the brunt of your intermittent sadness or moods. You answer, "How are you feeling? Is anything wrong?" with a shrug of your shoulders and a wistful, "Oh, I'm just in a funk—a lousy mood—I just feel down about things." Or, if you decide to deny it, "I'm just tired, I'm fine." Nonetheless, through the process of emotional osmosis, those close to you are likely to sense what you are feeling.

Your behavior in infancy and early childhood helps to identify your innate temperament. Your parents may remember
that you were prone to moodiness even as a child. When other
kids may have expressed their emotions outwardly and inten-
sively, you were inclined to mope a bit more, retreat into yourself. Luckily, the focuser child is also predisposed to discover
within himself inner resources that actually become assets. The
creation of imaginary playmates, for example, is highly related
to later creative thinking.

There is, in fact, a correlation between intelligence and being
a focuser. Studies indicate that bright people are more likely to
be pessimistic and depressed because they have a more accurate
picture of life and its troubles. Bright, creative, introspective
people have the somewhat dubious ability to focus on their concerns and worry themselves into a miserable state. This same
ability to concentrate and ruminate enables them to grapple
with complex intellectual pursuits. Abraham Lincoln and Winston Churchill undoubtedly were focusers, given their well-
documented moods—what Churchill called the "black dogs"
—so you are in good company.

MISLEADING MESSAGES

All his life the focuser has been told that he is too pessimistic or
apprehensive. When younger, he was told he was too gloomy.
As he got older, he became influenced by society's messages of
why people feel the way they do. Conventional therapists tell
the focuser that some loss or withholding of love must have
caused his intermittent bouts of feeling melancholy.

As a focuser, if you sought counseling or psychotherapy, the
therapist likely said, "Let's work through the losses you obviously must have experienced." Well-intentioned professionals
urged you to focus on these inner feelings to try to connect
them to childhood experiences. What they did, unfortunately, is
reinforce your predisposition to self-focusing and rumination.

Most therapies imply that if you only do what they suggest
you do, you will never feel this emptiness again. And that's
where they really mess you up. They unwittingly encourage
ruminative behavior, the endless rehashing of old wounds—a

process that only promotes more ruminative behavior. Even antidepressants promote this false message—that is, if you take this pill for a while, you'll get over this painful episode of moodiness and (implicit) you'll probably not feel it again (subtext message: and if you do, there's probably something seriously wrong with you!).

My more hopeful message is that once you understand that your temperament is also a mood forecaster, you won't be thrown by your feelings, you won't become a captive to them, and your self-esteem won't be undermined by them.

THE FOCUSER'S NATURAL SELF

HIGH THRESHOLD OF AROUSAL

Unlike the sensor and the discharger, focusers have a high threshold of arousal. As a result, they tend to feel less arousal, and thus are prone to feeling empty and bored.

ACTION TENDENCY: INTROVERTED/RUMINATION

As a focuser, when you sense this lack of arousal, your innate reflex is to try to raise it to generate some sort of feelings, to feel something, in order to feel alive again. Because your action tendency is inward oriented (like the sensor, you are introverted), you become self-focused and self-absorbed. In simple terms, you look inside and wonder why you feel nothing. On a subconscious level of awareness, you ponder your lack of bodily sensation, which may be experienced as hollowness. Gradually, this becomes more conscious. You become acutely aware of feeling nothing. And, as your attention increases, the sensations are consequently magnified. Next, the interpretive function kicks in: "I'm feeling empty because . . ." You're likely to focus on some painful loss or disappointment in your life, and you start to feel sad. Emptiness becomes sadness.

As we'll see, what breaks this pattern is not ignored or repressed feelings but distraction—a new activity that will short circuit the fixation. This can be as simple as returning a phone call or leafing through a magazine. Distraction is the focuser's corrective task.

The focuser is inward oriented to a fault. There is a growing body of psychological research that demonstrates the negative and depressive effects of self-focusing styles. This research has not taken the step I have, which is linking this action tendency to temperament and biologically based the thresholds of arousal.

THE GIFT OF INTROSPECTION

The propensity to look inward can be a very positive attribute. It allows for insights that the outward-looking individual never discovers. Graham is a history professor who has also published several university press history books. His area of expertise is the Civil War. Graham has a labyrinthine mind and memory. In his popular lectures, he brings to life entire Civil War battles, replete with biographies of generals and foot soldiers, military strategy, and all the raw, cataclysmic carnage of that tragic era in American history. Like Shakespeare or Gore Vidal or William F. Buckley, Graham leavens his often dark views with his wry, laconic humor and his sense of irony about humankind's doomed grandiosity.

Though he has many private moments of moodiness and even occasional bouts of sadness, Graham is a sought-after dinner party guest because of his brilliant and quite funny analyses of political issues, movies, and social trends. His gift for introspection allows him to make connections and find the ironic twist in topics.

Oddly enough, this link between humor and moodiness is rather common. Many comedians are focusers. It is said that all humor stems from the pain of being human. Great comedians, such as Charlie Chaplin, George Carlin, Richard Pryor, and Lenny Bruce, share dark perspectives. They all possess or possessed the gift of taking painful experiences, reflecting on them, looking at them from new angles, and discovering the ironic twist that turns the pain into insight and humor.

Studies on people prone to depression and pessimism find

they are often much more accurate perceivers of life. They are certainly not prone to fantasy or undue optimism. This capacity for accurate insight and introspection, when appreciated, lends a fascinating facet to one's personality.

THE FOCUSER'S DARK SIDE: DEPRESSION AND OBSESSION

Sadness is normal. No one is immune to the hurt of a disappointment, whether it's a love affair that fails, a personal ambition that's thwarted, or sadness for other people's misfortunes. If you're alive, you're going to hurt sometimes. The focuser experiences sadness too, but he worries about the feeling itself. Again, it's what we do with these inevitable despondent moments—whether we grieve and recover and risk again or whether we go into a decline—that shapes how we move through our lives.

Like sadness, worry is normal. Life is certainly filled with enough uncertainty that there are concerns to worry about. None of us has enough control over our destiny to be worry free. It is temperament which determines *how* we deal with worry. For the focuser, the progression from mild apprehension to worry to painful and unrelenting rumination can be subtle. An avalanche can begin with a rolling pebble. If you do nothing to stop it, worry can snowball into obsession.

The focuser is often misunderstood, mislabeled, and misdiagnosed. When focusers are in extreme distress, they are labeled as having mental or emotional disorders because their daily functioning is impaired. But these so-called disorders need a fresh look. I believe entrenched theories have been off the mark. The elemental questions that may point to solutions are: Why do some people deal with worry and sadness so much better than others? How are people different who have trouble snapping out of depression?

OUTDATED THEORIES OF MOODINESS

We're going to take a detour into the theories that have evolved concerning depression and obsession. Most doctors and therapists use these theories to guide you. It is mandatory that I caution the reader at this point. In order to understand the dynamics of sadness and worry, one must study the research on the extreme forms of these states, that is, depression and obsessional behavior. But keep in mind that the focuser is not necessarily ill. The extreme form of this temperament is what has been most documented, which is why we are exploring it now.

There is no more comprehensively documented illness than depression. It is said to affect more of us than any other mental illness. Statistics tell us that clinical (severe) depression will affect 20 million Americans at some point in their lives. Clinical depression can be marked by persistent sad moods, feelings of hopelessness and worthlessness, a lack of appetite for any of life's pleasures, sleep problems, difficulty concentrating, and irritability—the list is long.

A much smaller percentage of us suffer from uncontrollable worrying and ruminations labeled as obsessive disorders. Obsessions are defined as recurrent and persistent thoughts. For some people, this mental fixation leads to physical behaviors known as compulsions, which are defined as repetitive and purposeful actions. The purposeful behaviors are designed to reduce anxiety or inner tension. For example, a man who has what he believes are bad or dirty thoughts can engage in compulsive hand washing as an unconscious way to expiate his guilt over his thoughts. The woman who is worried about a lack of control in her life keeps checking to see if she has her keys or if she turned off her stove.

LOSS THEORIES OF DEPRESSION

The first theories of depression were formulated by Sigmund Freud and his disciples. The key word is *loss*. Depression was said to be the emotional reaction to a real or imagined loss. More specifically, the loss of someone important to us, someone who provided love and emotional security. There are unlimited ways in which this loss may occur: death, separation, abandonment, rejection. If this loss occurred early in life, the sufferer was said to be prone to depression all of his life.

Later psychoanalytic theorists elaborated on loss as a way to explain the role of anger, or anger-turned-inward in depression. The survivor was said to mentally incorporate or internalize the person he lost, and then vent his rage toward this abandoner, through self-hatred or self-loathing. Very esoteric, very interesting, and for the most part, I believe, quite useless in treatment. Yes, it is important to work your way through loss, and it is important to grieve, then to let go. But the loss theory could not account for all the sadness, melancholy, and depression experienced by people who hadn't lost anyone or anything!

COGNITIVE THEORIES OF DEPRESSION

In time, Freud's loss model was eclipsed by other theories of depression. These theories emphasize how we think—they are cognitive theories. One is called the helplessness theory. Psychologist Martin Seligman at the University of Pennsylvania hypothesized that depression hit people who attribute their helplessness to their own lack of skills. They blame themselves for not coping better, and they carry the belief that they will remain helpless into every new situation.

Psychiatrist Aaron Beck, the father of cognitive therapy, theorized that childhood failures and bad experiences led to the development of negative schemas, or belief systems. These are dysfunctional attitudes that say, "I can't control my environment," or "Bad things tend to happen to me." Not surprisingly, these attitudes undermine self-esteem like termites in your foundation. People who hold negative schemas or belief systems can become seriously depressed in the face of any setback—not just tragic or crisis events but normal, everyday pressures.

The weakness in cognitive theories such as these, in my view, is that bad thinking doesn't adequately explain people who are intermittently blue, in spite of the fact that they're doing wonderfully by objective standards. They may be successful, stable, and have supportive families! Cognitive theories come up short, I believe, because they insist on learned ways of thinking as causes when oftentimes moods are simply biochemical effects of one's innate temperament.

THEORIES OF OBSESSIONS

In contrast to depression, theories of obsessionalism or excessive worry focus on thinking disorders in which over-intellectualization is the predominant symptom. Obsessive thinking is said to be a maladaptive strategy people employ in order to reduce anxiety over some feared thought or action. The glaring inadequacy of this theory is that clinicians cannot explain why tranquilizers or antianxiety drugs don't seem to work. If obsession is an anxiety condition, tranquilizers should soothe obsessive thinkers, but they're not effective at all. In fact, it is antidepressants that deliver relief from obsessions—a puzzle that can be explained by my temperament theory.

CURRENT BIOCHEMICAL THEORIES OF DEPRESSION

Discoveries about brain chemistry in recent years have led to a revolution in thinking about depression. The great successes with antidepressant medication led biopsychiatrists to redefine depression from a purely biochemical standpoint: a mood of affective disorder caused by a chemical imbalance, plain and simple, with no causality laid to personal history. These new beliefs were helpful in many ways. Sufferers no longer had to shoulder the blame for causing their illness by their negative thinking; there was no need to explore or work through unhappy childhoods or losses.

The latest family of antidepressants focuses on the neurotransmitter called serotonin. Perhaps the most publicized new drug, Prozac, is what is called a serotonin re-uptake blocker—that is, instead of serotonin being absorbed by a particular receptor as it travels along its path, Prozac blocks this soaking-up action and therefore allows the serotonin to travel unobstructed along the pathways in the parts of the brain that control emotions.

The exciting results from Prozac and other antidepressants led to many trial-and-error studies. As antidepressants were used randomly and blindly to treat a variety of problems, including depression, eating disorders, and obsessions, their success rate for a wide spectrum of disorders led to confusion in diagnosis. Because these disorders were helped by antidepressants, are these problems merely different faces of depression? Some biopsychiatrists think so, but such a global conclusion flies in the face of logic and intuition. Surely there is a better answer than lumping these disorders together as depression. What is the biochemical common denominator?

In conventional therapy, in clinical practice and theory, depressions and obsessions are thought to be unrelated in any way. They are approached as different classifications of ailments with different causes and different treatments. Significantly, I believe they are related both in their cause and their correction.

SELF-FOCUSING AND FIXATION: THE MISSING LINK

The real truth, in my view, is that antidepressants are not antidepressants. I believe it is more accurate to define them as arousal activators! This is most clearly seen in the success of Prozac with both obsessional behavior—which was thought to be an anxiety condition—and depression, which was classified as a mood disorder. What these two conditions have in common is underarousal and self-focusing. Obsessives are thought to be chronically overaroused because they are thinking all the time. It's my belief that the opposite is true: obsessives are underaroused, like depressives.

According to my temperament theory, both sadness (depression, when extreme) and worry (obsession, when extreme) are caused by high thresholds of arousal that result in fixation, or an inability to break away from self-focusing. Focusers are prone to fixate either on loss and emptiness (depression) or worries (obsessions).

What do antidepressants like Prozac do? Such serotonin re-uptake blockers boost the flow of serotonin. They wake up or activate the arousal systems of depressives and obsessives (as long as they continue on the drug). More serotonin means more arousal. The aliveness redirects people's attention to the outside world, away from themselves; it serves to allow them to release or distract from self-focusing and fixation.

Another class of antidepressants are known as monoamine oxidase inhibitors (MAOI). They inhibit MAO, an enzyme that influences serotonin. Depressed people may have high levels of MAO. By inhibiting MAO, these antidepressants act as psychic energizers.

These, then, are the underlying theories. Again, don't be thrown by the discussion of pathology (illness). The research on emotional illness sheds light on our normal moods. The crucial difference is, obviously, in degree. We took this detour in order to understand the focuser's normal natural self, which is illuminated by the key theories that deal with the focuser in extremis.

THE GENDER GAP

Women, in general, are more emotional (perhaps partly due to hormonal factors) and are more aware of their emotions than men (certainly due to cultural conditioning). It follows that women focusers are likely to be more sensitive to their inner arousal or *lack* of inner arousal. The female focuser is likely to play out her need for emotional stimulation in romance and marriage, searching for the perfect exciting partner, looking to her boyfriend or husband to provide enthusiasm and spark. And she is likely to focus her worrying and her tendency to fixate on her love relationship or marriage.

Men, typically, are less likely than women to pay attention to their inner emotions. The typical male focuser is likely to be less consciously aware than the female focuser of his lack of arousal and his tendency to fixate and worry. He is likely to play out his need for stimulation in the arena of work, career, success, and money. These are the magnets, as well, for his worrying and analyzing.

THE FOCUSER IN RELATIONSHIPS

ROMANTIC CHEMISTRY

Love and romance are ideal fantasy solutions to the focuser's fear of lack of aliveness. What better antidote than the excitement of a new romance? Indeed, for many of us, the word *excitement* conjures up romance and the powerful feelings we experience as we fall in love.

If you are a focuser, the quest for love and for someone who will change everything is likely to be the solution to your internal lack of arousal. Your unconscious wish is for someone who will save you from your moodiness or boredom. You are usually drawn to people who excite you, including the exciting seeker and the emotionally explosive discharger. You may be attracted to passionate types: opinionated, emotionally expressive, even volatile personalities, men or women who make you feel emotionally alive. Or you may be attracted to partners who are doers, active, even hyperactive, in sports, outdoor activities, hobbies, politics, religious or spiritual quests—you love their passion and enthusiasm.

Your craving for emotional stimulation can lead you down more twisted avenues, unfortunately. You are vulnerable to relationships with people with problems. You get a contact emotional high from their emotional chaos. You get to star in your own personal soap opera. It gives you good reason and ample material for what terrifies you—worrying about their problems and your relationship. And you can can analyze, criticize, counsel them, and try to fix them, playing out all the facets of your temperament. You may have a pattern of chasing elusive or rejecting lovers or getting involved with married or otherwise unavailable men or women. The bad or difficult relationship provides a generous supply of emotional stimulation.

The single focuser is likely to date long and hard, searching for the perfect, exciting mate. The fantasy of mate as savior is played out endlessly in the focuser's love affairs. As you gradually come to realize your partner cannot provide continual stimulation, you may feel resentment, even hostility. You conclude that he just wasn't right for you and you move on to someone new, vainly searching for an external solution to what is an internal biochemical dilemma that cannot be solved by anyone but yourself!

In dating, you may be overcritical. And you may have problems with intimacy, in allowing anyone to get too close to you, for fear they'll reject you when they experience your moodiness.

Marriage commonly gets hyped as a source of joy. Many marriage advisors hold out the implicit promise that, if you work on your marriage in the right way, your marriage will make you feel alive in ways you never thought possible. This advice feeds into the focuser's rich fantasy life, as well as into the focuser's predisposition to ruminate. You can ruminate endlessly about what's wrong with your marriage, how to improve it, or how you can turn your mate into a fantasy lover.

CONFLICT IN RELATIONSHIPS

Blaming your husband or wife for failing to provide that missing spark in your life is scapegoating. Unfortunately, it is sanctioned by scores of books, magazine articles, and talk shows that encourage people to look outside themselves for solutions to their personal dilemmas, such as expecting your partner to make you feel more alive.

Whereas for other temperament types boredom is an emotionally neutral gear, focusers read boredom as a prelude to sadness. Not surprisingly, focusers are especially resistant to the reality that periods of boredom are natural and inevitable in any marriage.

Wendy and Jack entered marital therapy at Wendy's insistence. After twelve years of marriage, she felt they had gone adrift. She felt a sense of routine and predictability that she found dreadful. "We act like we're old already," she said.

Jack, on the other hand, was like many married men I see, basically quite satisfied. "I love her. We have a great family. Our sex life is okay, I guess. Maybe we could communicate more, but, frankly, I get so pissed off at her complaints that I don't really feel like talking." They sounded like hundreds of other couples I've seen in my office.

In couples therapy, I try to find out what is going on with the partner who is most dissatisfied, in this case, Wendy. What does she really want? And why does she want it? Most people who take the trouble to come into treatment are hurting in some way. They rarely just want to improve their marriage—they're usually motivated by urgent emotional distress.

Talking with Wendy about her inner emotional life, it became clear to me that she was a focuser. She had lots of friends, lots of interests, and appeared upbeat. But inwardly she was a worrier. This manifested as perfectionism. If things weren't done just right, she felt vaguely unsettled. Especially when her children were infants and toddlers, her worries had dominated their family life.

The more I probed, the more I began to get a feel for the frequency of her worries, and when they became obsessive. It was during these times that she felt most "turned off inside," as she put it. "I do have a tendency to feel real pessimistic at times, but I usually snap out of it. Lately, I know I really don't have a lot to worry about, yet I don't feel happy. I feel a kind of sadness unless I'm preoccupied with projects. I think the cause of what I'm feeling really is our marriage. It's sort of stagnant."

I told Wendy there were two dynamics at work. One was a marriage that certainly could use some revitalization. The other was her lack of awareness of her own temperament. She was confusing the two issues. I told her that she had to forget her husband as a remedy to her occasional underarousal. Jack hadn't created her biological temperament, and he couldn't cure it. Her marriage could indeed be better, but first they needed to set aside blame and accusation. If she told Jack, "Look, I have this tendency to feel a little morose and worried at times. It would help me feel happier if you and I could try to have more fun together," this would be a positive communication. Her two-hour harangues on the theme, "You are so boring," weren't helping.

I asked Wendy and Jack not to communicate at all about the relationship. Wendy's task was to research and plan new activities and interests that she and her husband could do together, and new interests she could do alone. She was *not* to work on changing Jack, or look to him to solve her problem.

Once you start obsessing about ways your mate can be improved or helped to grow, the sky is the limit. Why stop at nagging your husband to lose ten pounds, or to pick up his wet towel from the bathroom floor? Why isn't your wife more interested in your work? Why isn't she funnier or nicer in the morning?

Thinking about ways someone can improve is similar to becoming annoyed by a particular quality or mannerism in your mate, then thinking about it all the time. That obsessive concern is not only difficult to shake but it magnifies the irritating quality until it is all you can see. This blaming in the guise of improving backfires hugely on the focuser. The more the focuser criticizes, blames, and accuses, the more likely her mate is to withdraw emotionally. Then the focuser gets even less stimulus from her mate.

The focuser is likely to view communication as the lever by which the marriage will be captapulted into something more alive and stimulating. Focusers are victims of pop-psych thinking. "Get in touch with your feelings" and "talk it out" are two prescriptions they eagerly embrace. If any temperament type is qualified to engage in excessive self-absorption and endless talk, it is the focuser. Unfortunately, when she announces to her mate, "We have to communicate more," what she is really saying is, "Join me in my rumination to feel more alive." The person on the other end of such a request is saying, "No thanks," as he withdraws.

Another common behavior in the focuser is sexual fantasy. It is easy for a focuser to get caught up in fantasy. For example, a focuser may get obsessed with a bank teller, or a tennis partner, and may secretly ruminate about having an affair. Usually this fantasy will not be acted on but instead will remain safely within the realm of fantasy. Why don't focusers act on their fantasies? Because these fantasies are more about excitement—filling up their emptiness—than about sexual hunger or lust. Sometimes I work with focusers who compulsively masturbate, and this is often the key to what is going on. They feel deadened inside, and masturbating to a fantasy momentarily counteracts this deadness. At its most basic level, they are looking for any sensation in order to feel more alive.

As a focuser, before you can build a sound love relationship, you must first deal with accepting and honoring your temperament. When you can acknowledge that other people are not going to fix you, and that it is up to you to cope with the difficult aspects of your temperament, a relationship or marriage can serve as a healthy distractor, in the best sense of the word. I have emphasized the focuser's dilemmas, but focusers can make warm, attentive, giving mates.

FRIENDSHIPS

Focusers are certainly good friends. They do sometimes have difficulties trusting their friends. They are inclined to experience emptiness and begin ruminating about the quality of their friendships and the degree to which their friends care about them. In these instances, just as in marriage, a fear they are not getting enough back from their friends will trouble them and even plunge them into endless rumination about possible neglect.

THE FOCUSER PARENT

Parents worry, and focuser parents probably worry a whole lot more than other parents. If you recognize in yourself this tendency to worry, you will have to be extra cautious and work on sorting out normal worries, normal parental concerns, and excessive worry due more to your temperament. The good news is that focuser parents are also very conscientious and consistent in their loving and protectiveness.

THE FOCUSER AT WORK

AMBITION AND CAREER

In America, our favorite fantasy and antidote to boredom, sadness, or worry is money and success. The hope of a win or a score or a successful deal makes anyone feel excited. While the female focuser may look to romance or marriage to provide excitement, the male focuser is more likely to look to the work arena to play out his need for vibrance.

Arnold is a successful entrepreneur who happens to be a focuser. His entire life has been spent on a quest for financial success. He came to see me at age forty-six because all his years of intense striving had not made a dent in his daily emotional state. Prone to dark depressions that could last for weeks, he finally had come to the conclusion that something was wrong with him. In recent months he had become increasingly despondent. He spent many hours just sitting around the house. His company could now run quite well without his constant presence. His wife suggested that he seek therapy. She was quite sure he was seriously depressed; whenever she tried to coax him out of his moods, he just became more irritable with her.

Arnold was clearly a focuser. From childhood on, he had been a somber and sometimes sad person. He remembered his teenage years; many hours were spent alone, dreaming but also worrying about school, girls, getting into a good college. And, in later years, he had worried about law school, then choosing to go into business. "It's been rather joyless most of the time," Arnold admitted.

Arnold tried to convince me he was having a midlife crisis. "My values are like junk food," he said. "That's where I went wrong. I should have become a marine biologist, like my brother. He doesn't have a pot to piss in, but he's happy." I agreed that he had missed out on a lot—friendships, community involvement, spiritual development—as a result of his pursuit for money. But I urged him to delay any major changes, such as buying a sailboat and setting off for the South Pacific until he learned more about himself.

Arnold did become more acquainted with himself. He developed new and creative interests that are providing both distraction and gratification for him. It turned out that this self-knowledge was more important to him than intense striving to make money. He came home to himself.

So many men and women find themselves disillusioned when they finally taste the long-sought rewards of success. Focusers are the most susceptible to this disenchantment. They finally get the job, the house, money in the bank—whatever is their personal totem of success—and they crash. They had always hoped that success would make them happy. Forgive me if I borrow the cliche that, "It's an inside job." Nothing and no one—nothing external—can assure your happiness. But by learning to orchestrate your emotional life—how you react to whatever life deals you—you can become more comfortable, more resilient. Once you learn to work *with* your temperament, work and achievement can serve as terrific distractors.

THE FOCUSER EMPLOYEE

You can be an outstanding employee. You are likely to be analytical, precise, and attentive to details. Rumination and the ability to concentrate, after all, is what enables scientists, writers, scholars, and inventors, among others, to explore all the facets of a project before they begin their creative problem solving.

You may be prone to getting bogged down in details, getting overanalytical, and losing sight of the cost effectiveness of dealing with a problem the best you can and moving forward. You may lose time fixating on problems. You need to remind yourself often that rarely does any project in the business world go as planned or approach perfection.

The focuser can easily be thrown by ordinary setbacks in the business or work world. All of us can become discouraged or worried in the face of real adversity, but it is usually the focuser who stays in a funk longer and who is liable to be overwhelmed by feelings of helplessness and pessimism. Since your worry and despondency can be infectious, and your gloom can spread faster than the flu, you probably know all too well that your coworkers are likely to pull away from you when you fall into these moods. You can quickly build a spiral of failure when sadness, pessimism, or indecision caused by excessive worry erode your work relationships or productivity. For this reason, knowing how to cope with your temperament and short circuit its negatives is imperative for your economic survival, at the most basic level.

THE FOCUSER BOSS

Heads of companies are often focusers. They are able to analyze a project, asset the competition, develop strategy and procedures, set goals, and stay on track. There is a link between leadership and focusing. Remember our focuser, Winston Churchill, who was said to struggle with major bouts of depression. He understood his temperament, and when the "black dogs" came over him, as he knew they would, he would seclude himself in his study and think and write. He kept his inclination to be obssesive within his control by giving it a clear, positive outlet.

FALSE PATHS TO EMOTIONAL RELIEF

As a focuser, your dislike of underarousal may be so powerful that your visceral instinct is to get rid of the lifeless feeling at any

cost. For that reason, focusers often are black-belt therapy consumers. You'll eagerly read any book, try any therapy, attend
any growth seminar, join self-actualizing organizations—anything that promises emotional relief, psychological change, or
aliveness. Let's look at why and how these avenues can turn out
to be false solutions for you.

UNENDING INSIGHT PSYCHOTHERAPY

For the focuser, insight or traditional psychotherapy has built-in
pitfalls. Such therapy is predicated on getting in touch with
your feelings, on self-focusing, which is your problem! You end
up with a partner in your rumination—the therapist! You can
remain in therapy for decades and, although you'll accumulate
a great deal of intellectual insight, you're likely to feel no better,
no happier. For you, countless hours of introspection and
analysis are destined to fail to deliver the emotional relief you
long for.

ADDICTION TO PERSONAL GROWTH SEMINARS

In my experiences with men and women enamored of the new
twelve-step recovery groups based on the AA (Alcoholics Anonymous) model, I find focusers to be easy converts. This is especially true of therapies whose pivotal concept is the wounded
inner child. The spontaneous, trusting, vibrant inner child is
fantasied to be the source of potential aliveness. The promise is
that once your inner child is acknowledged, loved, and its childhood wounds are healed, you will be rejuvenated by your awak-
ened inner child. Your inner child will become a source of joy,
play, and inner contentment—a perfect antidote to brooding
and endless concern. Like a crab shedding its shell on a beach in
the moonlight, you will cast off your old moody persona and
dance away in a new guise.

Johnny is a young assistant professor of theater arts at a local
college. We have known each other for a number of years and
have had an ongoing dialogue about therapy techniques and
changes in my field. Astute and analytical, he won his post at the
college on the basis of a brilliant reappraisal of the plays of one
of America's darkest playwrights, a dissertation that was re-

worked as a college dramatic arts textbook. He's a gifted direc-
tor and dramaturge who guides his students to the essence of
their characters.

But when it came to his moods, Johnny hated himself. Prone
to inexplicable "funks" that came out of the blue, he had at one
time flirted with cocaine as a solution. This led to an empty
pocketbook and a serious depression. That depression set him
on his self-actualizing quest. He told me he believed that his
seminar treks—a number of them over the span of six years—
were a search for self-acceptance. I told him I thought he was
driven by self-loathing; he couldn't stand who he really was and
he was trying to change into someone different.

As we explored each of his experiences, Johnny conceded
that the positive effects, the honeymoon of hope and love and
connection with the seminar leader and other members, faded
after a few months. He would get bored and eventually cut
down his participation from an intense two or three times a
week meetings, to once in a while. Then he would start looking
for something else to fix him—to minimize his downs and increase his periods of aliveness. But invariably he would settle
back into his basic temperament—the focuser.

After I helped him explore his temperament, and he learned
not to be frightened by underarousal, he gradually learned how
to recognize what his body was saying. Johnny learned to accept
his underarousal, not analyze it. He learned to calmly and deliberately distract himself not in a morning meditation or at a
weekend seminar but *as it happened.* The whole process took
only minutes. He enlarged his emotional comfort zone by short-
ening his periods of melancholy and elongating his periods of
aliveness. By fighting his temperament, he had turned it into his
enemy. I believe the quest of an inner child can be helpful for
some people, but not when the search is for an idealized fantasy.
My goal is to help you reclaim your genuine self.

ANTIDEPRESSANTS AS AN AROUSAL CRUTCH

Conventional treatment approaches for depression and obsessional worry have had limited success, for several reasons. In
the long run, drug therapy precludes you from learning to

lower your threshold on your own. However, it can be helpful as a short-term aid. For example, to relieve an acute episode of depression or fixation, or to boost a chronically sad or worried patient to a comfort level at which he or she can benefit from talking therapy. Unfortunately, most people remain on the medication well beyond the point at which they're stabilized in their emotional comfort zone: the patient may be fearful of a relapse; the doctor may be unaware of when to stop the drug treatment.

Some focusers who take antidepressants (or arousal activators, in my opinion) may at first feel more vibrant. If your experience with antidepressants was typical of most people, you may remember that within a few weeks you felt better and started to recover your interest in activities, which in turn boosted your confidence and self-esteem. Sooner or later, you felt "cured," and, when your prescription ran out, you didn't renew it. "I don't need the pills anymore. I pulled out of it." Within a few weeks, you may have felt your energy and enthusiasm evaporating, and you may have started sliding back into that gray and gloomy mood.

Typically, when this happens, and it's very common, people make another appointment with their doctor and ask for another prescription. Now, unfortunately, they begin to identify themselves as mentally or emotionally ill and begin to feel ashamed of their condition. I have read many studies in which psychopharmacologists, noting this common pattern, conclude that it might be better for the patient's self-confidence if he remains on the medication continually—presumably forever! This opinion is an implied admission that medications don't cure an emotional disorder; they just manage it. You can't cure a temperament. But you can learn to manage it without perpetual prescriptions.

SELF-MEDICATION: STIMULANTS AND FOOD

Unlike the sensor, who craves sedation and tranquilizing, if you're a focuser, you crave arousal and aliveness—you crave stimulants. Whereas you may find the sensor at a bar, the discharger at a soccer game, and the seeker on a mountaineering

expedition, you will find focusers in their natural habitat: cof-
feehouses and cafes. In any setting, the heavy smokers and
persistent coffee drinkers are likely to be focusers. They love
the buzz, the charge, and the boost that caffeine and nicotine
deliver. Focusers are vulnerable to all stimulants, including
strong ones such as cocaine.

Food is a self-medication of a slightly different sort. Whereas
sensors may overeat to soothe and sedate themselves, focusers
may engage in binge or compulsive eating to fill up their inner
emptiness. Jane, a high school science teacher, found that emotional upset threw her into a state of self-absorption. "What did
I do wrong?" she worried. "How could I have said that?" She
would isolate herself and engage in endless worry; usually this
happened when a love relationship failed. Then she would
binge on sweets and bakery goods. The fantasy of putting more
stuff inside always seemed to fill her up momentarily. But the
boost in her emotional state lasted only a few minutes, and her
moodiness would return. Now, to compound her moodiness,
she had another thing to hate herself for—overeating and gaining weight. Jane was a bulimic, off and on, for twelve years. This
vicious cycle may be familiar to many of you; eating disorders
are among the most common dilemmas we face in therapy.
Both sensors and focusers are prone to such self-defeating solutions, since food will soothe anxiety and fill up emptiness, at
least temporarily. Sugar and its momentary high will also make
one feel alive.

EXPANDING YOUR COMFORT ZONE: DISTRACTION

For the focusers, the first step toward orchestrating their emotional life is self-acceptance, which is an especially tough step for
focusers to take. They've made a habit of thinking that, if only
they continue to worry or ruminate about their troubles, they
will discover a solution. Like other types, what they reflexively
do in the face of too little or too much arousal is often the very
response that exacerbates their emotional dilemma. Helping
them become aware that they have a natural self operating below their conscious self is the first, and most difficult, task for
anyone counseling a focuser.

The task for focusers is to master the step-by-step distraction process that I will describe in detail in part III of the book. Remember that the key concept for the sensor was desensitization and for the discharger, benign release?" The key concept for the focuser is distraction. Distraction leads to a release of the fixation and a boosting of aliveness or arousal. This is what psychotropic medication does, as well. Based on what we know about the chemical actions of certain antidepressants, it's my view that when serotonin is stimulated, arousal is activated, fixation is released, distractions occur, and the depression lifts. Happily, we can learn to employ distraction without medications.

My goal is to teach you how to lower thresholds on your own. You'll feel more alive, and you'll have the energy and the desire to engage in positively distracting activities: work, social life, sports, and so on. You will break the habit of depression and develop what I call a distraction reflex. In time, action rather than rumination will become second nature.

FOCUSERS: LIBERATION FROM TOXIC MYTHS

1. The myth of uniformity: No one is free from worry or even despondency. Most people hide these emotions, but they still have them.

2. The myth of good and bad: Worry and sadness are certainly not desirable, but to regard them as bad is to open yourself to shame and feelings of inadequacy.

3. The myth of control: Believing you can dominate your worries or control the possibility of sadness will make you focus interminably on the lack of aliveness you feel. Attempting to control that over which you feel helpless will only make your life more unhappy.

4. The myth of perfectibility: In the best of all possible worlds, there are always future events to worry about, disappointments to absorb. Do not delude yourself into thinking a life can always be blissful.

5. The myth of emotional illness: To experience worry and sadness is to experience the most common emotions in life.

Even when such feelings make you unhappy, that doesn't mean you are ill. To define yourself as ill may be what is needed to give yourself permission to get some help, but in the long run, it is a label that harms more than helps.

6. The myth of positive thinking: The focuser may not be helped at all by positive thinking; in fact, it may produce the opposite effect. Focusers think too much, and the antidote is not thinking but taking action.

THE FOCUSER IDENTIFICATION CHECKLIST

Rate the following statements by making an "X" on the blank line next to the response that best describes you:

1. I often experience periods of sadness.

   _____ 1 Not at all true
   _____ 2 Rarely true
   _____ 3 Somewhat true
   _____ 4 Always true

2. When something bothers me, I tend to ruminate about it.

   _____ 1 Not at all true
   _____ 2 Rarely true
   _____ 3 Somewhat true
   _____ 4 Always true

3. My ability to concentrate is very good and I am able to focus for long periods of time on getting tasks done well.

   _____ 1 Not at all true
   _____ 2 Rarely true
   _____ 3 Somewhat true
   _____ 4 Always true

4. I experience much boredom in my life.

   _____ 1 Not at all true
   _____ 2 Rarely true
   _____ 3 Somewhat true
   _____ 4 Always true

5. Once I begin to even briefly think about past mistakes

and painful experiences, I often continue to think about them for a long while.

_____ 1 Not at all true
_____ 2 Rarely true
_____ 3 Somewhat true
_____ 4 Always true

6. When I worry, I tend to build up my concerns into huge worries that interfere with my thinking about other things.

_____ 1 Not at all true
_____ 2 Rarely true
_____ 3 Somewhat true
_____ 4 Always true

7. I usually think that if I concentrate on thinking about whatever is bothering me, I will find a way to feel better.

_____ 1 Not at all true
_____ 2 Rarely true
_____ 3 Somewhat true
_____ 4 Always true

8. I have used caffeine (e.g., in coffee, cola, or chocolate), cigarettes, or stimulant drugs to help me feel invigorated.

_____ 1 Not at all true
_____ 2 Rarely true
_____ 3 Somewhat true
_____ 4 Always true

9. I get bored quickly in relationships.

_____ 1 Not at all true
_____ 2 Rarely true
_____ 3 Somewhat true
_____ 4 Always true

10. The people close to me have avoided me when I've been in a sad mood for a while.

_____ 1 Not at all true
_____ 2 Rarely true
_____ 3 Somewhat true
_____ 4 Always true

11. When people criticize me, it bothers me a great deal.

_____ 1 Not at all true
_____ 2 Rarely true
_____ 3 Somewhat true
_____ 4 Always true

12. I tend to focus on my inner feelings to the extent that I ignore the things that go on around me.

_____ 1 Not at all true
_____ 2 Rarely true
_____ 3 Somewhat true
_____ 4 Always true

13. I pay close attention to details in my work.

_____ 1 Not at all true
_____ 2 Rarely true
_____ 3 Somewhat true
_____ 4 Always true

14. I get angry at my partner when he or she does not do the things I need to make me happy.

_____ 1 Not at all true
_____ 2 Rarely true
_____ 3 Somewhat true
_____ 4 Always true

15. When I feel blue, I fixate on my negative feelings and think that I will never feel better again.

_____ 1 Not at all true
_____ 2 Rarely true
_____ 3 Somewhat true
_____ 4 Always true

16. I feel that the future is hopeless.

_____ 1 Not all all true
_____ 2 Rarely true
_____ 3 Somewhat true
_____ 4 Always true

17. I am dissatisfied with myself.

_____ 1 Not at all true
_____ 2 Rarely true
_____ 3 Somewhat true
_____ 4 Always true

18. When I feel bored or sad, I feel like eating, but once I eat, I continue to feel empty and unsatisfied.

_____ 1 Not at all true
_____ 2 Rarely true
_____ 3 Somewhat true
_____ 4 Always true

19. I seem to cry all the time.

_____ 1 Not at all true
_____ 2 Rarely true
_____ 3 Somewhat true
_____ 4 Always true

20. I have difficulty sleeping because my mind is preoccupied.

_____ 1 Not at all true
_____ 2 Rarely true
_____ 3 Somewhat true
_____ 4 Always true

21. I blame myself because my life is a failure.

_____ 1 Not at all true
_____ 2 Rarely true
_____ 3 Somewhat true
_____ 4 Always true

22. I have trouble making decisions.

_____ 1 Not at all true
_____ 2 Rarely true
_____ 3 Somewhat true
_____ 4 Always true

23. I am often too exhausted to even move.

_____ 1 Not at all true
_____ 2 Rarely true

_____ 3 Somewhat true
_____ 4 Always true

24. I am frequently troubled by guilt.

_____ 1 Not at all true
_____ 2 Rarely true
_____ 3 Somewhat true
_____ 4 Always true

25. I often feel lonely or unimportant and I think that no one cares about me.

_____ 1 Not at all true
_____ 2 Rarely true
_____ 3 Somewhat true
_____ 4 Always true

26. I am very worried about physical problems (e.g., aches, stomach problems, constipation).

_____ 1 Not all true
_____ 2 Rarely true
_____ 3 Somewhat true
_____ 4 Always true

27. I feel tense much of the time.

_____ 1 Not at all true
_____ 2 Rarely true
_____ 3 Somewhat true
_____ 4 Always true

28. My dreams are often frightening.

_____ 1 Not at all true
_____ 2 Rarely true
_____ 3 Somewhat true
_____ 4 Always true

29. I get easily irritated by people or events.

_____ 1 Not at all true
_____ 2 Rarely true
_____ 3 Somewhat true
_____ 4 Always true

30. I often worry about small events or details that others would consider unimportant.

_____ 1 Not at all true.

_____ 2 Rarely true

_____ 3 Somewhat true

_____ 4 Always true

Be sure that you have responded to each of the items. Calculate your score by adding the numbers next to the responses you have marked. Record the sum here: _____.

80 and above: a definite focuser

70–79:many focuser characteristics

60–69: some focusers characteristics

60 and below: few of these characteristics play an important role in your temperament.

Chapter 8

SEEKERS: FROM CRAVING TO CONTENTMENT

A LONGTIME FRIEND and I are taking a stroll after having dinner. James and I have known each other since childhood, and we talk about our lives, our values, our dreams. He tells me that he's finally thinking of retiring, of stepping down as chairman of a company he started twenty years ago and developed into a multimillion-dollar company. He is probably the most aggressive and determined person I have ever known personally.

James talks about moving to Greece or to Italy. "I'm going to lay around in a hammock under a big, shady tree and do nothing but read—history, the Greeks, Faulkner, Henry Miller, Proust from start to finish." He then describes the difficulty in letting go of the quest he's been on for so many years. I know what's coming, for I know his temperament. He likes excitement, and relaxing is something he fantasizes about but doesn't do.

In a more hushed voice, he tells me, "I'm tired. I'm going to be fifty-four, and I've been doing this for decades. But you know me. I'm like a fighter or an athlete. I can't imagine not having the excitement I'm used to. That's why I became a runner (he runs marathons), because I feel like the action and the sensation is defining who I am at the moment. The idea of just relaxing is . . . I'm having a hard time with it." He has always defined himself by what he does, and the idea of slowing down makes him feel unsettled, even scared.

James is the quintessential seeker. He described it perfectly: the sensation itself defines him. It is the state of craving sensation and then seeking and striving toward a goal; striving creates the seeker's emotional comfort zone.

James wants to downshift to a more reflective third act in his life, but he's apprehensive. Years ago, when he felt restless, he would shift to another venue for sensation seeking: drugs, a love affair, running (marathons, of course), or another escalation in his business dreams.

My friend James epitomizes the destiny and dilemma of the seeker. He knows his unfortunate potential for addiction of any sort. He knows that he is quite capable of going after sensation, becoming satiated or habituated, and always needing more. Unlike many seekers, he now wants respite from the various games that have dominated his life. But in our talks he's told me he knows that simple bromides like, "Give yourself a break," or "Stop and smell the roses," don't work for him. What he was asking of me on our walk was how he could get off the treadmill and still be comfortable in his own skin, with his demanding temperament. "Am I going to be able to hack if it I retire?" he asks me.

Janet is a recovering alcoholic and cocaine addict who came into treatment with me initially saying she wanted to work on her self-destructive tendencies. After five years of sobriety, she had come close to relapsing after a one-night stand with her former boyfriend, Nigel, with whom she had hit bottom before she went into a rehab clinic and turned her life around. She was frightened and confused by her near relapse. "I've been doing so great in AA and my job for five years. What's wrong with me that I feel so bored and empty when I'm doing everything right? I thought I had grown out of that phase."

In exploring her life experiences and her emotional dynamic, it became clear that Janet was a seeker who was at war with her natural self. She felt ashamed and morally defective for secretly missing the drama and excitement of her past. She was unaware that her innate emotional biochemistry set up her craving for adventure and sensation. And temperament is not something you outgrow.

Janet remembers being bored and restless while growing up in a small farming town in Iowa. "From the time I was twelve or fourteen, I was a rebel, hanging out with the hippie crowd—it was the sixties even in Iowa. I gave my parents a lot of grief. They blamed themselves and could never understand why I was so wild." She moved to Los Angeles after high school. Warm, funny, and energetic, Janet had always done well as a sales representative.

Janet described herself as a "recovering crazed drama queen" in her relationships with men. "I was like a chain smoker with men. I went from one actor or musician to another. I usually was paying all the bills, but I didn't care. All that mattered was passion and drama. All of it magnified by coke and drinking, of course."

I asked Janet to describe her normal weekly schedule now. She said, "Since I've been sober, I've gotten totally disciplined." She gets to the gym for a 6 A.M. aerobics class, then goes to her office and works to six or seven in the evening. Unless she has to work late, she attends a twelve-step meeting. On weekends, she works out, puts in additional hours at her office, and tries to take in a movie on Saturday night. She hadn't dated anyone for the past year, and had not taken a vacation, other than to visit her parents in Iowa, since she got sober.

"When's the last time you really had fun, Janet?" I asked. She protested: "I have a lot of fun with my friends. We go out for coffee after meetings. . . . We laugh a lot." "When's the last time you felt passionate, intense, really excited?" I pressed her for an answer. "I'm trying to *not be* a thrill junkie. That's what screwed up my life for so many years," she argued, annoyed.

I suggested that her black and white thinking was screwing up her emotional life now. Like so many alcoholics, or criminals, or sexually promiscuous people who reform, Janet had flipped to the opposite extreme, to severely conservative behavior. At some level, Janet was doing penance for her past destructive behavior. She was full of self-hatred and was operating out of fear. A victim of the myth of perfectibility, she was trying to become someone totally different than the Janet of the past.

Because her craving for passion and excitement had led her into drugs and chaotic relationships, she was now denying herself any ardor or exhilaration—they were bad feelings (the myth of good and bad emotions). It's my view that this kind of black and white thinking is a sure setup for relapse into damaging behavior. I reassured Janet that there was nothing morally or mentally defective about her hunger for intensity and aliveness. This was part of her temperament. Her task was to learn to honor who she was, to feel good about herself, and to begin finding healthy ways to reintegrate passion and just plain fun into her life.

THE SEEKER: THE RESTLESS TEMPERAMENT

Seekers are the least common of the temperament types. The seeker feels the least discomfort with his temperament; he is the least reluctant to accept who he is. He is the least prone to self-hatred and the least likely to deny or disguise his emotional predispositions. Due to their dynamic and intense natures, seekers feel special, and it's a feeling that fuels many of their activities.

If you're a seeker, your emotionality is craving linked to goal-oriented action, and your relentless drive often translates into success. Your temperament causes you to seek. You are emotionally hungry in the sense that you live in a perpetual state of craving—this is how you experience your natural self.

You are the classic extrovert: gregarious and assertive. You are driven by conscious intentions to reach goals you set for yourself. Purposefulness is a pivotal quality to the seeker. In a society that values achievement and action, you are often held in high regard. As a seeker, you can be quite unique. Because most people are less directed, less motivated, you are admired, even envied.

However, not all seekers are admirable. For every self-made entrepreneur or sportsperson or dynamo whose volunteer work makes a difference in his community, there is probably a seeker who is a compulsive gambler, romance addict, or drug addict. There are also seekers who have never found their niche in life—people with big ideas and too little luck or opportunity.

SOCIETY'S SHIFTING APPROVAL

For the seeker, his cultural context is critical. During the 1960s and 1970s, when our social and psychological values emphasized being laid back, seekers were at a disadvantage. The 1990s are a golden era for the seeker. Today, society loves the man or woman of action and ambition. Seekers who are workaholics can throw themselves into their business or careers with total cultural approval; after all, everybody is working more hours these days, competing for tight money in a down economy. Work provides reinforcing moments of satisfaction and an unlimited opportunity for striving. As seekers put in more and more hours and create ever-expanding territories to conquer, they can regulate their emotional life in a way that is sanctioned by current values.

The seeker is a rather complicated type, full of positives, and always tempted by negatives, in his search for relief from his relentless inner cravings. Seekers aren't easy to know, for they are always in a state of flux. Their natural self doesn't allow them much internal contentment.

PASSIONS OR ADDICTIONS?

Because of the seeker's craving for sensation, many are viewed as possessing addictive personalities. They can be addicted to anything that leads to a high: challenges, risks, dangers, even stormy or difficult love relationships. But beyond the indisputably harmful addictions such as drugs, the more appropriate word to describe seekers is *passion*, not addiction.

In my view, the term *addictive* is overused. The seeker is often a passionate person. And passions come in all shapes, sizes, and degrees with attendant degrees of danger. If I say I'm addicted to reading, I feel good about it. I even feel good about being addicted to watching sports on television; I derive a great deal of pleasure from it. I use the term *addicted* wryly. Naturally, if these passions or addictions begin to interfere with my life in a negative way, then I will have to reexamine them. But to disparage all addictions is to suggest that balance and moderation is always a virtue, which I don't believe it is. Perhaps passion crosses the line into addiction when some activity becomes destructive to yourself or to others, or when the passion is characterized by fear or compulsion instead of enjoyment. It isn't always an easy call to make.

MISLEADING MESSAGES

If you're a seeker, from childhood on, you probably were told things about your temperament that led you astray. As a child, you were told you were too restless, too self-centered, and never satisfied. When you grew up, people were always telling you to settle down as though your quests were a sign of something wrong within you.

As adults, seekers are often suspected of compensating for some inner feeling of worthlessness. It is believed that they never feel they're enough, and so they must always pursue something they don't have and that will presumably make them feel whole. In therapy, the seeker is urged to discover the root cause of his lack of self-esteem. Therapeutic strategies with seekers usually focus on what seems to be missing in their personality. "You always have to prove yourself" is the epithet that is laid on them. They are told there must have been something missing from their childhood that they are now trying to make up for. In fact, none of these messages are necessarily valid or accurate. The seeker is driven much more by innate forces than anything he learned or did not learn, lacked or did not lack, while growing up.

THE SEEKER'S NATURAL SELF

HIGH THRESHOLD OF AROUSAL

Like the focuser, seekers have a high threshold of arousal—that is, they are prone to underarousal; they feel too little. At times they are inclined to feel nothing. What they feel as lack of emotion or aliveness in itself can be quite distressing.

ACTION TENDENCY: EXTROVERTED/SENSATION SEEKING

Unlike introverted focusers who immediately turn inward when they sense underarousal, the seeker's action tendency is outward. Seekers are extroverted—their visceral reflex to boost their arousal is action itself. Because they feel too little, seekers need intense experience in order to feel alive. Like moths to a flame, they're drawn to passion, challenge, risk, and even danger to counteract their underarousal.

The seeker's arousal thermostat is such that action momentarily lowers the threshold. But soon after seekers experience an arousal high, their threshold rises again—they have to seek again and again. Action doesn't seem to sustain arousal because it habituates (wears off) and then the seeker needs more. The seeker lives in constant restlessness, endless desire. The action tendency to strive continually is both a blessing and a curse—a blessing because seekers often do find worthy challenges, and a curse because seekers can misdirect their craving into destructive avenues.

THE BIOCHEMISTRY OF THE SEEKER

As I have been developing my theory of temperament, studies have been conducted in the United States and in Britain on sensation-seeking and impulse-driven behaviors. These studies are the closest I have found to my ideas about the seeker. Additional scientific support for the seeker temperament comes from the new research on behavior genetics that indicates many traits (including activity level, shyness, and aggressiveness) are inherited. Indeed, the proof is in studies of newborn infants: some are active, striving, restless, and aggressive, already exhibiting seeker-type temperament. Finally, there has been exhaustive research into the addictive personality. Indeed, new evidence coming from a number of standpoints supports my theory of the biochemical basis for the temperament of the seeker.

Among the most impressive studies that have been done on sensation seekers are those conducted by Marvin Zuckerman at the University of Delaware. His work points to low levels of MAO (monoamine oxidase). If you remember, when we looked at the biochemistry of the discharger in chapter 6, low levels of the enzyme monoamine oxidase are thought to be instrumental in the discharger's aggressiveness. If follows that the aggressive seeker's temperament is also partly determined by low levels of MAO. The seeker and the discharger may have different thresholds of arousal, but they share extroverted, aggressive action tendencies.

Professor Zuckerman also found that the people he called sensation seekers have high levels of the neurotransmitter dopamine. Although his definition of the term *sensation seeker* is not exactly the same as mine, there are enough similarities that his research clearly sheds light on the emotional temperament type I call the seeker. Professor Zuckerman believes the combination of low MAO and high levels of dopamine beget activity, impulsivity, and sociability.

Research into extroverts also finds high levels of dopamine. Another piece of the puzzle locks in when you consider that dopamine receptors in the brain are linked to pleasure and reward systems. This is biochemical evidence that the seeker, an extrovert *cum laude,* is biologically disposed to both action and the seeking out of rewards or pleasure.

Taking it one step further and incorporating these findings into my theory, seekers are, in essence, arousal seekers. My threshold theory goes on to assert that seekers must have high thresholds of arousal, making them experience unwanted times of underarousal. For example, the reason they abhor boredom is because it is a state of underarousal. It is this unpleasant underarousal that sets their seeking tendency in motion. Seekers have innate stimulus-seeking reflexes. Their mission? To find stimuli to raise their low arousal.

The seeker's arousal is typically so low that he's constantly seeking stimuli. And he's satiated easily. The process of satiation means that the seeker quickly wears out the power of an activity or substance or person to arouse him, so he continually must find something newer, more novel, more exciting, more dangerous. The seeker is like a Ferrari whose gas tank is shot full of holes—it roars from gas station to gas station, continually refueling, and needing higher and higher octane gas to make its motor turn over.

MANIC DEPRESSION AND CYCLOTHYMIA

The seeker is sometimes misdiagnosed with manic-depressive behavior or bipolar depression. This label refers to extreme mood swings that alternate from agitated and impulsive manic behavior to states of apathy and depression. Many manic-depressive individuals are highly creative and successful in certain fields, but they cannot control their emotions enough to stay out of serious trouble. In the manic phase, they can become so grandiose and outrageous in their behavior that they exhaust themselves physically and emotionally, land in jail, go on spending sprees, or launch impulsive business ventures that border on self-destructiveness. In the depressive phase, they can become suicidal.

The seeker, similarly, seems manic at times and exhausted at others. However, the degree is muted in comparison to manic-depressive disorders. Clearly the later represents brain chemistry gone awry, which is why a powerful drug like lithium is needed. Although I cautioned against the illness model of emotions, there is a minor version of manic depression that is appropriate to the seeker temperament. It is the cyclothymic character. Cyclothymia means milder swings between periods of apathy and disinterest, and periods of intense extroverted behavior. I believe cyclothymia is at the extreme boundaries of the seeker temperament; the swings represent failure to adequately regulate the emotional thermostat. More specifically, if you look at the chart on page 65, you will see there is a point at which the focuser and the seeker may be close together. It could be that a manic-depressive individual exists where the focuser and seeker (both people who struggle with underarousal) merge—that is, a mixed and very extreme type.

THE GIFT OF STRIVING

Of all the temperament types, the seeker's special gift is the most highly rewarded one in our society. To seek challenges, to take risks, and to do so with a sense of excitement is the hallmark of many successful men and women. They are the objects of envy and admiration.

Seekers obviously do well in careers in which aggressive pursuit pays off. Wherever you look, you will see seekers in business, in athletics, in any work that rewards intense striving. But there are also seekers in the sciences and the humanities—men and women enlivened by the sensations inherent in the pursuit of new ideas, the testing of new theories. And, of course, the politican is often a seeker. President Clinton was initially attacked for being too single-minded in his ambitious pursuit of the presidency. One might argue that many fine men and women who are not successful in their political ambitions may falter because they do not really have the seeker's temperament.

THE DARK SIDE OF THE SEEKER: RESTLESS SELF-ABSORPTION

NARCISSISM

Because of their constant craving for sensation, is it appropriate to ask whether the seeker is also a narcissist? Since the seeker is so powerfully oriented to self-satisfaction, there is a high correlation between being a seeker and having a narcissistic personality. The narcissist is self-absorbed and constantly attuned to whatever might satisfy her emotional cravings and, thereby, make her feel whole. But narcissists are not necessarily selfish, in the narrow sense of that term; they can be loyal and generous in their interactions with other people. The seeker is excessively concerned with bolstering his self-definition. Without argument, the seeker tends to be a self-centered person.

FEAR OF BOREDOM

A concern for one's sense of self also explains the seeker's most secret fear: boredom. My friend James always has been terrified of the possibility of being enveloped in boredom. Typically, boredom occurs when there is little or no sensory input—we are underaroused. We're vulnerable to unpleasant internal sensations and thoughts welling up into this vacuum: old anxieties, fears, sadness, even existential aloneness—the dread about our very existence on this planet.

A secondary apprehension about boredom stems from our mind telling us that, if we're bored, we're probably boring to other people, and no one will love us if we're uninteresting. Boredom thereby stimulates social anxiety—we'll be rejected, unwanted. Ask anyone what they fear the most when asked how others perceive them—"Oh, she's so boring." Some of us would even rather be judged a bad person than a boring person. Bad can be intriguing; boring is just, well—boring. To experience boredom is to experience your aloneness. And to experience aloneness can lead to feeling lonely, and can again raise self-doubts about how lovable we may be. Given these consider-ations, it's easy to understand why the emotionally hungry, self-centered seeker fears boredom above all else, and why you seekers are so driven to pursue excitement and passion.

THE GENDER GAP

There's a wide gender gap between male seekers and female seekers. These gender differences are probably not biological or innate; I believe they're dictated more by stubborn cultural ex-pectations of what is appropriate for each sex. The female seeker has been suppressed more in our society. Extroverted, aggressive, ambitious, adventurous behavior has been labeled unfeminine in the past. Recently, we saw the first female driver compete in the Indianapolis 500 race. As you can imagine, when she was growing up and displayed an interest in cars and racing, she certainly went against the grain of what people think women should aspire to. It is a wonder that, in the past, the female seeker could even partly accept her temperament, given all the prescriptions for appropriate femininity.

Thankfully, today the female seeker is freer to pursue her ambition. Nevertheless, in my professional experience, I still see a marked difference between the goals of male and female seek-ers. Although there are exceptions, women, whether partly due to biology or not, gravitate toward relationships as an avenue for fulfilling their emotional craving. Men gravitate toward money, power, and sports. Most male seekers do not become love or romance addicts, and most female seekers don't harbor fantasies of athletic prowess and dominance.

THE SEEKER IN RELATIONSHIPS
ROMANTIC CHEMISTRY

The feeling of being loved, and the longing to love and be loved, are among the most common ways we have of regulating our emotional life. As psychologists will verify, the search of love dominates most of their patients' lives. The absence of love is often why people enter treatment.

Of the four temperament types, the seeker is the most driven by the quest for love. As a seeker, you are the most inclined to use romance to regulate your emotional life; romantic or sexual intensity is a sure boost to your underarousal. Once your arousal increases, your interpretive brain takes over and you invest your partner with wonderful qualities: "She's so sweet and affectionate!" "He's so exciting, yet so loving!" The way you weave a romantic story around your emotional/sexual arousal is the grist of every seeker's romantic fantasy.

One could say seekers seem to be love-starved. It's more precise to say that seekers are emotionally hungry in general. When we think of hunger, we think of putting something from outside of us inside us. What better stuff than the emotional ups and downs and inside-outs that we all know can be derived from a love affair? Emotionally hungry seekers see love as the encompassing solution to their lack of feeling and aliveness.

Again and again, I hear seekers confide some version of, "My real problem is that I haven't found the right person. If I could find the right person, I would be happy. I could feel at peace." They believe the right lover, loving them the right way, will fix them—and that's an incredible demand to make on anyone. Again, the seeker instinctively looks outside himself to find the answer he needs.

When I say the seeker is especially preoccupied with love, I want to narrow the definition somewhat. I'm not speaking of mature love, or the idea of love, or the ethical/moral concept of love. It's the emotional/physical sensation of love that preoccupies the seeker. Often confused, the sensation of love is different from the idea of it. Love as sensation or intensity is something I have studied for many years. It never ceases to amaze me how much we—especially women in general and female seekers in particular—are conditioned by novels, pop songs, or movies to believe that love is a solution to emotional unease. We are socially conditioned to regulate our emotions with fantasies of fusion or oneness. Love is a state of excitement that has great power to arouse us. Conversely, if we feel we are losing love, it has the power to deaden us. It's this emotional/

physical sensation on which the seeker becomes fixated. As we'll see, this craving for passion often costs the seeker deeper, lasting love relationships.

From the outside, Beth looks like she has it all together. She's slim and athletic, and she always dresses well. In casual conversation, you would surmise that she's a warm, intelligent, competent woman whom most men would find quite attractive. Although that's true, her relationships with men have been terrible. At age thirty-two, she hasn't had a relationship that has lasted more than two months. "Men are just totally disappointing to me," she said angry and frustrated. "They're too self-centered. Sure, they can be romantic for the first few dates, and I get so full of hope, thinking I've finally found *the one,* but then they turn out to be total duds."

Beth was quite specific about what she wanted from me as a therapist. "I want to know, is it my fault? Am I doing it all wrong, or should I just give up on men?" As we explored Beth's attitudes and behaviors with men, it emerged that Beth had a seeker temperament and she had enormous expectations about what a love relationship should provide. She wanted grand passion, storybook romance, total devotion—and she wanted it from the first date on.

She dated only very successful, accomplished men (probably other seekers) who had demanding careers. But she quickly became angry and resentful when these men could not (or would not) provide the passion and attention she craved. Beth had set a standard of what she wanted from "Mr. Right" that was so high she was repeatedly rejected when men realized what her agenda was.

I explained the seeker temperament and her need for sensation and intensity to Beth. I suggested that her task was to diffuse her need for passion into several new arenas. I suggested that she find a more challenging job. (Although she had a college degree, she had had a succession of dead-end jobs.) I recommended that she find a competitive sport about which she could become passionate and get involved with a cause or a charitable organization. I advised Beth that no man could provide the standard of continual passion and attention she had set for herself. She had to fulfill at least some of her needs herself, in other areas.

Beth didn't say anything for a long moment. Then she stood

up. "I guess you've answered my question. Men can't give me what I want. I'm going to take some of your suggestions and find some new interests, but I'm just going to give up on dating for a while. I'll never settle for just feeling bored." That was my last session with Beth. I sometimes wonder how she's doing and whether she's still alone. The seeker who asks too much of a love relationship inevitably drives the other person away.

Most of us come to understand that mature love takes over after the intensity of romantic love subsides. This, however, is bad news for the seeker. The seeker craves only the romantic intensity. Infatuation provides thrilling arousal, but as the lover becomes known and familiar, arousal diminishes. The seeker interprets this diminution as boredom, disinterest, even sadness. The power of someone else to stimulate us is not infinite.

Any of you who have been on a long weekend with a new lover know the feeling of satiation. You begin to find fault, he begins to get on your nerves, and what started out as passionate bonding changes to a feeling that you can't wait to get home and be alone again! The seeker is likely to feel this way in any dating relationship.

CONFLICT IN RELATIONSHIPS

If you're a seeker, you can be a true challenger as a husband or wife. Your intense emotional hunger sends out powerful messages that you cannot be satisfied by one person for long. Your mate can easily fear that you will abandon her. In time, she may sense that she is not providing sufficient excitement to meet your needs. She begins to wonder, "What will happen when he no longer finds me intriguing? If I stop playing hard to get, will he lose interest?" As a seeker, you don't have to communicate your propensity for satiation explicitly; everything you do implies it.

Mitch and Dinah hadn't spoken to each other in more than a week when they arrived, in separate cars, at my office for their first session. They sat down at opposite ends of my couch without glancing at each other. The tension between them buzzed like an electric fence. "So, what's the problem?" I ventured. "She's acting crazy," he said, bewildered and frustrated. "He's making me crazy," she said, accusingly.

Mitch, who had made the appointment with me, explained

that he had gone on a business trip to Costa Rica for two weeks. When he returned home, "Out of the blue, Dinah won't say a word to me. She has lost at least ten pounds, and is out jogging or at the gym or playing tennis all day. She's sleeping in the guest room. She leaves the house every night when I get home from work, won't say a word to me, won't tell me what's wrong, where she's going—anything."

Dinah turned to look at him for the first time, livid with rage, and said, "If you're just such a coward, I'll say it. I want a divorce. It's not working out—there!"

Through the tears and accusations and counteraccusations that followed, what emerged was that Dinah felt that after only eight months of marriage, Mitch had tired of her and was having an affair with his attractive assistant who had been in the group of five people from his company that had gone to Costa Rica. Dinah felt that his passion for her had shriveled. A discharger, she was trying to work out her fear and anger with nonstop exercise. She had become so livid, so imploded with emotion, that she had become mute.

Mitch denied he was having an affair. He insisted that he loved her, saying, "You're my wife. I wouldn't have married you if I didn't love you." Dinah countered, "I know what I feel, and I know you're not excited by me like you were." In a private session later, Mitch said he wasn't having an affair with his assistant, but admitted, "I'd love to." A seeker, Mitch wasn't sure he wanted to stay married. Dinah's perceptions were prescient; his feelings for her *had* cooled. While he had not yet been unfaithful, he had begun to think about it.

Due to your restless nature, your mate can come to fear that you'll be unfaithful. She senses your craving for that kind of excitement. She knows you are a sucker for what's new and intriguing. I would say that the seeker is the most likely temperament type to be sexually unfaithful not because he is less ethical but because the male seeker is like a shark—if he stops moving, he thinks he will die.

If you are seeker, and you wish to allay the fears of your spouse, it is important to be aware of the impact your temperament has on your marriage. Your mate may need reassurance, even though you are totally committed to the relationship and you conduct yourself in a totally faithful manner. The seeker who is involved with a sensor or focuser should be especially sensitive to his spouse's anxieties.

Jim is unusual. Most male seekers do not tolerate humiliation—they move quickly to a substitute goal. Jim has been satisfied with pursuing rejecting women. He has been driven by sensation seeking and novelty all of his life, whether it be buying one car after another or changing jobs repeatedly as the newness wears off. In his mid-forties and never married, Jim was a sucker for any woman who rejected him. He would continue to call, have presents delivered to her, and generally humiliate himself. He was relentless in his pursuit.

Because he obsessed about women to no end, he had been diagnosed with obsessive-compulsive disorder by several psychiatrists, but none of the medications usually prescribed for such disorders worked for him. I concluded that the reason the medications had no effect was that Jim was not a focuser but he was a seeker with a seeker's biochemistry. His pursuits were not compulsive acts but behaviors designed to achieve a high. He derived a high from the hope of conquering the women's objections. His action tendencies were impulsive and sensation seeking, not compulsive.

He had a deep resentment toward women due to problems with his mother. He didn't like women, so any genuine relationship was beyond his capacity. Because he didn't care about having a real relationship, he did not experience the normal frustration or shame that would cause other men to quickly cease a dead-end romantic pursuit.

I've described a number of seekers and the predicaments they encounter. In spite of these warnings, however, let us not overlook the fact that most seekers do not fall prey to unhealthy solutions. Most do find ways to find stimulus that is healthy. The seeker needs to be highly aware of his impact on his mate and must make sure he gets excitement in work, or sports, or community activity. If they commit themselves, seekers can be faithful and loving companions.

FRIENDSHIPS

The seeker gathers friends in a rather effortless fashion. She looks for others who are engaging and enlivening. Indeed, initially, the seeker appears to be the kind of person who makes good friendships because they happen so quickly. But in time, the seeker may tire of the relationship if it appears that it is becoming dull or routine. The initial rush of engagement and chemistry that seems to be a predictor of a deep friendship in the making results from the excitement the seeker feels when she finds a new source of excitement and intensity. New ideas and new activities are relished by the seeker. But, as in all relationships, what at first was novel, may in time become old hat—at least intermittently. The seeker has no patience for these predictable lulls in any relationship.

Jerry, a young public-relations executive certainly does not regard himself as a dull guy, but he also gravitates to intense buddies who are typically the seeker type. In one such relationship, he ruefully acknowledged that what he thought was a great buddy, had evolved into a sparse now-and-again friendship. "I feel as as though he used me up and then just got tired of me." It is not that seekers are disloyal, it's just that all too often their cravings do not leave room for the more mundane moments that occur in any relationship.

THE SEEKER PARENT

The seeker parent is both dynamically engaging to her child and a bit of a burden because she has so little time for quietude and patience, the hallmarks of good parenting. Yet, most seekers probably end up being interesting parents in that they provide a level of intensity and stimulation that engages children and teenagers. Provided the seeker parent does not move too quickly in his own hunger for intensity, he often finds that the novel experiences of child rearing are other interesting sources of pleasure and involvement.

THE SEEKER AT WORK

AMBITION AND CAREER

The seeker proves outstanding in career situations that are goal and results oriented. Seekers prefer to work in situations where their energy remains unfettered; micromanaging seekers is a sure way to lose them as employees. Because they tend to be energetic, dynamic, even magnetic, seekers do well in leadership roles.

Seekers thrive on competition. The excitement of clear-cut winning and losing bring out their best efforts. They love to take risks and may end up being entrepreneurs. The seeker can easily become a workaholic. Seekers find the excitation and sensation rewarding, but it can get out of control. They intensify their work efforts, set higher goals, and begin working ten-hour, then twelve-hour, then sixteen-hour days. As workaholism progresses, they think only of work. After all, there are always new challenges on the horizon.

It also follows that routine is deadly for the seeker. Whenever novelty fades, she has to move on. This explains why the seeker will often job hop from company to company, position to position, even from one career to the next. Show me a person with a twenty-year pension and I'll show someone who's definitely not a seeker. Seekers will to go great pains to list their reasons for moving on, but the bottom line is change, novelty, and the sensations associated with new challenge.

In my experience, many people who are viewed as having a fear of success are not worried at all about success. More precisely, they are fearful of routine, of achieving something, of feeling satiated and sliding back into a state of underarousal. The quest, the pursuit of success, is what makes them feel alive. They don't want to actually "arrive" at success. So, while they appear to run from success, they are really running from the anticipation of emotional deadness.

"It's like each new job has a beginning, a middle, and an end for me," explained Doug, a manufacturing executive who had grown weary of changing jobs and moving every year. Thirty-eight, he had been married and divorced twice, partially as a result of moving around so much. He wanted help in finding stability in his life. "I go in, all excited—a new team, a new project to organize and implement. That's the beginning. The middle is overcoming all the obstacles, hiring and firing and getting the right mix of people working well together, getting the bugs worked out, getting the product shipped. And that's the second act, until I have everything under control. The third act is total boredom and a kind of depression. And I put my feelers out and get the recruiters looking for something new."

Doug thought his problem was that he was a control freak who lost interest when he got things battened down. In the recession, he thought he should learn to be comfortable staying in the well-paying, secure job he now held. My diagnosis was that he was a seeker who had habituated himself to an annual sea change in his life. My prescription was for him to buy a house and put down some roots in his community; and to satisfy his need for novelty, challenge, and sensation in arenas other than his career. What wound up helping Doug was joining a softball league. He derives marvelous challenge and passion from his team, and he has found a satisfying social life and sense of belonging with his teammates.

THE SEEKER BOSS

The seeker is not always up and excited. The seeker boss can be mercurial. Because of their hunger for stimulus, seekers can be impatient with others. They may be well liked but also exhausting as you struggle to keep up with them.

Helena was just such a boss. After twenty years of working her way up the ladder of a leading swimsuit firm, she said, "Enough!" Within a month, she rounded up the capital to launch her own line of clothing. Creative, savvy, and engaging, Helena lured five up-and-coming executives away from their jobs to join her. As her venture capital vice-president characterizes her, "She's manic one day, and sort of moody and inscrutable the next. I think she stays awake at night reading the trades and getting ideas. She calls meetings and throws out as many as ten ideas for whole new lines of products. We're supposed to find out everything about the competition, etc., and let her know, always 'by tomorrow.' As if we weren't already pushing fourteen-hour days just trying to keep up with our day-to-day responsibilities. I admire her, and I am excited working with her, but I sometimes feel like she's going to go over the edge. She just wears everybody out."

THE SOCIOPATHIC SEEKER

The seeker may be overly political in the work environment, saying or doing anything to advance. Seekers may even be mildly sociopathic, bending the rules in order to get what they want. They may feel superior and special. Initially, they seem dynamic and charming, but when they feel satiated, they may go beyond the usual limits. They may go beyond the law to meet their needs.

Dana was thirty-six when she started working for Stuart. She admits that she was aware of all the laws governing mortgage banking; her state certificates and licenses hung on the walls. Stuart made her a vice-president and gave her an impressive office overlooking the marina. Dana says, "I thought if he could get away with what he was doing for years and years, and still be sitting at the head table at fund-raisers for senators and big charity events, I could too." Dana had made a comfortable living working as a bank officer previously, but, "When I was passed over for promotion to president in favor of men, again and again, I guess that set me up for wanting to beat the system."

After the first few fraudulent loans she approved and signed off, Dana stopped worrying about going to prison. "It was all set up, everybody was making a lot of money, and our clients were the so-called pillars of the community." Inflated appraisals and lease agreements that showed 100 percent tenancy in office buildings she knew were only half full were rationalized by Dana's belief that many people were doing business this way. She reveled in the glamour and the sense of having arrived, as she lunched at expensive restaurants, rode to meetings with Stuart in his Rolls Royce, and entered into the social scene of the wealthy and powerful.

Dana came into therapy when the pervasive fraud began to unravel. It took two years before Dana was actually indicted, and another year before she made a deal with the various district and state attorneys and the Justice Department. The scandal toppled several large savings and loans and sent some thirty people to prison. Dana is now doing a twenty-month prison term.

In the past few years, we've seen scams and scandals that reach all the way to the heads of Wall Street firms and the White House. In his pursuit of power, money, and success, the seeker who thinks he's above the law is a danger not only to himself but to the people whose trust he betrays.

FALSE PATHS TO EMOTIONAL RELIEF

SUBSTANCE ABUSE

Due to their propensity for seeking and their ability to derive great pleasure from this seeking, seekers are much more prone to use substances that deliver immediate sensation or pleasure. They are active consumers of caffeine, nicotine, and stimulant drugs. They are victims of addictions. And nothing is more tempting than drugs in their promise of an instant high or euphoric state. Anyone who has experienced drug addiction is familiar with chasing a high—doing more and more to get that initial wonderful feeling.

It goes without saying that not all addicts are seekers. But temperament does indicate who is biologically predisposed to addiction, and what kind of drug they're likely to choose. Like the similarly underaroused focuser, the seeker is drawn to stimulants: coffee, nicotine, speed, and cocaine. The overaroused types—dischargers and sensors—are more likely to be tempted by sedatives.

While both the seeker and focuser have low arousal, the seeker's biochemistry may be dominated more by dopamine. As noted, dopamine is involved in the pleasure centers in the brain. The seeker is a pleasure seeker whereas the focuser is a pain avoider; the difference is critical. The focuser is more likely to get addicted and stay addicted because of the pain-relieving qualities of substance abuse. The seeker will also get addicted, but because she is more pleasure oriented, she is also more likely to quit or detach from the addiction as it becomes less pleasurable and more painful—which is how most addictions progress. The seeker is therefore healthier in many ways. Time after time, I have seen seeker patients of mine who simply quit abusing on their own when the drugs are no longer pleasurable.

Seekers will go on binges, eventually find them unsatisfying, walk away from the drug, and shift to another substance or to another activity that will provide a new intense sensation. Seekers are always looking for either new challenges or new behaviors to replace ones they've just let go of. That's why in AA meetings, seekers who have learned to control alcohol or drugs will be sitting in meetings consuming large amounts of coffee and cigarettes—they still feel a need for sensation.

SEXUAL ADDICTION

Being easily habituated to a lover and losing interest after the infatuation phase is typical of most seekers. It's one of several dark sides of the seeker temperament. Another dilemma occurs when the seeker chooses to have love or sex as the primary source of emotional regulation. In those cases, the possibility of sexual addiction looms large. Sexual addiction refers to normal attachment needs that are magnified and distorted. If there is no balance in her life, the seeker can focus exclusively on the sensations of questing after someone. Having sex becomes the goal. When seekers achieve this goal, they are then satisfied and they have to move on. The anticipation of a date or sexual encounter is intensely stimulating, but this excitement wears off as the novelty no longer engages them. They don't savor a relationship or allow it to evolve into something deeper and mutually nourishing. The so-called Don Juan character is another way of characterizing male seekers who have chosen to use women as arousal elicitors.

EXPANDING YOUR EMOTIONAL COMFORT ZONE: ALTERNATION

When the seeker is not in motion, actively seeking sensation, she feels underaroused—and she loathes this dead feeling. Her innate action tendency to escape this underarousal is to seek external stimulus. Therefore, her primary task for modulating her emotions is to learn to tolerate periods of calm and relaxation, and to alternate these periods with healthy, constructive, challenging activities that will satisfy her need for stimulus. Her task is to balance rest and seeking.

My prescription for the seeker is the search for behaviors that will provide a counterbalance to sensation seeking. The only real answer for the seeker to find emotional relief is alternating between moderate sensation and calm. The seeker needs to feel enough sensation to feel vibrant, but not so intensely that he falls into addictive behavior. He needs to discipline himself to feel good as a result of moderate activity, whether it's sexual activity, romance, working, or sports. While the advice sounds simple, implementing it is more difficult, yet attainable, as you will discover in chapter 10.

SEEKERS: LIBERATION FROM TOXIC MYTHS

1. The myth of uniformity: Stop comparing yourself to others; enjoy the complexity of your nature.

2. The myth of good and bad: When some seekers grew up, they were criticized for their intensity. Now it's time to honor and enjoy your intensity.

3. The myth of control: To attempt to even out your emotional fluctuations is foolhardy and even destructive.

4. The myth of perfectibility: The seeker who yearns for a serene existence will be disappointed. Your nature is such that emotional rhythms rather than constant calm are your destiny.

5. The myth of emotional illness: To have cravings and powerful desires is a sign of aliveness, not illness.

6. The myth of positive thinking: You will never talk your nature into quieting down and being mellow. Listen to your nature rather than talking it into submission.

THE SEEKER IDENTIFICATION CHECKLIST

Rate the following statements by marking an "X" on the blank line next to the response that best describes you:

1. I would do almost anything to avoid being bored.

_____ 1 Not at all true
_____ 2 Rarely true
_____ 3 Somewhat true
_____ 4 Always true

2. I am always striving for money, power, or some other goal.

_____ 1 Not at all true
_____ 2 Rarely true
_____ 3 Somewhat true
_____ 4 Always true

3. I enjoy being spontaneous.

_____ 1 Not at all true
_____ 2 Rarely true
_____ 3 Somewhat true
_____ 4 Always true

4. I sometimes do things to see the shocked reaction of others.

_____ 1 Not at all true
_____ 2 Rarely true
_____ 3 Somewhat true
_____ 4 Always true

5. I enjoy riding in fast cars.

_____ 1 Not at all true
_____ 2 Rarely true
_____ 3 Somewhat true
_____ 4 Always true

6. My impulsive actions get me in trouble.

_____ 1 Not at all true
_____ 2 Rarely true
_____ 3 Somewhat true
_____ 4 Always true

7. I am most attracted to sexy, physically exciting persons.

_____ 1 Not at all true
_____ 2 Rarely true

_____ 3 Somewhat true
_____ 4 Always true

8. When I go to an amusement park, my favorite rides are the roller coasters.

_____ 1 Not at all true
_____ 2 Rarely true
_____ 3 Somewhat true
_____ 4 Always true

9. I get a rush from the competition.

_____ 1 Not at all true
_____ 2 Rarely true
_____ 3 Somewhat true
_____ 4 Always true

10. I am a very assertive person.

_____ 1 Not at all true
_____ 2 Rarely true
_____ 3 Somewhat true
_____ 4 Always true

11. I get quickly bored in my romantic relationships.

_____ 1 Not at all true
_____ 2 Rarely true
_____ 3 Somewhat true
_____ 4 Always true

12. I like to dress unconventionally.

_____ 1 Not at all true
_____ 2 Rarely true
_____ 3 Somewhat true
_____ 4 Always true

13. I enjoy a challenge.

_____ 1 Not at all true
_____ 2 Rarely true
_____ 3 Somewhat true
_____ 4 Always true

14. I like trying new or different things.

_____ 1 Not at all true
_____ 2 Rarely true
_____ 3 Somewhat true
_____ 4 Always true

15. I have held many jobs.

_____ 1 Not at all true
_____ 2 Rarely true
_____ 3 Somewhat true
_____ 4 Always true

16. I am an impatient person.

_____ 1 Not at all true
_____ 2 Rarely true
_____ 3 Somewhat true
_____ 4 Always true

17. I have frequently used or abused caffeine, nicotine, or other drugs.

_____ 1 Not at all true
_____ 2 Rarely true
_____ 3 Somewhat true
_____ 4 Always true

18. Once I finish a project or achieve a goal, I immediately move on to my next venture.

_____ 1 Not at all true
_____ 2 Rarely true
_____ 3 Somewhat true
_____ 4 Always true

19. I am very energetic.

_____ 1 Not at all true
_____ 2 Rarely true
_____ 3 Somewhat true
_____ 4 Always true

20. I sometimes like to do things that are a bit frightening.

_____ 1 Not at all true
_____ 2 Rarely true

_____ 3 Somewhat true

_____ 4 Always true

21. I enjoy a good argument or controversial discussion.

_____ 1 Not at all true

_____ 2 Rarely true

_____ 3 Somewhat true

_____ 4 Always true

22. I get quickly tired of doing the same task for a long period of time.

_____ 1 Not at all true

_____ 2 Rarely true

_____ 3 Somewhat true

_____ 4 Always true

23. Traveling to different places excites me.

_____ 1 Not at all true

_____ 2 Rarely true

_____ 3 Somewhat true

_____ 4 Always true

24. I have difficulty relaxing.

_____ 1 Not at all true

_____ 2 Rarely true

_____ 3 Somewhat true

_____ 4 Always true

25. I enjoy meeting new people.

_____ 1 Not at all true

_____ 2 Rarely true

_____ 3 Somewhat true

_____ 4 Always true

26. I consider myself to be a "partyer."

_____ 1 Not at all true

_____ 2 Rarely true

_____ 3 Somewhat true

_____ 4 Always true

27. I perform well in leadership roles.

_____ 1 Not at all true
_____ 2 Rarely true
_____ 3 Somewhat true
_____ 4 Always true

28. I like to do things with a variety of friends.

    _____ 1 Not at all true
    _____ 2 Rarely true
    _____ 3 Somewhat true
    _____ 4 Always true

29. I get a thrill from taking risks.

    _____ 1 Not at all true
    _____ 2 Rarely true
    _____ 3 Somewhat true
    _____ 4 Always true

30. I usually have at least a couple of drinks when I am socializing.

    _____ 1 Not at all true
    _____ 2 Rarely true
    _____ 3 Somewhat true
    _____ 4 Always true

Be sure that you have responded to each of the items. Calculate your score by adding the numbers next to the responses you have marked. Record the sum here: _____.

> 80 and above: a definite seeker
> 70–79: many seeker characteristics
> 60–69: some seeker characteristics
> 60 and below: few of these characteristics play an important role in your temperament.

PART THREE

MASTERING YOUR
EMOTIONS

Chapter 9

RECONSIDERING COMFORT ZONES

By now, you should have identified your temperament type and should have a good working knowledge of it. In this final section of the book, we'll learn how to work with your temperament, to become more emotionally alive, to short circuit bad moods, and to broaden your comfort zone so you can enjoy a greater range of experiences.

Our first step is to figure out what your emotional life is like now, and to look at the rules and assumptions from which you're operating. You may be distanced from your feelings, you may be in denial or confusion, or, like so many people, you may be emotionally shut down or numb to some degree. Each of us makes a thousand choices and decisions each day based on remaining in our emotional comfort zone. It operates behind the scenes, in the dark. Let's illuminate and explore your own idea of emotional comfort.

For most of us, emotional comfort is the absence of distress, not the presence of passion, ecstasy, joy, or delight. We crave safety and tend not to have exaggerated expectations about the more positive emotions. Perhaps that is the result of our being preoccupied with survival—a basic concern that never changes. For most of their time on this planet, humans did not expect wonderful things to happen to them. Survival was uppermost both in our conscious minds and in our instinctive responses to stressful situations. It is only in recent history that our pursuit of fulfillment and emotional well-being has taken center stage.

Comfort, of course, is a relative concept. Each of us has a life philosophy expressing just how emotionally safe or comfortable our life must be in order to declare ourselves content or happy. For some, these expectations are quietly implicit; for others they are explicit and consciously pursued. My point of view is that since your own idea of comfort exists whether you acknowledge it or not, why not make it a deliberate set of choices? Why not decide which emotions you wish to enhance or encourage in your life, rather than being passive or blind to those that biologically well up within you. Emotional self-deception and denial only lead to your being imprisoned by your emotions.

WHAT IS YOUR IDEA OF COMFORT?

People differ in their attitudes about life. Some people are pessimistic. For them, an absence of emotional distress is enough. When they take stock of their lives, their questions are, "Is everything okay? Do I have anything to worry about?" If their loved ones are alright, if their job is secure, if their bills are paid, they are extremely comfortable. Focusers are like this.

Optimists expect more out of life. For the optimist, often exemplified in the seeker, the mere absence of distress is not satisfying; they crave intense emotions such as excitement, joy, and passion. If, for some men and women, comfort is merely relief from pain or danger, for others, comfort is about the capacity to savor emotional potentialities. Depending on your outlook, then, the term *comfort* or *comfort zone* takes on a very different meanings.

Comfort zones refer to the specific range of emotionality we are accustomed to feeling. Comfort zones are not even necessarily comfortable—they may just be familiar and predictable. Declaring that you wish to enlarge your comfort zone is tantamount to saying you are willing to take more risks in life in order to live more fully and less fearfully. You are choosing to move beyond what you are accustomed to feeling, to forgo safety and embrace potential.

There's another, perhaps more important, reason for expanding your emotional comfort zone. If you don't work to expand it, it shrinks on its own! Like arteries that harden and clog over the years, you can gradually find your comfort zone becoming smaller and more restrictive. For example, the anxious sensor who consistently avoids being overaroused finds himself retreating farther and farther from life's challenges. The seeker who cannot tolerate underarousal finds herself caught up in unrelenting craving and sensation seeking. To remain within the zone of familiarity is to dramatically limit your life experiences. Moreover, as we get older, our habits become more rigid; our character tends to harden. In other words, our emotional comfort zones become constricted whether or not we are even conscious of this occurring.

First, let's examine what happens when people decide that feeling in itself is threatening and dangerous. For them, comfort is essentially a life devoid of the experience of emotions. There are three different types of people who are unaware of their emotions. Some are not aware of ever having made a choice at all—they are just emotionally shut down, numb. Others make a conscious, well-thought-out choice. And the third group chooses to act as if they are feeling appropriate emotions even though they're numb. All of them want to avoid painful and bad feelings.

WHEN COMFORT IS NOT FEELING AT ALL

I would estimate that at least one-third of my patients come into therapy because they feel numb, cut off from their emotions. Many of them are sent in by spouses or other loved ones who feel frustrated and estranged.

Hugh, an aerospace engineer, was emotionally numb and he wasn't aware of it. To his wife, he seemed emotionally dead. She insisted he come into therapy. "I'm tired of being alone in this marriage," she told him. Hugh didn't think there was anything wrong with him. "She's always at me for not feeling this or that. Hey—she's a woman—they're built like that. I'm an engineer—this is the way we're built."

To most people, Hugh would appear pleasant and engaging,

if somewhat bland. Unless we probe as a therapist might, we do not necessarily know what others feel—or whether they feel at all. It is the therapist's task to listen and probe the intricacies of inner emotional life. Let me describe what a therapist sees and senses when he is confronted with someone, like Hugh, who is not conscious of feeling or has so numbed himself that he truly has no feelings.

In clinical terms, feelings are described as *affect*. We describe someone who is lacking in feeling expressiveness as exhibiting blunt or flat affect. Either there seems to be no affect or the range of feeling is extremely limited. The most obvious sign of numbness is the refusal to say anything that suggests a feeling state. Every therapist has had the experience of talking to someone like Hugh for an entire session without once hearing a sentence or word with emotional coloring, even when the patient is describing the most horrendous events or concerns.

Hugh told me about being laid off from a downsizing aerospace firm, and being unemployed for eight months. He had to sell off his prized collection of baseball cards and wound up living in a cheap motel before a job offer came through. He recounted this matter-of-factly, using no emotional words. He simply shrugged and said, "That's part of life. You got to roll with the punches."

Naturally, the skilled clinician tries to ask the right questions, or to hazard guesses after the patient's statements. For example, "I would imagine you felt kind of angry when she did that." Or "That must have been a huge loss, selling your baseball cards." Depending on if, and how, the patient acknowledges our guess, we have further clues as to whether they are feeling anything. More clues emerge in a person's choice of words to describe his emotions. When I asked Hugh how he felt about his wife threatening to divorce him, instead of saying, "I feel sad," or, "I feel scared," he answered, "I feel weird."

We say a person like Hugh is *alexithymic* when he is unable to label his emotions or even to describe the various bodily sensations he experiences. Hugh was also what we label *anhedonic*, that is, unable to feel pleasure or any other positive feelings. It is the opposite of hedonism. The anhedonic person initially intends to shut himself off only from unpleasant feelings, but there's a poor payoff for the attempt. Because pleasure and pain use similar physiological pathways, he is unable to experience pleasurable emotions as well. Shutting off unpleasant feelings shuts down the entire spectrum of emotions, as it did for Hugh.

These verbal clues are usually accompanied by a lack of emotional expressiveness in the patient's voice. In Hugh's case, he spoke in a bland monotone, without the inflections and rises and falls that would accompany emotionally laden speech. His body language was equally unexpressive. He sat on the couch, relaxed but virtually motionless. He used no hand gesturing and his facial expression was deadpan.

A patient's body provides meaningful clues about his emotional energy. Obviously, someone who is relentlessly tapping his fingers on the arm of a chair, or twirling the tassels on a pillow, is portraying nervousness or distress. Squirming in a chair, tapping one's foot, bouncing a leg, or shifting repeatedly are signs of energy seeking expression.

Hugh had all the signs of someone who is emotionally numb. He used few emotionally toned words. His voice, facial expressions, and body demonstrated blunted affect and no emotional range. Although he was intelligent and pleasant, I could understand his wife's frustration and estrangement. Apparently at work he was a competent and valued engineer and did well in that setting. But at home his wife needed emotional connection in order not to feel alone. Hugh wasn't resentful or angry at his wife. He wasn't punishing her by withholding his love. Hugh was just empty. He felt nothing and had nothing to give. His wife was like a thirsty woman who stands cursing and crying at an empty well.

CHOOSING TO THINK RATHER THAN TO FEEL

Nina finally entered therapy at age forty-four because she was tired of being unfeeling. Her entire life had been spent cutting off her emotions because of a painful childhood marked by the loss of both her parents in an auto accident.

When she went to college, she chose a philosophy major. She reasoned that the world of ideas, void of emotion, would be a safe haven for her scarred psyche. Nina did, in fact, survive and function, but one aspect of her life suffered greatly—intimate relationships. She could not allow anyone to really know her or to know how she felt, because she didn't know how she felt herself.

After receiving her doctorate, she chose to remain in the academic world. It was harmonious to her psychological well-being. She was comfortable dealing with lofty ideas at the expense of basic feelings. By her early thirties, she was on tenure track as a history and philosophy professor. As her loneliness grew, she finally decided to enter therapy in the hope that she could get in touch with her emotions and perhaps learn to relate to others well enough to finally begin a love relationship.

After Nina had been in therapy with me for a few months, she began dating someone and had high hopes for this relationship. But she had picked a man who, in contrast to her, was very much in touch with his emotions. When she discussed each date in our sessions, I felt that he was desperately trying to know her better and was becoming increasingly frustrated at what he perceived as coldness on her part. Unfortunately, we had not made enough progress in therapy, so as the relationship ran aground, Nina was so filled with shame and discouragement that she stopped treatment. I speculate this happened; she didn't tell me. I only hope she resumed therapy later, for she was living half a life.

THE "AS IF" CHARACTER

Another psychological strategy to ensure comfort is the suppression of genuine emotions, followed by the pretense of socially appropriate feelings. This is rarely a conscious decision. The "as if" character does this. Rachel was such a patient, and described her moment of realization about her nonfeeling state.

"At the funeral, I was sitting right in the front pew of the church, with my cousins on either side of me, hearing the minister talk about my aunt's life and what a wonderful person she had been. And she was—a warm, very sweet, happy person who was always terrific to me. Yet in the midst of all that sadness, I caught myself thinking about a client's project I'm working on.

"My cousin, who's seventeen, started crying, and I put my arm around him and tried to comfort him, but I felt removed from the whole thing, like it was a movie and everybody was acting. I felt embarrassed and kind of annoyed by everybody's crying and their wet faces. I said the right things and acted sad, but inside, I just felt . . . nothing. And when I think about the last year or so, since Matt [her ex-husband] moved out, I think I've been sleepwalking through my life since then, acting like I'm fine, but inside, I think I'm a mess."

Men and women like Rachel have lost such a sense of their real selves that they learn to behave as if they are experiencing certain emotions. They don't intend to be fake, but they fundamentally are. They may express sympathy or grief because they know that's what you are supposed to do, but they don't feel it inside. Even when they seem happy, they are not—they know the event calls for happiness, so they act as if they feel that emotion. At least Rachel was aware of her "as if" tendencies. Many people live "as if" lives without any awareness that their expressions are no longer even connected to real feelings inside. You've undoubtedly met people like this. You hear what they're saying, but somehow you just don't believe them; you are not touched by them.

THE PITFALLS OF DENIAL

Denial of one's emotions is a progressive process. First, surface feelings diminish, then the denial burrows deeper. In the first stage of denial, we refuse to label our feelings or we label them improperly, but we still feel some basic inner arousal. But in time, if we are prone to denial, we even express our awareness of arousal. Denial is a coping and survival technique. It's just like going into physical shock and not being able to feel pain when we're seriously injured. Sometimes numbing is actually adaptive. If we didn't go numb in certain extreme circumstances, we would go insane or die.

Bruno Bettelheim, the psychologist who studied concentration camp behavior, noted that very few people fainted in the camps in spite of the horrors taking place. He concluded that sometimes, in the face of stress, it can be advantageous to lose sight of what you feel. The camp inmates shut down emotionally—to feel the pain and misery and sheer horror would have been overwhelming. They sealed off, or insulated, their emotions in order to survive. Soldiers in battle cope this way. They go numb and suppress emotional responses; it's the only way they can tolerate the stress of the battlefield. They force themselves to think, "It can't happen to me," as they see death all around them. People who risk their own lives to rescue others report the same kind of detachment at the instant they must summon great courage and strength.

In some emotionally extreme situations, people depersonalize themselves. They become so detached and dissociated that they feel as though they're watching themselves from a distance. This process is common in near-death experiences, and for children who are molested. It is a survival mechanism that keeps us alive until the immediate danger has passed. However, few of us will experience such actual life and death situations in which detachment is adaptive. For most of us, detachment and denial are usually not constructive strategies; they lead to the most self-deceptive and self-defeating narrow comfort zones. Ultimately, denial, detachment, and nonfeeling rob us of our sense of self.

CHOOSING TO EMBRACE YOUR EMOTIONS

I believe that once you have learned to deal comfortably with negative emotional states, you feel your energy for more positive ones. It's like clearing the brambles away from a dormant rose garden. Understanding that you can orchestrate your emotions and enlarge your comfort zones has a liberating, magical effect. Every temperament type has its dark side, but also its inclination to positive emotions. By virtue of how we are psychologically constructed and because of social conditioning, we automatically begin to want more out of life and to experience the higher emotions that relate more to pleasure than to pain.

Today, people who wish to enlarge their comfort zones find this task consistent with an overall health-enriching outlook.

Two of the new terms in health care are *wellness* and *hardiness*. For me, wellness smacks of dubious standards of normalcy. But hardiness, or resilience, connotes an ability to roll with the punches, to engage and cope effectively with the inevitable adversities that come our way. Hardiness implies an enhanced tolerance for stress and pressure. It suggests an adaptability and flexibility that is the mark of those who overcome setbacks and seek out challenges. In sum, hardiness is about the ability to master (not control) your emotions.

So, if you have been living a life of emotional denial or numbness, or even just with a little too much emotional safety, hopefully you are now willing to entertain the possibility of living differently, of expanding the range of emotionality you will allow into your life.

THOUGHTS AND FEELINGS: THE MIND/BODY DUALITY

In order to be aware of yourself as an integrated mind/body organism, let us examine each side of this duality. Your mind, or interpretive brain, is essentially the content of your thoughts. It is the part of your brain that monitors, appraises, and interprets your arousal. It is what interprets fear arousal as you watch a scary part in a movie and it tells you, "It's only a movie," then reinterprets the arousal as excitement. The same process would take place if you were on a roller coaster. It enables you to separate real fear from imagined fear. In a more general sense, how you interpret your arousal is a product of your life-long conditioning.

Ideally, the highest level of functioning occurs when your mind and body are fully integrated in a feedback loop: (1) You experience arousal plus your action tendency. (2) Your mind assimilates this information. (3) You then choose to regulate your emotions in a way that is consistent with your temperament (as we will explore in chapter 10).

But the beginning of awareness is about bodily sensations. It may be helpful to think of your body as a musical instrument. The unique music it plays is your temperament. It can be played with love or with indifference. By using these images, I am implying that it is a beautiful instrument, even though some of the sounds may at first seem harsh and discordant. If you think back to the first time you heard Oriental, Indian, or modern atonal music, you may have found it jarring and strange. So, too, with the sensations that can arise from your body.

For many people, learning to listen to and understand the music of their bodies enables them to see themselves in a new way. Often, the discovery that you have a natural self is a similar experience. Learning your instrument, the notes it plays, its range, its rhythms, is a prerequisite for orchestrating your emotional life.

DISCOVERING YOUR NATURAL SELF

Mastering your emotions requires that you learn to hear and understand the emotional signs your body is constantly broadcasting. This means cutting through all layers of old ideas, all the shoulds and should nots, all the layers of ingrained old habits and thoughts about your social self—right down to your core, to the more basic natural self that operates in your body. You must experiment with yourself to discover what your natural self feels—how intensely it feels, whether you've numbed yourself to a state of not feeling. The best context for becoming aware of your natural self is spending time alone.

When I suggest this to patients of mine, they often protest that their emotions don't occur in the context of being alone; they occur in social context, in the heat of encounter or clash with others that trigger their emotions. My response is that we must first become aware of our natural self in solitude, then address our emotional interactions with others. Indeed, the only way we can discover ourselves is in a state of aloneness, a time-out for ourselves. Not reading, not thinking about work or relationships or chores, just being alone, quiet. You can do this in a quiet room. The context should be free of external sensory input—no talk, no people, no distractions.

Spending time alone in quiet can be difficult. We may feel guilty that we're not doing anything when we've got so much to do. And, as we shut out sensory input, nagging thoughts or worries may arise: work worries, family problems, disappointments, resentments. Unfortunately, negative concerns tend to rise to the surface more easily than positive ones.

Some of my patients say this exercise, at first, can lead to a poignant awareness of loneliness and, thus, sadness. Loneliness is obviously a state most of us work hard to keep at bay. Usually, when we spend time by ourselves, we busy our senses with talk on the phone, television, radio, cleaning up, organizing, making lists, and other busy work—anything will do so long as it staves off isolation. In this exercise, acknowledge your feeling of loneliness, and refocus on your body's signals.

You may find that your mind begins racing with thoughts. As one patient described it, "I feel as though my mind is just a clutter of thoughts and emotions jumbled together. I just keep going from one to another until I can't sort them out." Don't try to sort out your thoughts. The point of this exercise is to become aware of your body and the emotional signals it is sending out. It takes practice and concentration, but simply allow your thoughts to race along while you focus instead on what you are feeling. You can do this on a weekly basis, at random times, for a half hour, but I've found most people choose to do this at times when they feel burdened by unpleasant emotions. When you have done this exercise three or four times, you will find yourself familiar with the predictable nature of your emotionality.

Allow your thoughts to drift through your mind. Don't focus on them; don't fight them; let them drift in and drift out. This technique is aimed at disconnecting sensations with old interpretations of the sensations.

First, focus on your extremities: your hands and feet. Become aware of any tension, sweating, or nervousness. Next, focus on your chest (tightness). Your stomach (gripped, knotted, butterflies, trembling, unusual hot or cold). Your face and head (flushing, headache). Become aware of any impatience, agitation, deadness, emptiness, sense of nothingness. All of these sensations are the music your natural self may be playing.

Emotions begin in the central nervous system (the brain) and then travel through other peripheral bodily systems, such as the autonomic nervous system, and may be expressed by sweating, muscle tension, and so on. This explains why we must first become aware of the peripheral signals and work our way into the center of our body: our chest and stomach.

Finally comes the recognition of arousal or the lack of it. What words come to you as you experience these sensations? It could be anything. Focus on whatever terms come to you, then focus on one term at a time, and make it three-dimensional. Allow more images to come, for example, "light" as what? As a balloon? What does "lightness" mean to you? Then, work your way down into the basic emotional labels such as fear, anxiety, happiness, contentment, or other feelings. The process is awareness of sensations, awareness of your interpretations of the sensations.

This exercise is more difficult for some temperament types. The sensor finds it easy to tune into his body. By his very nature—sensitivity—he is more attuned to his body. So, too, is the focuser. Both are introverted and, thus, more inner oriented. The discharger and seeker are extroverted, more action oriented. For these latter types, slowing down enough to tune into themselves is more unfamiliar.

I feel confident in telling you that if you allow yourself the time to become acquainted with the source of your emotions, the payoff is well worth the initial discomfort: an awareness of the unique rhythms and flow of your emotional arousal. As you become familiar with the flow of this arousal, it becomes less surprising, less unsettling, less unexpected. This awareness eventually becomes your foundation for self-acceptance and emotional self-confidence.

BECOMING AWARE OF YOUR COMFORT ZONES: PREPARATION

Obviously all temperaments have to cope, in varying degrees, with all of the basic emotions, including anxiety, anger, sadness, and impulsivity. Temperament refers to the predominant emotional response of an individual. Let's review the three areas you need to explore to discover your emotional identity: acknowledgments, awareness, and self-inquiry.

ACKNOWLEDGMENTS

What is my temperament? By now you will have taken the quizzes and identified what type you are. You should know:

- Whether your typical arousal level is high or low.
- What your action tendency is.
- The general situations that trigger arousal and you should have an idea of what your corrective task is, that is, what you need to do to reset your thermostat.

AWARENESS

I have discussed awareness of bodily sensations, but here I would like to be more specific. First, there is the awareness of emotional discomfort in its various forms. There are the consciously obvious painful emotions like anxiety. There are physical manifestations like sweating, breathing heavily, tension, and fatigue. And finally, there are cognitive manifestations of distressing emotions, such as a lack of concentration, slowed motor or physical behavior, freezing or clutching, and blocking of thought processes such as forgetfulness.

SELF-INQUIRY

You can ask yourself the following questions in order to further the process of emotional awareness:

1. Do I have an accurate identification of my own innate predispositions or have I denied them? If I have disguised my temperament, why? Am I ashamed?
2. Do I allow myself to feel whatever wells up in me? Do I quickly scramble to alter it? What are the self-defeating ways I regulated my emotions in the past?
3. How do I interpret arousal? What emotions am I aware of?
4. Can I first accept what happens inside me in the sense of accepting arousal or lack of it, and then watch passively to see what happens? If I choose to reset my thermostat, what is my task?

EMOTIONAL TRIGGERS

There are two types of events that affect your thermostat: internal only, where the mere ebbing and flowing of neurotransmitters raises or lowers your arousal; and, of course, interactions with your external environment, including exchanges with other people.

It can be important to determine whether the trigger is internal or external. To distinguish where it's coming from, you have to work from the outside in. First, take stock of what is going on around you at that moment, and what is going on in your life in general. If you can't find any obvious provocations in the external world, the arousal may be occurring solely as biochemical "burp," a change in your "brain soup." Women who are subject to the heightened emotions that accompany premenstrual syndrome can remind themselves of the hormonal influence on their feelings. Similarly, when you experience a sudden mood change, you can consciously choose to go about your business.

When you are aware of emotional discomfort, of being out of your comfort zone, ask yourself the following questions:

1. What am I conscious of? What thoughts are going on in my head?
2. Do these thoughts or feelings seem connected to events going on right now?
3. Are these thoughts disconnected to the outside world? Are they vague yearnings, fears, or worries?

Next, go through your temperament checklist of possible triggers:

Sensors: "Something feels threatening" (overarousal):

- Feeling nervous about the performance of a future event or task.
- Feeling nervous being with other people right now (social anxiety), including what feels like a performance in front of others.

- Feeling nervous about fear itself, fear of panic.
- Fear of symptoms: bodily arousal, sweating, breathing, shaking.
- Fear of potential blows to self-esteem.
- Fear of helplessness in threatening events.

Focusers: "I'm feeling or anticipating some emptiness" (under-arousal):

- Feeling hopeless about some external situation.
- Feeling actual loss of ego and self-esteem.
- Feeling sad about a loss.
- Having constant worries, ruminative thoughts.
- Worrying and feeling helplessness about some future loss.
- Feeling helplessness about controlling outcomes.
- Feeling empty, sad, or worried for no apparent reason.

Dischargers: "I'm tuned into an aversive or negative target" (overarousal):

- Interruption of any goal-directed behavior.
- Any frustrating events or people preventing you from achieving something.
- Perceived attacks on your self-worth and self-esteem by others.
- Inability to control your environment or other people.
- Arousal welling up for no reason leading to nonspecific irritability.

Seekers: "I feel a craving for something" (underarousal):

- Boredom and lack of newness or novelty.
- Familiarity of situation.
- Satiation due to repeated experience with same situations or activities.
- Temptation for new and novel situations or activities that promise sensation.
- Potential pleasure in some anticipated event or situation.

As you monitor your feelings and thoughts, and identify the provocation, you can then employ the corrective task specific to your temperament. Calmly becoming aware of what you feel and what the trigger might have been is usually sufficient to set you in motion toward this task, which, in turn, will result in your feeling more comfortable. In time, you will expand your comfort zone this way, because awareness makes what was once unpleasant, now less unsettling.

EMOTIONAL EXPRESSION AND INDIVIDUALITY

For many people with whom I've worked, the discovery and acceptance of temperament is the final missing piece in their search for a complete identity. Most of us have a sense of who we are by virtue of ideas we have about ourselves. But it is our very uniqueness and individuality that we often fear. We want to be individuals, but we don't want to be thought of as different. We are torn between wanting to stand out and wanting to blend into the crowd. For many of us, this is a constant struggle.

It is essential that you understand you are taking the chance of expanding your identity. New emotional choices lead to new behaviors. New ways of conducting yourself lead to new perceptions of you by others. For some, this is welcome; for others, this new identity can create some anxiety about being accepted by others.

To affirm and express your emotions means you must choose to be who you are. The notion of choice is difficult for many of us. It is a lot easier to say, "I can't show this or that feeling because my friends can't handle it," or "I will be misunderstood" (meaning your friends will no longer buy into the image you've been trying to project). Acting on the courage of your convictions means you are making a decision as to how you will live your life, a decision to not waste your energy on creating bogus impressions. When it comes down to it, trying to be the person you think others want you to be, or trying to be the person you think they will like, is nothing more than a shadow dance.

If there is going to be a real you, you have to shed the myths we have discussed. To strive to be emotionally perfect will only cause you to feel terribly inadequate. To try to express only "good" emotions and to suppress "bad" ones will drain you of energy in a quest that is doomed to failure. Being an individual means that you accept and honor the full range of emotions that reveal all of your humanness. To be an individual means that you will not allow trendy theories of what is considered "healthy" and what is considered "dysfunctional" to be your emotional guideposts.

It goes without saying that to be an individual means you do not have to fit someone else's mold of what is "normal." The litmus test of accepting your temperament is setting your own standards, not allowing yourself to be defined by external standards. No matter how independent you are, the people around you, and society on a larger scale, are conveying messages about how you should behave, what emotions are appropriate, and what it takes to be regarded as likeable.

Oddly enough, the man or woman we find to be truly admirable is a person who has the courage of his or her convictions. This is a truth you need to grasp. As you work to expand your emotional comfort zone, you are likely to discover that your greatest fear is not the temperament-specific emotions that you need to experience but will people like you if they see these facets of your personality that you have denied or kept hidden for so long? There are no guarantees, of course, but people usually are more accepting of us than we are! Now you are ready for the specific courses of action necessary for you to feel more comfortable more of the time.

Chapter 10

RESETTING YOUR EMOTIONAL THERMOSTAT

As WE HAVE LEARNED, we cannot change the visceral, biological determinants of our feelings. What we can do is change the way we relate to our emotions and modify the ways we respond to them. That is where change begins, focusing on ourselves as catalysts for change.

Any desire to alter our psychological existence starts with an acceptance of the unchangeable. By accepting our temperament and our emotions, we bring about something that is rather odd, paradoxical, yet enormously powerful. At the moment of acceptance, we automatically alter how we experience our feelings. This is the magic of the existential moment—the moment at which conscious choice is made. When we choose to be aware of and accept our feelings, we affirm and respect our self. (Self-deception and denial makes us lose our sense of who we really are and leaves us emotionally adrift and confused.) Acceptance is an active process. It is not passive, nor is it resignation. Acceptance is the first step in emotional empowerment and mastery.

YOU ARE THE AGENT OF CHANGE

Most of us are stuck in old patterns more deeply than we realize. The familiar feels safe even when it is upsetting. I know this sounds paradoxical, but that's just how we are constructed psychologically. I've described how even the notion of comfort zone is based more on what is familiar and expected rather than on that which is truly pleasing and comfortable. Changing your responses and behavior requires letting go of old patterns that are making you miserable.

Declaring that you can be self-determining is to affirm that you are the agent of change. This is what the eminent psychologist Albert Bandura characterizes as self-efficacy, the essence of what is more commonly known as confidence. Self-efficacy means that you view yourself and the world as a feedback system: you cause effects in the world, which in turn influences you and how you feel.

Bandura believes we are always processing information from our environment telling us how to adjust our thinking and behavior in order to maximize our effectiveness. He believes that we process expectations and, when they are discrepant from what we want, we then make adjustments. In my terms, this means processing the information that tells you how to adjust or reset your emotional thermostat: the task you can employ to enlarge the comfort zone dictated by your temperament.

We must believe in our personal power or self-efficacy before we can deal with outside stressors or emotional triggers. Our degree of self-efficacy predicts which challenges we will seek out, which we will avoid, and whether we can overcome obstacles. Blending Bandura's concept into my theory of the natural self, we can say it is possible to develop a form of emotional self-confidence.

In chapter 9, we looked at the process of awareness in general: the recognition of your temperament and how it dictates the ebbing and flowing of your emotions on a continual basis. Now let us review the general steps that apply to all temperaments.

1. Awareness. Accepting the arousal, flowing with it without shame or judgment.

2. Disengagement. Accepting the underarousal or overarousal and halting the instinctive action tendency. This means seizing a moment in time: if a sensor, before you avoid; if a discharger, before prolonged expression; if a focuser, before prolonged rumination; if a seeker, before you pursue new sensations. By accepting arousal before you take action, you are automatically modifying the action tendency which, even though it is innate, is still subject to the general psychological laws of learning and conditioning. In other words, disengagement breaks the habit you have built up over the years. The instinctive response becomes diminished rather than reinforced.

3. Action. Now is the time to implement the resetting task for your temperament.

THE SENSOR'S TASK: DESENSITIZATION

First is awareness of arousal. Next is allowing yourself to simply tolerate it. Let the arousal, in effect, wash over you. This leads to desensitization, meaning that in time the arousal will subside and will be less likely to instinctively lead to avoidance or withdrawal. With repeated desensitization, you will more courageously expose yourself to fearful situations. The range of possible emotions as you learn the task are: terrified→apprehensive→anxious→uneasy→calm→nonchalant→effective→confident→courageous.

THE DISCHARGER'S TASK: BENIGN RELEASE

First, identify the provocation, remove yourself from the trigger, and briefly express your emotional energy (benign release). Then continue to shift your attention away from the target and begin self-focusing on your own arousal. The range of possible emotions as you learn the task are: hate→rage→anger→disgust→irritation→resentment→petulance→relief→release→contentment.

THE FOCUSER'S TASK: DISTRACTION

First, focus internally on the lack of inner arousal. Next, defuse from fixation and self-focusing. Shift to searching for distractors. Finally, change your focus via distraction. The range of possible emotions as you learn the task are: despair→ sorrow→depression→sadness→rumination→worry→serious-ness→relaxation→aliveness.

THE SEEKER'S TASK: OSCILLATION OR ALTERNATION

There must be a shifting between resting behavior and seeking. The seeker must learn to tolerate even relatively brief periods of rest, and concurrently must explore more adaptive sensation-seeking goals. The range of possible emotions as you learn the task are: exhausted→stressed→bored→disinterested→satis-fied→curious→determined→enthusiastic→excited.

In time, you will be able to visualize your threshold of arousal going up and down like a dam in a river. If you are a sensor or discharger, imagine the threshold slowly rising, damming in the water (arousal) so it doesn't overwhelm you. If you are a seeker or focuser, imagine the dam being lowered and allowing the water to flow freely and vitally.

SENSORS: ENLARGING THE COMFORT ZONE

You can live more comfortably as a sensor. Notice I say *live more comfortably:* trying to eliminate disturbing emotions is what gets us in trouble and is the reason so many sensors fail in their search for emotional relief. If you are a sensor, your attempts will fail if what you're really trying to do is to bludgeon your temperament into submission.

The key to enlarging your comfort zone as a sensor is to modify your action tendency, which is typically your withdrawal from potential harm. By using desensitization, in which you experience the scary thought or situation and defuse it of its power, you can condition yourself to become less aroused. The less you avoid and the more you face threat, the more you will raise your threshold, having less arousal and thus an enlarged comfort zone. This process must be done in a conscious, systematic, and carefully orchestrated way.

Systematic desensitization is a term behavioral psychologists use. It means gradual and graded exposure to feared situations that give rise to anxiety. A classic example is snake phobias. If you expose a person with such a phobia to a snake, initially, he is highly aroused. But with repeated exposure to the snake over time, he gradually feels less arousal and can start touching, even holding the snake. In time, with gradual exposure to any feared circumstances, less anxiety is aroused. Often this work can take place in a situation other than the actual fearful one, for example, an office, employing mental imagery and visualization as a kind of rehearsal. If you have to give a speech, the more you rehearse it in your mind, the less anxious you may feel.

Psychologists are now focusing on the self-evaluations of people who become anxious. They find that the worst thing you can do is to try to control or subdue your anxiety. This only makes you feel helpless. When you feel helpless and you become anxious, you tend to magnify the pain and discomfort, because in fact you cannot control it. These researchers don't take the theoretical leap that I do in postulating innate emotional types, but implicit in their work is the conviction that arousal exists not because you are neurotic but because of your temperament.

The most important thing you must keep in mind is that the more comfortable you become with your natural self, the easier it is to begin readjusting your emotional thermostat. You may want to return to chapter 2 on the emotional myths and clear your mind of unrealistic beliefs and foolish expectations. Stop looking around you in the old way. Stop comparing your insides to other people's outsides. Stop rejecting yourself.

STEP BY STEP

1. Don't try medication unless you are so anxious that you are not even able to consider other options. In the hands of doctors who don't educate you, antianxiety drugs will distance you further from your natural self. You will come to regard messages from your natural self as unwanted symptoms of illness. In the

hands of those few doctors who know what they're doing, they'll tell you the medication is just a booster for resetting a thermostat and lessening debilitating arousal. In either case, you will not have access to the emotional and physiological data necessary in order to live comfortably with your temperament. (In chapter 12, I will provide a set of guidelines on medication, and how to ascertain that a doctor is knowledgeable about medication.)

2.   Don't think that simple meditation or relaxation is the answer to unwanted aspects of your temperament. While these techniques may feel good, they were devised by people on lonely mountaintops, people who didn't have to deal with the continual onslaught of emotionally triggering stimuli on a daily and hourly basis. These techniques don't travel well from the quiet room to the noisy world. You must learn how to find comfort in stressful situations.

3. Become aware of your body and its signals of arousal. Be able to describe it in vivid detail, including breathing, sweating, jitters, lack of concentration, fearful thoughts, the content of those thoughts (i.e., the specific dangers). Begin looking at these outer manifestations of inner arousal as natural and commonplace. Start reminding yourself that they won't kill you. Awareness defuses the power of these signals.

4. Become aware of arousal sequences, how one awareness leads to the next. Allow the sequence to happen. Ordinary distress leads to apprehension, concern, anxiety, even panic. Review the sequence and discover how natural it is, and how irrational your fear is.

5. Rehearse in your mind situations that typically trigger your arousal. Close your eyes and think about that scary date, the talk you have to give, or a boss criticizing you. Now focus solely, cooly, and deliberately on your arousal—what you feel in your body. Some desensitization will occur. Arousal will tend to decrease as you are now raising your threshold, paradoxically just by your attention to, and acceptance of, your arousal. And, of

course, you may feel you are in a state of overarousal with no apparent trigger.

6. Next, do the last step in real life. Pick out a scary situation. Maybe it's a phone call you've been avoiding. Let arousal wash over you as you deliberately face the anxiety-provoking situation—let it happen. You'll find you're not overwhelmed. You'll also find that you are now, in effect, creating an enlarged comfort zone. The next time you face that situation, your anxiety level won't be so high.

7. Expose yourself to scary situations and to scary thoughts as a way of becoming more familiar with your threshold of arousal. Thresholds of arousal for all temperaments tend to float more than we think. This float comes from brain chemistry flux, the ebbing and flowing of neurotransmitters. The exercises I'm suggesting are in effect modulating the flow of these chemicals.

8. Inventory the situations and people that overstimulated you and take them on. Don't expect to have lost your temperament; it's still there. Get a feeling of your temperament in all the situations that bothered you. Without powerful expectations, it will be easier to do this. This is a way to know yourself.

ANDREW: A SENSOR

Andrew is married, but even with his gregarious wife at his side, he still feels nervous when he meets new people or attends a large party. In the past, Andrew's solution was to attempt to ignore his anxiety and talk nonstop with a nervous torrent of words when he found himself in social situations. He would become exhausted, but he would feel pleased that he had averted a disaster if people saw how nervous and shy he really was. Invariably, he would leave these occasions early and then return home to relax . . . and be himself.

After learning how sensors feel and what they can do about their feelings, we worked two exercises for him:

1. He was told to visualize or rehearse what it was like to walk into a room with everyone staring at him. When he did this, he felt his arousal elevate. He did this a number of times with the

instruction to just feel the arousal. With repeated rehearsal, his arousal diminished, even when I upped the ante: he was to imagine people ignoring him or finding him uninteresting and walking away after a few moments of conversation.

2. Andrew went to a number of social events without his wife. I instructed him to pause before going into the room and experience his arousal, his nervous anticipation. I told him to feel it, let it subside, then go in. Once inside, he was told to be aware of his arousal, without suppressing it or talking nervously, without doing anything—just let it happen and feel it. In fact, I told him if he really wanted to enlarge his comfort zone, he had to try and desensitize himself to all the triggers that made him nervous, which meant he had to tolerate sitting by himself, not talking to anyone, and take the chance of being perceived as shy or noncommunicative. This exercise really aroused him at first, but in time, his threshold drifted higher and he was able to feel relatively comfortable.

After months of experimentation, Andrew found himself with a generally higher threshold, and thus less arousal in public situations. He also discovered that he felt more comfortable just because he was no longer ashamed of being seen as shy. Interestingly, he also found that certain other longtime anxieties were real but solvable. Secretly, he felt that he didn't have a lot to talk about. He started reading more, keeping up with current events, and generally being more knowledgeable. Sometimes there are reality considerations behind fears that were masked by temperament struggles.

Andrew learned to accept that he was always going to be predisposed to feeling overaroused in certain situations. But he learned how to work with his temperament instead of fighting or denying it. He learned that the ebbing and flowing of his sensor's arousal could be orchestrated and modulated. He grew more emotionally self-confident as it became more manageable.

DISCHARGERS: ENLARGING THE COMFORT ZONE

You will be unable to expand your comfort zone if you're angry at yourself or in a state of denial. You must set aside excuses, rationalization, and self-deception. You have to toss the myths out the front door, too. Reframe your feelings about yourself. Remind yourself of the desirable facets of your temperament: the energy, the dynamism, the spontaneity. Think of emotional regulation as an exercise in empowerment.

The task for the discharger is release or benign catharsis: shifting attention away from the target and back onto the arousal. Catharsis has an inherent appeal for the discharger, for release is partly what he or she needs. But dischargers usually do not realize that simple or brief expression will do the job, rather than fixating on a target and lashing out at it. By benign catharsis, I mean the expression of emotion in a way that does no harm to others or yourself. You don't hit people or things, you don't insult others, and you don't tell off your boss or your best friend. Those are all self-defeating strategies. Venting anger briefly while you are alone is sufficient to vent the arousal. There are safe and ethical ways to deal with the explosive component in anger.

This advice does not imply that you can never get angry again. You may still get angry with the same frequency as you do now, but it can last seconds rather than minutes, hours or days. Remember that beyond a brief catharsis, all the research evidence suggests that the chronic and prolonged expression of anger creates an anger habit.

What the discharger needs to realize is that the majority of the time, when he or she is aroused, the arousal comes from within. It often has no meaning or purpose: it is a biological phenomenon. Without argument (so to speak), dischargers are good at finding targets—they are off and running before they realize they've been triggered by internal "noise" in the biological system. Part of the solution is to reverse the discharger's natural tendency to go outside himself by refocusing and developing inner awareness. The basic process is expression followed by self-focusing.

STEP BY STEP

1. Identify the triggers in your life. Most are familiar and need no analysis: your spouse, a boss, a friend, a family feud,

even a political figure. The spark may be internally generated with no apparent trigger.

2. Don't stifle your anger. It only builds up because your arousal will build, but don't just let it blow. Follow the next step.

3. Allow yourself some release or catharsis. Move away from the target—leave the room, go for a walk. Even if the target is not physically present but in your mind, change locations and take a brief walk. As you walk, clench your muscles, breathe deeply, expel your anger with your breath, yell, walk vigorously, and swing your arms. This is what I mean by benign catharsis. You have to do something with the energy, or it loops back into your arousal. Benign release raises your threshold and the arousal-caused anger drops. By the way, you don't have to do a lot; running five miles may pump you up and get you more agitated. What I'm suggesting is five minutes of exercise.

4. Distract your thoughts from the target. Most dischargers naively believe, "If I focus (chew on) on the target and think about it or him or her, then I'll find a new way to interpret the situation." You may have to analyze the situation later, but focusing on the target will typically make you angrier. You have to break the outward action tendency.

5. Self-focus on the inner arousal. When you feel yourself heating up, turn your focus away from the object and back on yourself. Focus on your physical sensations, what's going on in your body. You will relax immediately, because your threshold was raised immediately by the shift in focus. However, you will be drawn back to the target by your mind, and you'll have to refocus onto yourself.

6. Condition yourself using behavior therapy. As you focus on yourself, flex your muscles systematically from your head to your toes. Tense or flex your toes, hold it, then release, now your foot, etc., working upward. What you are doing is pairing relaxation with arousal, which tends to reduce the intensity of the arousal.

Remember, unlike the focuser, when the discharger self-focuses it is good for him, since self-focusing lowers arousal which is exactly what the discharger needs.

A word to the mate of a discharger. Just exactly how do you go about changing this person who can be so delightful and yet so difficult? Well, you are not going to change him! You are going to help him or yourself learn to modulate and orchestrate the arousal that erupts so frequently. Forget about change in the sense of a psychological lobotomy. Anger and impulsivity have been given a bad name in our society. As soon as we hear words like anger and impulsivity, we automatically think of spouse abuse, child abuse, heart attacks. Suppressed anger which evolves into chronic hostility is what is usually at the bottom of our ugliest behaviors and ways of relating. It is the suppression especially of your innate nature that does you in.

NANCY: A DISCHARGER

Nancy is a freelance marketing person for a group of physicians. She's full of energy and has a magnetic personality, which accounts for her success in this field. Her job is to aggressively drum up new business from hospitals and personal injury lawyers. Her only problem is that she's a discharger and she occasionally flies off the handle with a client.

When she came to see me, she said she used to think these outbursts were related to premenstrual syndrome (PMS). But when she reviewed her datebook and compared the incidents to her menstrual cycle, she saw that they were unrelated. She wanted help. "I used to laugh at myself, because a lot of people actually got a kick out of my temperament. They used to call me feisty. Now they call me bitchy. For years I defended myself, thinking some people just can't handle strong women. Now I'm kind of worried about my blowing up. I can see things deteriorating, both in my work and with the men I date. I'm just alienating too many people. Frankly, I'm scared mostly about my career—I'm starting to get a bad reputation."

As I explained the discharger's temperament to Nancy, she nodded her head a lot. She identified immediately; the descriptions hit home, especially when I pointed out how the discharger's low threshold creates arousal even without an external trigger or target. Nancy said, "Yeah, you're right. I'll be driving on the freeway, just listening to music, and suddenly I'm thinking about someone who hasn't sent any business my way for a while. Instead of thinking how to cultivate them better, I'm just grinding my teeth, ticked off. If I don't shake that feeling, it'll come out on the phone with them or anyone I talk to in the next hour or so." She was aware that by not understanding her temperament was susceptible to intermittent or random "noise" in the system, she would begin to justify her anger, explain it, rationalize it, and act on it. Here's the program I developed for Nancy:

1. First, we explored the provocations in her life. The triggers were primarily people frustrating her from achieving a goal. Since there was no particular trigger or annoying person she had to deal with, there was no need for an encounter with the target. I told her she was forbidden to discuss any gripe or complaint with anyone in her life. This was a task she had to do alone to cease contaminating her external world with her anger.

2. Next we practiced benign release. If she were alone, she was to shout or yell out anything. If she were in public, she was to take a brief, brisk walk, or excuse herself and take a short break. Going to the ladies room proved to be a plausible excuse in business or social situations. She had to discharge some of the energy rather than suppress it. She could still think about the target of her anger, but only for the five or ten minutes this release took.

3. Disconnecting from the target was the next step. She had to allow angry thoughts about clients to drift out of her head. This was easier than she had thought because I told her that we would explore her concerns together, in session, when we could look at positive actions available to her to realize her goals.

4. Then, after disconnection, she had to self-focus on her arousal. She had to allow thoughts to drift out of her head and focus only on her physical sensations. First in her face and jaw,

and then on her heavy breathing and constricted chest. She was told to do this for five minutes following her expression or release of anger.

Nancy learned this step-by-step process of release, disconnection, and self-focus, and her periods of anger diminished. She continued to feel arousal, but she dealt with it fluidly, on her own, without acting it out. She felt a lot better about herself. She realized that she still had all of her dynamic nature. If fact, she became more energetic, because she wasn't stifling herself or exploding.

FOCUSERS: ENLARGING THE COMFORT ZONE

The solution for focusers is to master the process of distraction. Too much rumination is like spinning your tires in the mud—it just digs you in deeper. There is an ideal balance between attentiveness and distraction. Many of us shift between the two instinctively. If we become too worried, we'll get up from our chair, take a walk, return a phone call. What we're doing is short circuiting the unproductive cycling. By using distraction, the focuser finds emotional relief.

When you learn to reset your emotional thermostat, you will find that the antidote to the discomfort of underarousal is the awareness that it is time limited. Much of the fear of not feeling alive, or getting caught up in endless rumination, comes from the gnawing apprehension that it will never end.

STEP BY STEP

1. First, have faith. Focusers often end up feeling very pessimistic. Many focusers have withdrawn from the very activities in their life that would prove to be distractors. They have pulled back and isolated themselves because they feel sad or worried. They are ashamed of their emotions: they feel weak, vulnerable. They don't want anyone to see them like this, and they don't want to infect others with their negativity. They attack themselves: "If only I had more self-control, I would be happy."

They shame themselves into solitary confinement, where they can work their way deeper and deeper into a rut.

2. Don't fall for common sense. Studies show that thought suppression or thought stopping actually works against you. It creates a link between the thought and the lack of arousal. This technique is destructive for most people, especially for sensors and focusers. The more you try to stop thinking about something, the more you will think about it. It's like trying to not think of pink elephants. Try it, they will keep dancing around your mind. If you're lucky, they waltz!

3. Deliberately focus, then distract. You must first defuse from your fixation before you can pursue, or be open to, distractions. By defuse, I mean welcome the moods and the thoughts associated with them, then focus briefly on the arousal or lack of arousal. Now you are ready to distract. You deal with your emotions head on, without fear. The chain of events is critical: deliberately focus your inner physical sensations, eliminate conscious thoughts (concentrate on pure feeling or lack of feeling; understand it is your temperament), and then willfully take action to embrace distractors. This becomes a learning chain, by which you break the linkage between arousal and reflexive self-focusing. (This process has been called paradoxical intention.)

4. It is important that you develop a repertoire of distractors: friends, sports activities, workout videos, movies, shopping. Even when distractors are only momentary, they can be effective, for they create room to break the fixation on self-focusing behavior and direct your attention elsewhere.

5. Take action on problems. In the case of actual losses and real worries, for example, like serious personal rejection or a failed work project, the appropriate action is to jump right in and find substitutes. If a romance ends, don't sit home and let yourself sink into sadness; stay busy with friends, nonthreatening evenings out with groups of singles, and so on. If you suffer a career setback or a layoff, don't sit home working yourself into feeling worthless. Get busy facing the problem.

LAUREL: A FOCUSER

Laurel is happily married, and has a number of close friends. Yet she finds herself feeling insecure about her friendships. Occasionally she finds herself feeling rather lonely or empty. In response to this underarousal, she begins ruminating about each friend: why hasn't Susan called recently, or why didn't Kathleen invite her to come on an excursion to the outlet mall. When she came in for a consultation with me, she thought that perhaps all this worry stemmed from residual loneliness from her adolescence, when she had similar blue periods, or maybe something was missing in her marriage.

Even though her husband assured her of his love and commitment to their marriage, Laurel remained distraught about the recurrence of these states. What upset her the most was something she was too embarrassed to share with her husband. She would become so obsessed during the day that she would carry on imaginary dialogues with her friends. To make things worse, she would act on them. She would call a friend and share her insecurities about their friendship. The friends acted surprised and would reassure her. But in the last few months, they had begun to pull away from her. Laurel's worries and the way she acted on them became self-fulfilling prophecies.

In working with Laurel, I described what focusers are like, how they can feel vaguely empty or underaroused, and how this leads to the focuser's habit of relentless self-focusing. That's what she was doing, and it was worrying her into a depression. To compound this, she had begun to spread her obsessions into the real world and create actual (rather than imagined) social difficulties. I developed the following program for Laurel:

1. First, I explained that she was going to learn to distract whenever she felt these periods of underarousal. She was not to share her feelings with anyone, including her husband. I also explained focusers to him and sketched out what we were going to do.

2. Laurel and I explored the myths about emotions because we first had to deal with her sense of shame and embarrass-

ment. She was a very capable, very bright woman who felt increasingly imprisoned by her moods.

3. Next, Laurel began to learn the corrective task of deliberately focusing, then defusing the fixation. Instead of these self-focusing moments drifting in and out during the day, we allowed two separate one-hour periods during which she could self-focus to her heart's content. If she felt a mood coming on, she was told to overlook it, knowing she could ruminate during one of her worry periods. During this period, she was to self-focus on her physical sensations and let the conscious thoughts drift out, to feel the lack of arousal until she could do it without feeling upset. Then she was ready to break the fixation link.

4. Initially, the best distractor for Laurel was magazines—everything from hobby magazines to gossipy tabloids. In time, other distractors included spending time with her friends, but not in an anxious encounter-like fashion. I had told her that every focuser's worry has some basis in reality. For Laurel, this meant that she should try to be the best friend she could be—healthy give and take, not dumping her anxieties.

Laurel learned how to orchestrate her emotions to the point that she expected periods of underarousal and lack of aliveness. And she developed a greater range of distractors that she could automatically fold into her life when the need arose. Incidentally, the periods of feeling blue or worried did lessen, but they didn't disappear—that's her temperament. Now she experiences these periods a few times a week; they last for a few minutes to half an hour.

SEEKERS: ENLARGING THE COMFORT ZONE

When the seeker is not in motion, actively seeking sensation, he feels underaroused—and he loathes this dead feeling. His innate action tendency to escape from this underarousal is to seek external stimulus. His task, therefore, is to learn to tolerate periods of calm and relaxation, and alternate these periods with healthy, constructive, challenging activities that will satisfy his need for stimulus. His task is to balance rest and seeking.

One aspect of my prescription for the seeker is the search for behaviors that will provide a counterbalance to sensation seeking. Left to their own devices, seekers usually trade off one sensational activity for another. Jake, a thirty-four-year-old electrical contractor, was elated when he walked away from four years of compulsive gambling at the racetrack. He rewarded himself by buying a huge, fast motorcycle, and he took up driving his bike at high speeds on mountain roads. Jake's "healthier" habit could wind up being more self-destructive (literally) than having a perpetually empty wallet.

The only real answer for the seeker to find emotional relief is to alternate between moderate sensation and calm. The seeker needs to feel enough sensation to feel vibrant, but not so intensely that he falls into addictive behavior. He needs to discipline himself to feel good as a result of moderate activity— whether it's sexual activity or working or sports.

Balance is the key for the seeker—not a static state sitting on the middle ground but a balance between calm and sensation. It is important for the seeker to find calmness on a daily basis. The seeker's task is to create enough balance so his threshold is easily lowered by seeking behavior. When he is overly intense, all the time, his thermostat becomes conditioned to register only intense sensation or emotions. The seeker can gradually reset his emotional thermostat so that he feels satisfied more of the time.

The seeker also needs a variety of sources for his excitement. He tends to take one involvement, work it for every drop of excitement it has, then go on to something else. With several diverse focuses—work, love, sports, community—he doesn't deplete individual parts of his life. Like the balance between sensation and calm, he needs balance in all areas of his life. This is possible, and looked for, only if he understands and accepts his temperament.

RICK: THE SEEKER

Rick, age forty-one, was a successful real estate broker who was getting married. And he was terrified. His friends thought he was "commitment-phobic," which is a rather misleading term.

He desperately wanted to be married, yet the thought of all the responsibilities, accommodations, and changed lifestyle was distressing him.

For most of his life, Rick was a sports and activities fanatic. He loved to ski, rock climb, and compete in mountain bike races in the mountains. His lifelong dream was to sail around the world. His fiancée, Lynn, loved the same mountain sports, but she also wanted children and a family. Rick tried to analyze his fear of the marriage, and talked it over with his male friends who were married, but their reassurances that Lynn would be terrific for him didn't soothe him.

Rick came to see me at the urging of a friend who was a patient of mine. After exploring his childhood and underlying personality, it was clear that Rick was a seeker and that he was very uncomfortable with periods of aloneness, quietude, and containment, which felt to him like boredom.

I explained that even though he had lived with women before, he had always felt free. But now, making a permanent commitment felt like he had no escape when he got into one of his moods. Moreover, he was afraid that if his wife saw these moods, she would take it personally and come to believe that he didn't love her. Here's how I helped Rick:

1. First, just by understanding his temperament, he was enormously relieved and actually looked forward to the marriage. We didn't have to do anything. Pure insight can be curative itself.

2. I then explained about alternation. In order to modify or orchestrate his emotions, he had to avoid scrambling for stimulation. I explained that most of his activities were good distractors and not harmful in any way, but he had to more calmly engage them, seek them out, and relish them. He had to move away from underarousal-driven impulsive behavior.

3. Rick could do this by savoring the quiet moments more, without having to run around in a sensation-seeking mode. As long as he learned to rhythmically alternate between rest and sensation, he would be okay. As long he integrated stimulating activities into his life, he would be fine. If he tried to become a

total homebody, the marriage was likely to dissolve quickly. I also suggested that an activity that was less filled with sensation but also led to satisfaction would be good for him—something not too physical. He laughingly talked about a time when he had rented a house and cultivated a vegetable garden. "It balanced me out. I really enjoyed it."

I haven't talked to Rick since the couple of sessions I had with him, but I hear he's married, happy, and doing fine.

LIFE'S EMOTIONAL CHALLENGES

Now you are ready to embrace your temperament and enlarge your comfort zones if you choose to. I add that caveat because I have found that many people are just satisfied understanding why they feel the way they do and have no need and/or discipline to systematically modulate their emotions.

I cannot emphasize too much the importance of pure understanding. So often in therapy, patients get impatient. As I explain my ideas or observations, they will say, "Yeah, okay. I get it. Now what do I do?" This happens in any therapy. What the patient is saying is, "I don't care about theory, I don't want to analyze and all that. I only want to fix things fast, and get rid of whatever it is I'm feeling." Some patients don't realize that any strategies or processes built on self-deception or self-rejection are doomed to fail—denial is the very core of their problem.

Ultimately, however, I feel comfortable with whatever makes my patients feel comfortable. I am not a savior and have no need for each temperament type to do their utmost to achieve the maximum comfort. As you assess your own ebbing and flowing of emotions and arousal, at work or in your personal life, it is your choice to do what you need to do.

I hope I've convinced you that a life in denial or suppression of temperament is a path of needless misery. You can learn to shape and design your own comfort zone by awareness of your response patterns. Remember that your biology is not about limits but about perimeters of comfort.

Chapter 11

OTHER PEOPLE'S TEMPERAMENTS

YOUR ABILITY to get along with other people is pivotal in both your personal and your business life. It's as crucial a survival skill as knowing how to read and write. Emotional communication is a huge part of what happens between people. Emotional communication is what underlies the expressions: "Rub someone the wrong way." "Personality conflict." "He's a nice guy, but I just can't work with him." "We speak the same language." "The chemistry between us is terrific." "We just don't mesh." "He's a boss who brings out the best in his team."

Communicating your own emotions is half of the equation. Put two job candidates with comparable educational and work backgrounds in front of a personnel manager. The warm, vibrant candidate who "connects" with the interviewer will win over the candidate who sits rigidly in his chair, speaks in a monotone, and makes no connection with the interviewer.

Emotional communication, of course, is a two-way process. We not only need to communicate our own emotions to others but we also need to experience the emotionality of others in order to trust them, to know them, to have a sense of what they're all about. In the absence of this essential communication, we remain cautious. "I don't know what he feels . . . about anything. I don't really know him," say wives about husbands in marital therapy. To have this void in a personal relationship is to feel lonely and estranged.

And in business a handshake can close a million-dollar deal if the parties feel good about each other, if their gut instinct gives them a comfort level with trusting each other. The need to make emotional judgments about business associates is why people fly all over the world for face-to-face meetings.

A few years ago, a friend of mine was in charge of a major telecommuncation corporation's project to set up the first satellite teleconferencing facilities in major cities across the United States. These are like two-way TV stations. For example, a group of people in Chicago could meet via satellite with their counterparts in Los Angeles. Nobody had to leave home. Companies could save loads of money and many productive work hours, but the project was a failure. Emotional context was missing. As my friend discovered, "People just didn't want to make deals with people they hadn't met face-to-face." Teleconferencing is used now mainly for meetings between branches of companies: associates who already know each other from previous personal contact.

EMOTIONAL FLOW: BOUNDARIES AND VULNERABILITY

When people learn about their emotions, they always act surprised when I tell them they are feeling all the time. There is a constant flow of energy from both our external world and our internal world. Even when we sleep, our brain is processing internally generated images. It's as ceaseless and, most of the time, as unconscious as breathing in and out. Perpetually, we are experiencing the flow of energy, and we are self-regulating that flow. This constant processing links us to our outside world as long as we are alive. There is an oscillation or reciprocity of energy: stimuli penetrate our boundaries, we process them, and we react.

The mere presence of someone sends our energy to us. We aren't talking about intimacy but a more basic underlying issue, which is that we do get "vibes" from each other. Emotions can be infectious or contagious through emotional osmosis. Consider the following expressions: "He's so gloomy that he brings everybody down." "Her laughter is infectious." "When he walks into the sales meetings, morale goes up twenty points." "There's something very creepy about him; you can almost smell his fear and insecurity." "That woman radiates tension; she gives me a headache just sitting at the next desk." "She makes everybody around her feel good—if she could bottle it, she'd be a billionaire."

We're all familiar with people like the ones described above. Without saying a word, they communicate their moods to us, good or bad, and we're apt to "catch" their moods when we're together. It's one thing to catch someone's sunny or gloomy mood; it's more confusing when the person is disguising his true emotions. For example, consider a boss who is acting upbeat and encouraging, but you sense underlying hostility; or a secretary who is behaving in an energetic and professional manner, but you sense melancholy and depression. We've all had contact with people who smile and make upbeat small talk but send out quite contradictory emotional messages with their eyes or body language or general energy. Their words or overt communication don't match the emotional cues that we're sensing on a more intuitive level. As you're surely aware, this is commonplace. The end result is we feel unsettled, distracted, unsure; we don't feel comfortable with them and we do not trust them.

What's at work behind these kinds of mixed signals? Knowing how to read and understand other people's temperament—direct or disguised—allows us to know what they're like, how they disguise themselves, what sets them off, what they're scared of, what they're ashamed of, and what they need to feel secure and confident. Remember that temperament is predictable. Each type has an understandable emotional dynamic and predictable responses. A solid, working understanding of temperament leads not only to greater self-awareness and emotional self-confidence, but also to more graceful interactions with other people, whether it's your cranky neighbor or your underconfident nephew or your erratic boss or your moody subordinate.

In this chapter, we'll focus on communicating your own emotionality in a genuine manner, and learning to read, understand, and cope with the emotional temperaments of others.

Later in this chapter, we'll explore what you need to know about the temperaments of others in the important relationships in your life: lover or mate, friend and child, boss or employee. Let's begin, however, with the more general attitudes and understandings you need to bring to any successful interaction.

In very simple terms, unsuccessful interactions with other people come from being unaware of your own temperament, and not understanding and accepting the temperaments of others. All discomfort and discord between human beings stems from this! Conversely, getting along well with other people can be accomplished by means of a step-by-step process of:

1. Understanding and accepting your own temperament.
2. Behaving in a genuine manner—communicating your emotions to others in an open and direct style.
3. Awareness of what you are feeling and awareness of what emotion the other person is feeling.
4. Understanding the temperaments of others and accepting them for who they are—not trying to change them.
5. Respecting and tolerating the differences between you and others.
6. Practicing positive detachment. Possessing a clear sense of personal boundaries: knowing where you end and the other person begins. This solid sense of boundaries enables you to allow or disallow the process of emotional osmosis, so you can choose to fuse with or catch their emotions, or choose to not catch their moods.

This new model for emotional communication begins with your own emotional self-confidence.

BECOMING MORE OPEN AND RECEPTIVE

I'm sure you've had the experience of being in an especially good mood, and it seems as though everything you encounter and everyone you meet seems positive and worthy of your engagement—even colors are more vibrant. A park looks prettier; the salesperson seems nicer.

We're not choosing to perceive differently; rather we are open to the world around us and thus our perceptions are enhanced. If we could simply choose to do this, most of us would. But if it is not attitude or choice, how does it happen? We experience life as though we are surrounded by invisible membranes or boundaries separating us from the world. Some of us are receptive, open, and accessible; others are guarded and insulated.

It's my belief that emotional self-confidence is the key. When we lack confidence or self-awareness, when we lack a solid sense of self, the world is a more dangerous place, and we have to be on guard. We feel frail and vulnerable. In relationships we fear that we might be engulfed not only by the other person's demands but by his very being, his energy or emotionality. For self-protection, we put up a hurricane fence around our frail boundaries. Our psychological boundaries thicken; we insulate ourselves. In time, this insulation can make us feel dead or numb. The expressions, "He is walled off" or "She has a wall around her," are visual images for these defensive strategies.

I believe the more confident we are about who we are (including our temperament), the more solid we are and the stronger we feel; consequently, the more open and interactive we can be as we move through the world. When you possess a good working knowledge of your own personality and your emotional temperament, you act and react with a sense of personal power and emotional self-confidence. You don't feel the need to be guarded. You can be open to other people and to experiences.

BEING A MODEL FOR GENUINE EMOTIONS

Few of us get feedback from others about ourselves, and we tend to be private about what goes on inside us. Even in these times when most people think they're fairly sophisticated psychologically, you may still be rather private when it comes to sharing your emotions with others. We all want to be known and accepted, but we all harbor secret doubts about the acceptability of deeper emotional truths about ourselves.

I believe that part of the acceptance of your temperament

entails allowing other people to know you more than you have allowed in the past. You have to let some people know you are scared, or sad, or angry, or emotionally hungry. Discretion about whom you choose to share yourself with is important, but if you cannot expose some of your emotions to others, you obstruct genuine emotional communication, intimacy, and trust both in personal and work relationships.

While we all have private faces as well as public faces, I find that reluctance to be open about our feelings is typically a reflection of falling prey to the myths about emotions. No matter how independent we think we are, we still like to fit in. We're all afraid of being judged negatively. But think back to situations in which you have revealed some emotion you usually keep hidden, perhaps some work anxiety revealed to a friend over a cup of coffee, a despondent moment confessed to a work associate, or an angry outburst when you typically keep such emotions under tight rein. It probably made the other person feel closer to you, or like you better. Why? Because we are all hungry for something real.

If you look at the politicians and leaders we are drawn to today, the common denominator is the character issue. We are not looking necessarily for good character, we're looking for *any* character. We are so hungry to find authenticity, or reality, in a world where so much emphasis is placed on image, that the person who is real is charismatic.

As you become more genuine in your emotional expression, people's perceptions of you will change. People who thought you were tough minded may be surprised if you reveal more of your sensor traits to them. The discharger who begins to behave in a more expressive manner will surely provoke comments from those around her. There will be a period of adjustment. But you'll find that your example of being real will allow other people to reciprocate, and you'll grow closer to others as a result.

In marriage or close friendship you would be remiss not to encourage the other person to share his feelings with you. But there is an appropriate place to draw a line between intimacy and acting as someone's therapist. Where does sharing become dumping your emotions on a friend? How much should we depend on our mate to make us happy, to regulate our emotions? It's my view that each of us bears primary responsibility for our own well-being. And we have the responsibility to set boundaries and limits on the demands and behavior we will accept from other people.

GETTING ALONG WITH OTHERS, OR CHANGING THEM?

The bookstores are packed with books that will tell you how to turn on the opposite sex, make your spouse more loving and caring, disarm difficult people who make you miserable, and win friends and influence people. When we look at what we truly want from others, we don't want to accept them the way they are and learn to cope with their quirks. We don't want to get along with them. We want to change them! Because so many of our emotional dilemmas involve other people, we try our best to find strategies to alter their behavior and reprogram their responses so they will give us pleasure or refrain from causing us distress.

As any psychotherapist knows, effecting change in a patient is difficult, no matter how motivated the patient is. Trying to alter someone's personality when she doesn't want to change is foolhardy. We try to change other people as a method to control our environment. But the world just *is*, for the most part, and people simply *are*—they're not there to make you unhappy and they cannot be controlled or manipulated as if they're malleable actors in your own personal home movie.

Not Taking Other People's Moods Personally

My first piece of advice to those of you who are inclined to "rehabilitation" projects is, "Don't take it personally." You may say, "How can I not take it personally when he does that to me? He makes me feel so angry and frustrated." To which I respond, "He is not doing anything to you; you are doing something to yourself in response to his behavior." One of my favorite sayings is, "What drives you crazy, keeps them sane."

Most people don't intend to make other people unhappy; they are just doing what they need to do for themselves—to express some emotion, to vent some grievance, to protect their ego or identity from pain.

If you sincerely try to not personalize what other people do, you will find yourself immediately more relaxed, more comfortable, and not hurt by the actions of others. Try to keep this in mind the next time someone really gets to you. Accepting others enables you to accept yourself. "Live and let live" is a credo about tolerance. The AA serenity prayer (taken from the theologian Reinhold Niebuhr) is quite instructive here: "God, give us the serenity to accept the things we cannot change, the courage to change the things we can, and the wisdom to know the difference." We all need to enhance our wisdom of human emotions. The power of tolerance and acceptance, like the serenity prayer, is enormous when put into action in our daily lives.

POSITIVE DETACHMENT

Your wife is in a rotten mood. She's slamming dishes into the sink, banging the cabinet doors, sighing, and grumbling, "This kitchen never gets cleaned unless I do it!" Your boss is grumpy, criticizing you unfairly. Your date is moody and remote; your Sunday drive in the mountains is proving to be far from the romantic afternoon you both had talked about all week. How do you react? Do you jump right into the fight your wife obviously wants to pick? Do you react to your boss's bad mood with irritability and start defending yourself from her unfair criticism? Do you catch the moodiness of your date?

We don't have to react to, fuse with, or catch other people's emotions. Consider the saying, "Don't bark back at a barking dog." The technique of positive detachment goes beyond merely walking away from a fight. By just walking away, you react internally to the other person's emotions and you feel new emotions in response; you just don't express them.

Even though you don't lash back or defend yourself or say anything, you very probably will walk away in a rotten mood and spend the next couple of hours upset or angry. Although you may forgive and forget the encounter intellectually, your emotional memory will record the encounter and how badly it made you feel. You will feel alienated and resentful of the other person.

With positive detachment, the emotions of the other person do not permeate you; you do not fuse with them or catch them; you do not react with emotions of your own. You communicate understanding and compassion to the other person; instead of that person drawing you into his negative mood, you acknowledge and respect his right to feel the way he's feeling without reacting to it. You may end the interaction at this point, or you may make the choice to help diffuse the other person's mood and draw him back toward calmness and comfort. Share your more positive mood with him. We see that understanding, acceptance, and tolerance lead to a win-win outcome without lingering alienation or resentment on either side.

Positive detachment begins with a solid sense of personal boundaries, being able to discern your own mood from the emotions or mood you are sensing from someone else. "I'm feeling quite content, but I'm sensing crankiness in my wife. I am feeling this; she is feeling that."

Positive detachment does not mean holding it in—that is, getting angry at your irritable wife but not saying anything, walking away, then silently resenting her for the rest of the evening. Positive detachment means choosing to not react to someone else's emotions, to remain in your own mood or emotion, to remain centered in yourself. In this situation, it does not mean that you keep the peace by offering to clean the kitchen yourself. What's at issue is your wife's bad mood, not the kitchen. Without saying a word, you can express your love and sympathy by giving her a hug. What she wants and needs is to be comforted. Your expression of love and comforting will immediately begin to diffuse her bad mood, and she'll likely be able to laugh it off as she tells you about the traffic jam on her way home, or her rough day at work—whatever truly triggered her bad mood. The payoff is that she'll feel loved and reassured and appreciative of you; you'll be able to spend a close evening together. Again, it's a win-win situation that leads to greater intimacy rather than estrangement.

ROMANTIC RELATIONSHIPS

Most problems in romantic relationships stem from the failure to understand and accept your partner's temperament. I have already described what each temperament type is like in part two. Now I would like to briefly touch upon some issues that arise when you fall in love with various temperament types.

THE SENSOR

The sensor's mate needs to provide limits on accommodating her partner's more sensitive style. A common dilemma involving the sensor happens when chemistry backfires. The very quality that fuels attraction, the promise of an expanded comfort zone, is unfortunately what leads to trouble. What initially seems promising can later become threatening. Opposites do attract, but differences can throw your partner out of a state of emotional equilibrium into discomfort. For example, a reserved sensor man finds a woman who is brash, daring, and adventurous. The sensor believes these qualities will rub off on him. But unless he feels secure in her love, her nature will, sooner or later, become a threat. He thinks, "She'll meet someone more adventurous and run off with him. She'll get bored with me."

Chances are that if you've been with a sensor, you've experienced this—a man or woman who initially is enthralled by your independence, your spirit, your spontaneity, then tries his or her best to extinguish these qualities and turn you into a docile person. It's unfair to try to dampen someone's spirit.

If you're married to a disguised sensor, she may appear withdrawn or edgy at times, but it's usually a mask for anxiety. Reassurance and acceptance will have immediate and positive effects. Safety is essential for the sensor to feel intimate, and to feel relaxed and secure during lovemaking. When the sensor's needs for love and security are met, he is a terrific partner.

THE FOCUSER

The focuser looks to an exciting partner to provide stimulus and distraction. You may find that focusers are moody, or they make too many demands to provide stimulation. They may pull you into lengthy talks about your relationship or marriage—talks that don't lead to solutions or make you feel closer. It's important to set boundaries on how much introspection, how much dissecting, how much worrying, you will listen to or join. You need to set limits on how much excitement you're willing to provide in the relationship, and how much your focuser partner should be responsible for himself. Most importantly, don't take the focuser's moods personally.

A patient, Sally, would talk about coming home from work and noting a glum expression on her husband's face. She told me, "I hate it. I always feel like I did something wrong or I'm not doing enough to please him. I feel like I'm failing him by not making him happy." I asked her husband to come in for a session. He turned out to be a focuser. When he looked a little glum, Rob didn't feel that badly and was easily distracted from his mood. When Sally asked him, "What's wrong?" and he replied, "Nothing," he meant it. But Sally read it as, "You're not making me happy. I'm disillusioned about the marriage; you've failed me as a wife." I cautioned her: "You can't take your husband's temperament personally—that's just him."

If you're close to a focuser, keep in mind that distraction is the task that releases her from fixation and brooding. If your focuser appears to be bored, or sad, or sinking into a pessimistic frame of mind, you may help to short-circuit that mood by distracting her with news about your friends or a home improvement project. Or you may suggest going for a walk or to a restaurant. Talking about the dark mood is not a solution.

THE DISCHARGER

The discharger needs a partner who is able to cope with her intensity, respond to her passion, and perhaps comfort her when she feels ashamed after blowing up at someone. What the discharger needs from you is the capacity both to enjoy her aliveness and to accept the occasional irritability and outbursts. You need to understand that she's not out of control, or impulsive, or difficult. She has a biological imperative to discharge (express) the high emotional energy she typically feels.

Understanding and tolerating does not equate with being bullied or emotionally terrorized or abused. You have no obligation to be a constant target for anger. You can and should set limits on how much you're willing to be used as a target. It is the discharger's responsibility—not yours—to cope with the difficult aspects of his temperaments on his own. The discharger's corrective task is benign release—that is, brief discharge of his emotional energy, usually alone. You can remind your discharger of this solution; a daily regimen of activities done in an easy and casual manner.

THE SEEKER

Seekers can be quite attractive as dates. They're usually successful and driven doers. But they can prove to be less than ideal if you want a more committed partnership. Seekers are restless; they're sensation driven, not security driven. Male or female, they can be captivated with you while they're pursuing you, then lose all interest once they're sure of you. Biochemically programmed to prefer infatuation to mature love, to prefer the physical and sexual sensations to faithful devotion, the seeker can be a real challenge as a mate.

Because of their dynamic nature, male seekers are often the charismatic men that women desire and lust after. They're often a foolish choice for women who want a lasting relationship or marriage. The seeker can be the Don Juan or the elusive lover I wrote about in my book *Smart Women, Foolish Choices.*

There's a reason why the seeker male is so troublesome and disappointing to women. This noncommittal male has a craving for arousal that is quickly satisfied. Just when initial passion becomes comfortable security, he loses interest and moves on. He is not commitment-phobic. More precisely, he deeply fears the unaroused emotional state that is inevitable for him. A seeker patient of mine explains, "After a few months, I actually felt kind of depressed or down around her."

Women who play hard to get with this type of man are actually intuitively savvy—like the fly fisherman wisping the lure right on the surface of the lake, they are tantalizing the seeker's threshold of arousal. They rightly sense that they have to keep this kind of man hungry and in pursuit to hold his interest.

POTENTIALLY PROBLEMATIC PAIRINGS

The Sensor/Seeker Couple

As far as romantic pairings, the sensor is easily threatened by the intensity of the seeker, but the sensor's intimidation is often overpowered by her fascination with the courageous, charismatic seeker. Chemistry pops and crackles when the timid sensor feels a contact high of boldness and confidence in connecting with the seeker.

The Focuser/Seeker Couple

The focuser is threatened by the seeker. Focusers are biochemically "allergic" to any threat of loss. The seeker's elusiveness, noncommitment, and inevitable abandonment can throw the focuser into a depression. The focuser can be easily shattered by a love affair with a seeker.

The Focuser/Sensor Couple

One of the most problematic temperament combinations is a focuser and a sensor. The sensor is predisposed to feeling anxious, while the focuser tends to criticize others and make demands. And the no-win battle is engaged. As the sensor withdraws, the focuser worries and becomes more critical. The bruised, embattled sensor withdraws even more. When you have one person who fears overarousal and another who fears underarousal, you end up with two people who cannot satisfy each other. Bad chemistry. But don't be overly alarmed if you're dancing this dance. People who are aware of their temperament and know how to orchestrate its difficult aspects can be quite flexible and resilient in almost any pairing.

The Sensor/Sensor Couple

Despite the danger of exacerbating the worst in each other, people with the same temperament do get together. There is a common sensor/sensor pair. The cautious sensor often marries a sensor who denies his own temperament and blindly reaches far beyond his comfort zone. Provided the more outgoing of the pair is at least partially open about his own secret emotionality, they may empathize with each other's anxiety and feel understood. The assertive spouse serves as a model or catalyst for the more timid or shy partner. They can be a great match—catalyst and confidante.

A problem they will encounter is contagious anxiety. The denier loathes and despises his anxiety—that's why he is denying his temperament in the first place. When he senses his wife's apprehension, he will pull away. His wife reads his withdrawal as rejection, and her apprehension doubles. She now feels anxious and rejected. The anxious sensor needs reassurance and soothing. Remember that rejection and abandonment are the sensor's worst fears.

The Discharger/Sensor Couple

The sensor will put up with a lot if he feels secure in a marriage or a relationship. It's not uncommon for the male sensor to be with a woman who seems loud, overbearing, and overcontrolling. One may cringe and think this woman is going to make him feel overwhelmed with arousal; she will push him over the edge. But it doesn't happen. Why not? If they've been together long enough, he feels secure in her love for him, even though others might not see it. Security can override a confrontational style, loud behavior, erratic emotions, and even criticism. He may be aroused by her behavior, but he doesn't feel threatened.

WORK RELATIONSHIPS

How open should you be about your deeper emotions in a work situation? When should you suggest that someone open up to you? This depends on the relationship and the degree of intimacy. Generally in work situations it is important to be aware of temperaments, but it is typically foolhardy to try to change someone else. Do you tell your boss that you sense she's depressed and ask, "Do you want to talk about it?" Probably not. As a boss yourself, do you suggest to an angry, disruptive employee that you'd like to talk it out and see what's going on.

Probably not. You are more likely to inform him that his out-bursts and disruption will not be tolerated, and perhaps refer him to professional counseling as a condition of probation.

Understanding the temperaments of others, accepting them for who they are, and not personalizing their moods can trans-form your work life. Again, the technique of positive detach-ment enables you to not get pulled into the emotions and moods of others. It enables you to remain focused on the job to be done and on building your career.

THE SENSOR EMPLOYEE

Since he fears being embarrassed by blushing, sweating, or get-ting rattled in front of others, the sensor prefers one-on-one discussions to big, noisy free-for-alls. Do not criticize him in front of others; it can threaten his confidence. He needs your faith in his ideas. The aware manager will give him the reassur-ance and security he needs to realize his potential. You may have to encourage him to take on new responsibilities, but he's a conscientious worker who puts in long hours to meet dead-lines and quotas.

The sensor who feels unappreciated or insecure can be a drain on his superior's energy. He can be moody, touchy, high strung, and may go into a resistant mode. He'll become so fear-ful and uncertain that he will refuse to make a decision without consulting four or five other staffers. If he feels he's being eval-uated negatively or unfairly by his boss, he's likely to quit. He really needs reassurance and security to blossom, and when he feels respected and valued, he's a terrific employee.

THE SENSOR BOSS

If you're loyal, respectful and honest with the sensor boss, he will eventually warm up to you and will be an empathetic, sup-portive boss who will encourage you and give you full credit for your efforts. If you do not communicate these qualities to him, he's likely to remain cool and aloof. You're either on his team or off his team.

It's wise to keep in mind that even the counterphobic or disguised sensor boss is very sensitive to criticism or rejection. Even though he may behave in a dynamic, thick-skinned fashion, you have an enormous impact on him emotionally.

THE FOCUSER EMPLOYEE

The focuser employee is methodical, precise, and focused in his work. These qualities lead to highly effective and productive employees. You may run into problems with her proclivity for worry and rumination at the expense of just getting on with the job. Managing the focuser can become problematic if a fixation on a particular problem becomes unyielding.

The smart manager will set deadlines for the focuser employee and say, "Do the best you can in this time frame," or "Why don't you let me worry about that?" The savvy boss understands the solution is not to become frustrated with the focuser but to help her to release her fixation, even if it involves switching her to another task.

THE FOCUSER BOSS

The boss who is prone to fixate and ruminate also becomes very perfectionistic. And, by virtue of his superior position, he can stay fixated and perfectionistic even though you, as an employee, know this can be counterproductive in the long run. Although it requires forethought and diplomacy, the focuser's employee needs to gently suggest anything that might prove at all distracting, so the workplace can become unblocked.

THE DISCHARGER EMPLOYEE

The discharger can be a real asset as an employee: warm, funny, full of personality, able to attract and retain clients or customers through personal magnetism. However, the discharger can be impatient, easily frustrated, and prone to irritable outbursts. She can intimidate or alienate other employees and earn the reputation of being difficult. It's crucial to let the discharger know if she is causing a negative impact on others; she may be unaware or in denial about her effect on others. But it's a bad idea to try to shut down the discharger too harshly. She's likely to become passive-aggressive, resistant, and hostile.

THE DISCHARGER BOSS

Don't think you'll be able to change a boss who is an explosive discharger. Don't spend your time complaining or gossiping about him or trading war stories about his temper or demands. This will only make you more resentful as you build a case against him. You're likely to get into "if only" scenarios: "If only I had a different boss, my career would be going much better." This sours your work life and only hurts you in the long run. Keep in mind that the discharger is usually ashamed of his outburst and his lack of self-control. If you communicate you understand that's just the way he is, and demonstrate your acceptance and loyalty, he is likely to appreciate and repay your loyalty. Staying detached and upbeat, focused on your responsibilities and goals, in general not reacting to your discharger boss's emotional ups and downs, is the sensible strategy.

THE SEEKER EMPLOYEE

The seeker employee is dynamic and goal oriented. She is apt to be very ambitious. Her enemy is boredom and routine. As a result, she may neglect to follow through on the nuts and bolts of a project—she's already on to a new challenge. The seeker may be overly political in the workplace, focused on her own agenda rather than the company's or her team's. The smart manager will provide comprehensive details on the seeker's responsibilities and what is expected from her.

THE SEEKER BOSS

When a seeker is your superior, he will ignite your enthusiasm and serve as a model for initiative taking. However, the daily running of an organization is not necessarily his strong suit. Seeker's can frustrate you by dumping all the details in your lap. As a result of their tendency to look beyond the present task, seekers do not delegate carefully; they neglect detail and are unaware that your pace may be much slower than theirs.

ACCEPTING YOUR FRIENDS' TEMPERAMENTS

In some ways, it's easier to accept our friends than our mates and children. It's a bit of a paradox that the more we love someone, the more entitled we feel to criticize that person and to place unrealistic expectations on him. With our friends, there is usually sufficient distance that we honor them and accept them. It is easier to tolerate our friends' quirks and flaws because we are not so emotionally dependent on them, and we don't live with them. But if you think back to the quarrels you've had with friends, you know that the trigger for these conflicts was some clash between temperaments.

The sensor is drawn to the seeker because he envies the seeker's apparent courage. Yet the envy may take the form of some growing criticism of the way in which the seeker finds relief and satisfaction. In time, the seeker (who may already feel guilty) can no longer tolerate this implied criticism and she distances herself.

Focusers can prove troublesome as friends. Prone to worry, they can wear out their friends with their insistent concerns and apprehensions. In this case, the dynamic that unravels so many friendships is that the focuser feels frightened that she may lose someone, and her fear becomes so emotionally depleting to those around her that she brings on the very thing she fears: people eventually pull away. In fact, though I have been advocating the freer expression of your emotions, for the focuser that advice is not a license for endless complaining. It's okay to do that with a therapist, but your friends might not be as accepting.

The most obviously difficult friend is the discharger. If you recognize one of your friends as a discharger, you've probably already learned to overlook or ignore the intermittent outbursts of anger and/or frustration. You have learned not to take it personally. If you have a sense of your own uniqueness and boundaries, not overreacting is easier than you may think.

In my experience, the greatest difficulty people have in accepting the sensor is that the sensor will put you in touch with your own fears. In your view, when the sensor is unduly nervous or apprehensive, she is usually just magnifying what you would find fearful also. With that in mind, be compassionate and understanding and try not to become caught up in the sensor's apprehension.

ACCEPTING YOUR CHILD'S TEMPERAMENT

As parents, we are more concerned, more loving, and yet often more unaccepting of the four temperaments as they reveal themselves in our children. Parents often see their children as extensions of themselves. We are so inundated with theories of child rearing that we may view our children as "projects": wet clay to be shaped and molded into the perfect children.

We take responsibility with pride, shame, and every emotion in between. We do this not only because of the myths we hold about emotions but also because we are still so ignorant of the genetic factors that mold our children. The bottom line is that we are not nearly as powerful as we think in creating our children's destiny. This is either good news or bad news, depending on how you view your children. I emphasize again that the power of children's temperament to influence their parents' behavior is truly the neglected story in psychology.

The parenting treadmill is our belief that our child's personality and achievements are in some measure a reflection and determinant of our own value and self-worth. If we have a nervous child, we did something wrong. Perhaps we were not loving enough to give him the self-esteem he deserves. If we have an aggressive or feisty child, perhaps we did not discipline her with the consistency the books prescribed. However, a significant portion of our child's emotional temperament is genetically determined. What we can do is honor and respect our children's nature and encourage them to do likewise.

The parents of the sensor must learn to let go of the wish that their child will be fearless in the face of new challenges and situations. As you now know, that is not how the sensor copes.

The path he takes is different, sometimes more distressing, and he has to pay his emotional dues. The good news is that courage and daring is still open to him provided he knows how to deal with the inevitable unpleasant emotions that will well up within him. If you give him the combination of reassurance and prodding he needs, he will grow up to become a confident and resilient adult.

Focusers mature later in life. It is rare to see a child younger than twelve or thirteen clearly display focuser behavior. It will be your task to show your child that worry and concern are not emotions to be dwelled upon endlessly but are predictable emotional responses that require distraction and refocusing.

The parents of a discharger are going to need exceptional patience. She may be diagnosed as hyperactive; she will test your patience with her tantrums and frustration. It is all too easy to yell at this child or to worry about her. It's tough to deal with the discharger child. But when you begin to regard her temperament as innate and view it without bias, you won't see your child as a bad seed.

The parents of a seeker will often be frustrated by his energy level and tendency to get into behavioral difficulties. Again, gender issues rear their head here. The seeker girl is culturally regarded as more of a handful than the seeker boy. The "wild" behavior of the seeker is more acceptable in males.

PARENTS AND FALSE MESSAGES

No matter how psychologically astute or how caring we are as parents, we still may send out double messages: "I want to hear what you feel, but please don't upset me with the depth or intensity of those feelings." Anger is an example of that distinction. Few homes tolerate angry expressions; they are usually met with swift punishment. Children are urged to put their anger into safe phrases, such as, "Mom and dad, I feel really angry about that." I don't mean to poke fun, but some child-rearing theorists who think they are supportive of emotional expression aren't; they are just supportive of the idea or verbal statement of the emotion, not the raw energy of the emotion.

In today's psychologically enlightened world, parents are

more accepting of expressions of fear or sadness. Yet in most homes we so quickly rush in to help our child get rid of these "negative" emotions that they barely have time to acknowledge them. By rushing to help our child find emotional relief we inadvertently communicate that, "What you're feeling is 'bad.' Let me help you get rid of it."

Even the young child with a seeker temperament, who typically arouses the least concern in parents, gets negative messages as a child. How many of us have seen parents with an overactive child try to tame her wild nature? Unfortunately, part of the job of being a parent is to manage our children as well as nurture them.

When parents are caught on the parenting treadmill, they want their children to be perfect. Anything less translates into parental anxiety. This anxiety is directly and toxically communicated to the child. The child senses something is wrong—that she's not good enough. She has failed her parents. This serves only to compound all the other normal childhood anxieties and struggles. Children and adolescents resent and fear this extra burden. As parents, we all have to mourn the loss of the perfect child we wanted and none of us has ever had. We must accept the child we do have.

A WARNING ABOUT CHILD THERAPY

Even though I may be casting some aspersions on my profession, I warn you to think more than twice about dragging your child into psychotherapy for what is essentially a nonproblem for your child but a management problem for you. It's okay to seek counseling yourself and, hopefully, to find large doses of reassurance, along with some helpful guidelines. But don't label your child with the stigma of being disordered, which may be exactly what he or she will feel if brought into treatment.

There are many fine therapists who deal with children and adolescents, and there are children who do need a less emotional adult to help them deal with an acute crisis or dilemma. But way too often I see parents who want their child in treatment because it's easier than looking at their own difficulty with acceptance. A rule of thumb is to see a counselor on your own a few times before bringing in your child. The best therapists will help you explore your concerns without playing into your fantasies of remaking your child.

The process of awareness, understanding, acceptance, and tolerance for the temperaments of others is one of those situations where you cannot help but gain and grow as a person. Without accepting others, you will never be able to accept yourself and your own emotional temperament. And, when acceptance occurs, you find yourself appreciating what is emotionally unique about yourself.

Chapter 12

GETTING HELP: PSYCHOTHERAPY AND MEDICATIONS

I'M A REALIST. I know that people who find themselves in emotional quandaries may be distressed enough that they feel a need for outside guidance and assistance in grappling with their feelings. You may be so distressed that you are unable to implement what I've suggested here.

You (not a diagnostic guidebook) are the sole judge of whether you need help. This chapter is for those who want or need guidelines on choosing a psychotherapist as well as guidelines on medications. It is also addressed to those who have sought help and were discouraged by a lack of results, as well as for those who are presently taking medications for difficult emotional states yet are unsure of why they need them, and when, if ever, they can be free from medications.

WHO DEALS WITH EMOTIONS?

I must issue a caveat here. Too many people believe that because someone is licensed by the state to practice medicine, law, psychology, accounting, construction, plumbing, or whatever that they are somehow qualified to deliver a good service in exchange for your time and money.

Whenever I speak to young psychologists who ask about graduate schools, I always tell them to get the best training possible in academic psychology even if they intend to only practice psychotherapy. Yet I always note that in the twenty-four years of my private practice, no new patient has ever asked where I did my academic and clinical training. Check out qualifications—it's a starting point—especially in the area of psychotherapy and counseling. Incidentally, a poor education shouldn't necessarily eliminate someone. There are outstanding therapists with relatively little formal training or education. The brilliant psychoanalyst Erik Erikson had only a B.A. degree—and it was in art! And I know of at least two nationally famous media shrinks who have Ph.D.'s from "diploma mills"; in spite of their natural and intuitive talents, they felt the need to have "Dr." in front of their names.

The first step is being familiar with the classifications of people who help those in emotional distress. There are a number of professions. Following is a brief overview based on years of experience and years of my evolving biases:

1. *Clinical psychologists.* A Ph.D. from a clinical psychology training program at a graduate school recognized by the American Psychological Association. Trained in the treatment, diagnosis, and study of mental disorders. In my view, the best all-around practitioners of psychotherapy because of their balanced education in both clinical skills and grounding in the behavioral sciences. A critical and inquiring educated mind is absolutely necessary to evaluate all the new findings in the field and to knowledgeably separate value from snake oil.

2. *Psychiatrists.* An M.D. who has completed a residency in psychiatry from a recognized hospital/university training program in addition to medical training. The only physician speciality trained in the diagnosis and treatment of mental disorders. More on his qualifications later, for typically he is either good at prescribing psychoactive medications *or* at psychotherapy—rarely both, even though the public has been conditioned to think so.

3. *Physicians.* M.D.'s. They are aware that 50 percent of all doctor visits are probably fueled by problems whose origins are psychological in nature. A caution here: the vast majority of *all* psychoactive medicines such as tranquilizers and antidepressants are prescribed by M.D.'s who are not trained in psychiatry, who are not updated on the latest research in psychopharmacology, who are not inclined to monitor your progress on the drug, and who are not inclined to get you off the drug. Your family doctor may prescribe antianxiety drugs or antidepressants, but she is basically treating an area she knows nothing about.

4. *Social workers.* M.S.W.'s trained in the treatment of mental disorders as well as other more traditional social welfare subspecialities. Usually well trained from recognized university schools of social work.

5. *The rest.* There is a virtual explosion of training programs across the country leading either to master's degrees (e.g., marriage, family, and child counselors) or to doctoral degrees (Ph.D.) in psychology. Many are good; some are fraudulent. Some programs are comprehensive; others are diploma mills. The consumer should be careful.

First, ask around for names. The best way to start is by getting a referral from friends or relatives who have seen a therapist they found helpful. Or ask your doctor for a referral. This is by no means always the best method. Typically he will give you the name of a friend who reciprocates in these referrals. But it's a start.

If you cannot get a personal referral, call the department of psychology at the nearest university or the department of psychiatry at the nearest university medical school. Do not look in the yellow pages: ads are not indicators of competence. You may also call a church or synagogue for information.

Don't worry too much about getting the "right" professional to help you, because you won't know whether someone is right for you until you've seen the person at least twice. Finding a good therapist may take time.

WHAT SHOULD YOU LOOK FOR?

See at least two or three therapists at least once. See how you feel. Are they understanding? Do they talk or merely listen? After one session, if a therapist has not given you a sense of what your dilemma is about, how he intends to help you deal with it, and in what time frame (even if vague), don't go back.

If you leave upset, why are you upset? Did the therapist tell you something you didn't want to hear? That could be the *right* person. Conversely, if someone is warm and supportive, but vague in his understanding and program for you, you don't need that. You can get it free—it's called a friend. There's nothing wrong with supportive therapy, but in time a good supportive therapist should point out your need to develop a support system *outside* his office.

Ask the therapist about her orientation or beliefs just to see if she is open to such questions. If she isn't, get out. You need to know the therapist has a concrete understanding and approach to the dilemma you're experiencing. For example, I tell people if the primary reason for seeking help is a marital problem, ask your therapist if he is married. If he isn't, his understanding could be paper thin as contrasted with someone who is married.

If you are upset primarily about your emotions, if you feel alarmed about anxiety, sadness, anger, or emotional hungers, I believe you must ask about the therapist's orientation and/or bias. Ask your therapist how she views emotions—specifically, the biological basis of emotions. Does she believe in innate emotional temperaments? If not, why not? Understandably, I feel if the therapist doesn't believe in my ideas about a natural self (temperament, arousal, innate action tendencies), then she's not as accurate in her point of view as she needs to be. If you are looking for someone who has a point of view similar to mine, show the person this book, and ask what he thinks of it. Obviously, he doesn't have to agree with everything in it, but does he ascribe to the notion of innate emotional temperament?

Next, if you are seriously emotionally distressed, to the point where it is significantly interfering with your life at home or at work, and you also have physical signs of distress that are beginning to alarm you, you should be open to the possibility of medication that might relieve your anxiety, depression, or rumination to a point at which counseling can be effective. Although I believe too many people are on medication for too long, there are instances where it is needed to boost someone to a point at which the person can benefit from talk therapy.

WHOM DO YOU SEE FIRST?

It would be ideal if you could find a professional who is good at psychotherapy and also skilled in the art of psychopharmacology—that is, finding the right medication(s) for you. That person doesn't exist. Psychiatrists might disagree, but I believe they're wrong. Psychiatrists are either well trained in psychotherapy (or psychoanalysis) *or* in psychopharmacology. To be an expert on medication, you must either be very well trained in recent years or must keep up at a level that suggests you are working only with patients in need of medication. Psychopharmacology is an art based on lots of experiences with different drugs on a daily basis. As I will discuss, it is not the exact one-pill-fits-all science you read about in magazines.

Psychiatry training programs increasingly deemphasize psychotherapy, for they feel too many other professions are skilled in this area. They are increasingly teaching only biopsychiatry, which emphasizes the biochemical basis of mental disorders. Today, virtually none of the outstanding psychiatric residency programs teach psychoanalysis: Freud is no longer welcome in psychiatry! As a result, young psychiatrists are either skilled at psychotherapy (which is becoming rare) or at biopsychiatry (the wave of the future in psychiatry).

Occasionally, you can find both people skills and psychopharmacology skills in the same psychiatrist. I am sure I may sound biased or cynical here, but the public is rarely aware that psychiatry has always been the black sheep or unwanted cousin in medicine. Psychiatrists are now embracing a medical or illness model with open arms. Incidentally, I think this development is good. I believe that the future of treatment will have to be tied to biological models of behavior. My only disagreement is that biological doesn't mean illness. The point here is that even if

you think you might need medication, and you also want counseling or psychotherapy, you will have to find two different
professionals, much in the same way you go to a specialist in
medicine and then a subspecialist depending on your problem.

Don't let this disturb or confuse you; the way you get help is
still a rather simple process. See a therapist of whatever discipline and explain, "Look, I really feel awful, and I want to be
confident that if I do need medication, you will be alert to that,
and will be able to refer me to a psychopharmacology-oriented
psychiatrist with whom you work so he can monitor my
progress." If the therapist is against medication, avoid him; he
is too rigid. Conversely, if you see a professional who immediately wants to prescribe psychotropic medications, see if he can
answer the following questions (or ask these of someone to
whom you are referred):

1. Why do I need this drug? If he says you have a disorder,
ask him to explain, and to explain why you didn't have the
disorder before. Ask him what the disorder is, what its course is,
and what kind of therapy treatment should accompany it. If he
says you only need medication, get out; he doesn't know what
he's talking about. If he says you only need to come in once or
twice a month, get out. Tell him you understand that in thousands of studies, none suggests that medication alone is sufficient, and that many studies show therapy to be superior to
medication. Don't get obnoxious or annoying, but if he can't
handle these questions, he's either arrogant or ignorant—neither of which you need when you're feeling emotionally distressed.

2. Ask him what the side effects of the medication are, and
how long they last. Most importantly, ask how long he thinks
you will be on this drug. If he says, "Until we decide you no
longer need it," don't leave it at that. Ask, "What will change in
my mind, my emotions, and my behavior that will indicate I no
longer need it?" Encourage the doctor to explain how medications work, and also to explain what goes on in your thinking
and behavior that causes you to no longer need the drug.

I believe the ideal combination for anyone seeking help for seriously distressing emotional turmoil is a good psychotherapist (of whatever discipline, but who is open to the possibility that medication is needed), *plus* a biopsychiatrist versed in the latest progress in psychoactive medications.

LIMITATIONS OF MEDICATION

As I am writing this, I have two documents in front of me. One is *Time* magazine, July 6, 1992, whose cover story is "Pills for the Mind," describing new drugs for schizophrenia and depression. I feel as though this is at least the fiftieth such article I've read in the popular press in the past year. I'm sure you've seen many of these articles as well. In this *Time* cover story, the authors note, "It is the treatment of depression . . . that represents mental health's greatest success story." I agree, but then they go on: "Today depression can be treated—quickly and effectively—in seven cases out of ten. If a second round of treatment is required, the *cure* [italics mine] rate jumps to 90 percent."

The second document I have in front of me is a 1992 reprint, "Course of Depressive Symptoms over Follow Up: Findings from the National Institute of Mental Health Treatment of Depression Collaborative Research Program." This was a long-term, very prestigious study comparing psychotherapy with antidepressant treatment. The authors note that earlier studies consistently show cognitive behavior therapy to be *more* effective than antidepressant medication treatment. And in this study they found that of those who recovered and had no relapse, the best results (only 30 percent recovery) came from cognitive therapy while the worst (19 percent) came from those who had antidepressants along with "clinical management" visits with the doctor.

I'm not trying to tell you to avoid antidepressants. If you are seriously depressed, they work to either help you recover from that episode or, preferably, to enable you to get benefit from psychotherapy. My opinion of the *Time* magazine article is that whenever you read an article about psychological disorders and you read the word *cure*, quickly use the article to wrap your garbage. There is no cure for one's temperament.

266   *Mastering Your Moods*

Most psychiatric drugs are more complicated, less precise in their actions, and far less effective than experts or the media would have you believe. Science and health writing for the public is to be taken with a very large grain of salt. Scores of "breakthroughs" are bannered in the press each year; when reexamined later they prove to be a flash in the pan. Human brain chemistry is so individual, so complex, and so fluctuating that we've found no miracle drugs. Psychotropic medication requires constant monitoring and adjustment on an individual basis. Many drug companies fund research that is rather poor, but it provides drug companies with good ads, and the doctors involved get nice supplements to their income.

Honest (as opposed to drug company's selective revelations) studies on psychiatric drugs are filled with many contradictory results, and also many results that are just not very impressive—that's why honest experts refer to the *art* of psychopharmacology.

For example, drug research must always compare the effects of the drug to a placebo in order to figure out whether the *tincture of time* is creating the relief. You would be shocked to know how the majority of these studies use inactive placebos, meaning pills that have no effect (a blank or sugar pill). After reading this book, you can imagine my reaction to this practice. I believe that many drugs often simply create their effects by being arousal activators like antidepressants, or arousal suppressors like antianxiety drugs. To not use an active placebo (e.g., caffeine) is to not really determine what is actually causing the drug's effects.

An active placebo is any ingredient that may produce effects in the same direction as the drug being tested, yet it does not have the same chemical structure as the drug being tested. For example, if a caffeine or adrenaline placebo has the same effects as an antidepressant, then the chemicals unique to that antidepressant may not be the specific curative ingredients. Anything that lifted the patient's mood might have worked.

In all of my research on medications, one book stands out. Written for professionals in this area, *The Limits of Biological Treatments for Psychological Distress,* by Seymour Fisher and Roger Greenberg at the State University of New York Upstate Health Science Center, is the most comprehensive survey one can find in the medical and psychological literature. Consider the following quote from the authors:

> As we learned more about the ubiquitous side effects, we have begun to speculate about their possible role in the recovery process. Obviously they can be very threatening and disturbing. However, we have also wondered whether the sudden creation of a body "symptom" by a medication might not in certain instances serve paradoxically as a *distractor* [italics mine] that can draw attention away from the immediate psychological distress and therefore induce a sense of "Yes, I have an acute physical discomfort, but my depression or my bad psychological state now seems less pressing."

My theory predicts exactly that distraction effect for the focuser. Fisher and Greenberg's detailed analysis of hundreds of studies concludes:

> Although we have been critical of the biological psychiatry modes, we are aware that the work of those invested in this area has been marked by good intentions, vigor, and an overall desire to become more scientifically rigorous. We are aware too that the widespread existence of psychological disturbance creates a pressure to create treatments that can be given *en masse*. People want quick solutions to their nagging anxieties, sadnesses, and feelings of alienation from reality. The medicalization of psychological distress has promised analogous "medical solutions." One particularly tempting aspect of such medicalization is that it conveys to the sufferers that they can be cured without any special efforts on their own part. They need only ingest a powerful agent and the biochemical impact will restore them.

MEDICATIONS AND THERMOSTATS

As I've emphasized earlier, resetting your thermostat with externally ingested chemicals is helpful in acute distress. But if you remain on medication, you will never learn to reset your emotional thermostat on your own. That's the major problem with drugs and why the relapse rate is so high: the patient doesn't learn a thing. Medications are like crash diets—quick, seemingly effective, but you don't learn how to alter longstanding habits, and before long, you're overweight again.

Indeed, as more and more studies are being done, on depression, for example, the experts are suggesting the *best* results are obtained when the person stays on the medication for years, rather than going on and off when depressive episodes occur. This is hardly encouraging advice or progress.

When I talk to my patients about using medication as a permanent solution, I use this metaphorical story. Gordon bought a farm in Kansas where tornadoes come whipping across the plains just about every year. His first year on the farm, a violent tornado hit his house. It tore the roof off and a beam crashed down on him and broke his arm. Gordon's fractured arm healed and was good as new in three months. But Gordon remained terrified of tornadoes. He bought lumber and nails and boarded up all the windows in his beautiful old farmhouse and he left them sealed. As the years went by, the seasons came and went. Barricaded inside, Gordon was safe, but he missed out on the richness of life around him. Remaining on medication is like keeping your storm shutters locked tight. You may be shielded from storm, but you also miss out on emotional participation in your life.

COMMON MEDICATION APPROACHES

SENSORS

Medications are frequently given to aid people in dealing with acute episodes of anxiety (panic attacks) or to help people who have chronically high levels of anxiety (generalized anxiety disorder) raise their threshold of arousal so they can cope with everyday events without being distracted by their arousal. Some commonly used antianxiety drugs include benzodiazepines such as Xanax (alprazolam) or Halcion (triazolam). These drugs are sometimes prescribed with the direction to "take as needed" for acute anxiety episodes. In the case of periodic acute anxiety, longer-acting drugs such as Ativan (lorazepam) or Valium (diazepam) may be prescribed to alter the person's biochemistry and raise his threshold enough to stave off these acute episodes.

The idea is that if a sensor's threshold is raised high enough, an experience that would otherwise produce massive anxiety (and possibly a panic attack) will instead produce little anxiety relative to the higher threshold, so that the person's threshold level of anxiety will not be surpassed; therefore, the person will not move out of her comfort zone. In the case of chronic anxiety, the longer-acting drug BuSpar (buspirone) is usually given. The medication is generally prescribed for a regular schedule that biochemically maintains the patient's threshold at a higher level.

Side effects of benzodiazepines include daytime sedation and drug hangover, as well as dizziness, uncoordination, lassitude, confusion, delayed physical reaction, disrupted REM (rapid eye movement) sleep, and amnesia. These effects can be lethally amplified when the medication is combined with alcohol. However, overall these drugs are safe and rarely lead to cardiovascular or respiratory depression.

FOCUSERS

There are three basic types of antidepressants. All three work by altering the amount of neurotransmitters available in the central nervous system to regulate nerve transmission. Tricyclics (e.g., Tofranil [imipramine] or Elavil [amitriptyline]) work by inhibiting the re-uptake of norepinephrine, serotonin, (or both) after their release, thereby increasing the amount of neurotransmitters available for nerve transmission. Serotonin re-uptake blockers work by increasing the availability of serotonin to facilitate transmission. Monoamine oxidase (MAO) inhibitors (e.g., Nardil [phenelzine]) constrain the action of an enzyme (MAO) so that it cannot modulate the amount of neurotransmitter present, and neurotransmitters therefore accumulate in the nerve terminals and increase transmission. In depressed persons, this increase in nerve transmission leads to elevated mood, increased physical activity and mental alertness, better appetite and sleep patterns, and reduced preoccupation with morbid thoughts.

Antidepressant medications have demonstrated general effectiveness for treating acute episodes of depressed mood, but these medications typically require two to three weeks to take effect from inception. These medications can also be helpful in preventing relapses of depressive episodes and are often used to maintain the individual's threshold of arousal at a lower level so that he or she is more likely to enjoy everyday activities and keep from falling into depressed mood when external stimulation levels are low.

Focusers (who are diagnosed as depressed because of their high thresholds for arousal and generally placid temperaments) may receive antidepressants from their physicians and find that their moods do seem to improve. However, while their moods may improve, their overall temperaments are not modified by the drugs. Once the medication is withdrawn, these focusers will revert to their self-focusing style.

There are some problems with antidepressant drugs. One problem is the necessity of long-term usage for maintenance of a lower threshold of arousal. These drugs are not stimulants and do not function as recreational drugs even in nondepressed individuals; thus, addiction in its usual sense does not occur. However, focusers who experience periodic depression may find that they need to continue taking these drugs because they have not learned alternative methods for regulating their moods. They have not learned to work with their natural temperament to stay within a comfort zone that can be expanded with further effort.

The usual side effects of long-term usage of antidepressants are drowsiness, hypertension, dry mouth, blurred vision, constipation, and decrease of REM sleep. Upon cessation of using these medications, individuals may experience some withdrawal effects. These may occur because the central nervous system has grown accustomed to having higher levels of neurotransmitters available to facilitate synaptic transmission. Individuals may find that they briefly feel more depressed in the immediate period following termination of antidepressant use. This experience in itself may perpetuate their tendencies to focus inwardly.

DISCHARGERS

No typical drug medication is available. Dischargers often resemble and in some cases may be adults with attention deficit hyperactivity disorder–residual type (ADHD–RT). Diagnosis for this condition is based on the adult having a childhood history of the disorder and currently experiencing hyperactivity and attention deficit plus other indications: poor organization, poor concentration or task persistence, or impulsivity.

SEEKERS

Seekers are characterized by impulsivity. Risk taking and searching for stimulation in their daily lives is an attempt (albeit often unconscious) to push themselves beyond their high thresholds for arousal.

Stimulant medications may help seekers regulate their temperament and control their impulsivity because, by stimulating the central nervous system, the medications raise arousal levels closer to comfortable thresholds of arousal. Hence, less outside stimulation is needed to keep these people in their comfort zones; they do not feel the need to seek extra stimulation or to act impulsively to maintain a comfortable level of arousal.

TRENDY DRUGS

Occasionally, new medications appear on the market that cause a stir among the medical and popular community. The usual pattern for these drugs is that they have an aura of being a "miracle pill" and are widely prescribed until their full side effects are revealed. The media usually plays a role in this process, initially publicizing the "wonder drug" at the beginning of its use, then criticizing it and blaming drug companies and physicians alike at the time of its demise—until a newer "miracle pill" appears to steal the limelight. Several drugs in recent years that have undergone this cycle are Xanax (alprazolam), Halcion (triazolam), and Prozac (fluoxetine).

Xanax is a benzodiazepine that has been widely advertised as the ultimate drug for treating panic disorder. However, Xanax has not demonstrated superiority to other minor tranquilizers and it has similar side effects, including confusion, depression, forgetfulness, paranoia, and hostility. Moreover, Xanax binds more tightly to receptors and acts quickly, so it is more likely than other anxiety drugs to cause addiction and intense withdrawal symptoms. Xanax has produced feelings of fear, restlessness, disorientation, and severe anxiety upon its cessation. Combined with alcohol or other sedatives, it may cause death.

Research has revealed that long-term use of Xanax may even lead to higher levels of anxiety and panic, to the extent that patients receiving a placebo did better overall by avoiding the medication and its side effects. Therefore, the popularity of this drug as a panacea for panic disorder is highly questionable at the present time.

Media reports have detailed the controversy surrounding Halcion, a benzodiazepine used for the treatment of insomnia. It is a short-acting drug that has demonstrated success in treating sleep problems when prescribed with appropriate dosages for short periods of time, with the constraint that no alcohol or other sedative-hypnotic drug be taken simultaneously. Halcion has similar side effects to other benzodiazepines and may also produce rebound insomnia upon cessation.

A frightening potential side effect of long-term usage of benzodiazepines such as Halcion and Xanax is brain atrophy. Some research has indicated that enlarged ventricles (fluid-filled spaces) in the brain have been correlated with long-term benzodiazepine use. Although more research is needed to substantiate this danger, these findings should promote increased caution in the prescribing of these drugs by physicians for long periods of time.

Prozac is currently the most extensively prescribed antidepressant drug. It seems to be as effective as other antidepressants for treating major depression, and some patients have shown quick and positive responses. However, some patients have shown incomplete or no improvement, and Prozac's side effects, while different from those of most antidepressants, are not pleasant. Nausea, intermittent vomiting, weight loss, diarrhea, headache, anxiety, and insomnia frequently occur. A feeling of having to move around (motor agitation) may also occur, and some patients have reported the development of agitation and obsessional ideation. Fortunately, few overdoses on Prozac have been reported; Prozac is pharmacologically more difficult to overdose on than other antidepressants.

Caution should be taken in the use of this medication. Prozac has been tested for treating such diverse conditions as bulimia, borderline personality disorder, panic attacks, and obsessive-compulsive disorder, but substantial evidence for its effectiveness has not yet been shown. In addition, it is popularly believed to be a successful approach to weight loss, in spite of the unappealing side effects.

To reduce the side effects, the dosage must be decreased or another drug must be given with the Prozac to treat its negative effects. Another problem is that Prozac may induce mania, especially because it has a long half-life and can accumulate in the body for longer periods of time than other drugs. Additionally, long-term usage may lead to other psychological dysfunction upon withdrawal, including depression and anxiety. All of these factors should be considered. Therefore, a long-term strategy for treatment should be implemented with Prozac. Overall, Prozac may not be any better than other drugs for treating depression, and side effects may make it worse for some patients.

As this book goes to press, the new replacement for Prozac is a similar-acting drug called Zoloft. The only reason for the shift is that Prozac came under so much attack (much of it fallacious) that doctors needed a similar-acting substitute.

ALTERNATIVES

I'm often asked about the various twelve-step recovery programs. I am generally in favor of them. They provide emotional support, a sense of shared understandings, and compassion for each person's dilemma. And you certainly can't beat the price.

The difficulty I sometimes have with these programs is that they may spend too much time blaming people in one's past. I believe there is too much blaming and not enough getting on with life. I believe that even when we have troubled childhoods, or are children of alcoholics, we still have our temperament to contend with. And to blame all emotional states on one kind of addiction is too simplistic.

In addition to recovery groups, there are many other growth seminars and special-focus groups dealing with life dilemmas. All of them may be valuable, but they neglect innate temperament, they are lacking a significant chunk of understanding.

All alternatives to therapy have one thing in common and that is a feeling of support and connectedness. If there is one thing that helps people find emotional relief, it's the feeling that they are not alone, that others care about them and for them.

As I stated at the beginning of this book, I want to encourage you to stop trying to become a better person if that means comparing your insides to other people's outsides and denying your own temperament. Instead, I urge you to reframe your intention and strive to become more genuinely who you are. Embrace the richness of your emotional fluctuation. Your awareness and respect of your temperament will give you true emotional confidence. You'll move through your world open to people and to challenges, alive to life's possibilities.

Index